THE POLITICS OF COMPROMISE

*A Study of Parties and Cabinet Government
in Sweden*

THE POLITICS
OF COMPROMISE

A Study of Parties
and Cabinet Government
in Sweden

DANKWART A. RUSTOW

GREENWOOD PRESS, PUBLISHERS
NEW YORK

Published 1955 by Princeton University Press

Reprinted by arrangement with Princeton University Press

First Greenwood Reprinting 1969

Library of Congress Catalogue Card Number 69-14067

SBN 8371-1959-6

PRINTED IN UNITED STATES OF AMERICA

TO

R. L. R.

PREFACE

THIS study is not intended as a complete survey of Swedish government and politics. The reader will find only a cursory account, for example, of major substantive problems of Swedish politics such as economic planning, labor relations, social welfare, and foreign policy. On many of these, specialized studies are available. It would have been tempting to deal at some length with party activities in the provinces or with campaign techniques. But an exhaustive account of these and other themes related to the central subject would clearly have exceeded the scope of the present work. A few topics, such as the monarch's role in foreign policy during the recent world war, have been omitted reluctantly because sufficient source material is not yet available to guide the observer through a maze of controversy. Thus, even within the narrower sphere of parties and cabinet government the treatment has of necessity been selective. It is hoped that the following chapters will afford some insight into the political processes by which Sweden has been able to arrive at her remarkable and well-known achievements in social and economic policy, in foreign and domestic affairs.

I should like to express my gratitude to teachers, colleagues, and friends who in many ways have contributed to this study. Professors Elis Håstad (Stockholm), Jörgen Westerståhl (Göteborg), Herbert Tingsten (Stockholm), Hugo Vallentin (Uppsala), and Eric C. Bellquist (Berkeley) helped me orient myself to the Swedish scene and provided specific advice and information. Mr. Yngve Fritzell, of the Central Bureau of Statistics (Stockholm), graciously came to my aid in supplying data on the latest election returns. Professors Willmoore Kendall, of Yale, who was the first to interest me in a study of Swedish parties, and V. O. Key, Jr., of Harvard, critically read earlier versions of this study. My friend and Princeton colleague Gabriel A. Almond gave valuable advice and criticism based on a reading of the final version. I alone am responsible for any shortcomings of this study.

PREFACE

I also wish to express my appreciation to the Social Science Research Council, whose fellowship grant enabled me to spend a year in Sweden, and to Princeton University and its Research Committee for financial assistance in subsequent research and in the publication of this study. Neither institution should be deemed, by virtue of these grants, to approve any of the opinions expressed herein. I am indebted to the American-Scandinavian Foundation and to Albert Bonniers Förlag for permission to reproduce Heidenstam's "Citizen's Song" in the form in which it appears in chapter II.

For her to whom this book is dedicated may it be a token of a year of common exploration and a small compensation for the trials of living under the cloud of authorship.

Princeton, New Jersey
August 1955   Dankwart A. Rustow

CONTENTS

CONTENTS

TABLES

FIGURES

INTRODUCTION

INTEREST in Sweden was greatly intensified some years ago as a result of that country's remarkable recovery from the Great Depression. By 1935 her production and balance of trade were back to their 1929 positions, and by 1937 unemployment had dropped to its normal prosperity level. A Social Democratic government was in power during most of this period, but there was no attempt at socialization. A large-scale program of public works, social insurance, and farm subsidies was carried out within the framework of a predominantly private economy. Elsewhere "democracy in crisis" was the topic of the day, and Sweden's neighbor to the south, Germany, had succumbed to a ferocious dictatorship. Yet Swedish experience showed that democracy can cope with the problems of an industrial economy. The choice, it was widely believed in hope or despair, was between capitalism, with its dismal cycle of boom and slump, and socialism, with its promise of security and plenty. Yet here was proof that another alternative was feasible. Sweden's economic and social policies appeared to have realized the fondest dreams of large masses in Western civilization—just as her course of neutrality in two world wars struck a sympathetic chord in a world yearning for peace. *Sweden: The Middle Way;*[1] *This Is Democracy;*[2] *Sweden: Champion of Peace;*[3] *Sweden: Model for a World*[4]— such has been the steady crescendo of panegyrics in the English language.

Perhaps it was at times forgotten amid the well-deserved praise that "the real Scandinavian [is] a human being with his full share of vices as well as virtues."[5] Yet thorough and well-

[1] By Marquis W. Childs, New Haven: Yale University Press, 1937; rev. edn., 1947; Penguin edn., 1948.

[2] By Marquis W. Childs, New Haven: Yale University Press, 1938.

[3] By David Hinshaw, New York: Putnam, 1949.

[4] By Hudson Strode, New York: Harcourt, Brace, 1949.

[5] As B. J. Hovde reminds his readers in the preface to his history of *The Scandinavian Countries, 1720–1865*, Boston: Chapman & Grimes, 1943, I, 7.

informed studies soon supplemented the travel books and journalistic impromptus, putting into perspective the role of conscious choice and good fortune in Sweden's return to prosperity. Still, the picture that American and English readers were likely to carry away remained somewhat incomplete. The literature, whether popular or scholarly, tended to concentrate on economic and social problems and their concrete solutions. Except for the border-field of labor relations,[6] the political processes which brought forth these solutions have attracted scant attention.[7] Politics is as yet far less of an international discipline than economics. The fact that the works of Swedish economists like Lindahl, Myrdal, and Ohlin are far better known outside Scandinavia than those of their colleagues in political science[8] has further accentuated the disparity. The present study of the development and functioning of the political process in Sweden is an attempt to fill part of this gap.

The antidepression program of 1933 marked a major turning point in that process. It was sponsored by the Social Democrats, who for the first time assumed undisputed leadership within the government. It was supported by the Agrarians, who for the first time emerged from the sidelines. Under the impact of

[6] See Paul H. Norgren, *The Swedish Collective Bargaining System*, Cambridge: Harvard University Press, 1941; James J. Robbins, *The Government of Labor Relations in Sweden*, Chapel Hill: University of North Carolina Press, 1942; and Charles A. Myers, *Industrial Relations in Sweden*, Cambridge: Massachusetts Institute of Technology, 1951.

[7] Brief treatments of Swedish government and politics are included in the following surveys: Bjarne Braatoy, *The New Sweden: A Vindication of Democracy*, London: Thomas Nelson, 1939; Ben A. Arneson, *The Democratic Monarchies of Scandinavia*, 2d edn., New York: Van Nostrand, 1949; Eric Cyril Bellquist, "Government and Politics in Northern Europe," in David Fellman, ed., *Post-War Governments of Europe*, Gainesville, Fla.: Kallman, 1946; Henning Friis, ed., *Scandinavia between East and West*, Ithaca: Cornell University Press, 1950; Franklin D. Scott, *The United States and Scandinavia*, Cambridge: Harvard University Press, 1950; Ingvar Andersson et al., *Introduction to Sweden*, 2d edn., Stockholm: Swedish Institute, 1951; and Royal Institute of International Affairs, *The Scandinavian States and Finland*, London, 1951.

[8] Among the few works by Swedish political scientists available in English are Nils Herlitz, *Sweden: A Modern Democracy on Ancient Foundations*, Minneapolis: University of Minnesota Press, 1939; and two by Herbert Tingsten: *Political Behavior*, London: P. S. King, 1937, and *The Debate on the Foreign Policy of Sweden, 1918–1939*, tr. Joan Bulman, New York: Oxford University Press, 1949.

the depression the workers relinquished their historic radicalism and the farmers their traditional conservatism. While the former turned from a doctrine of socialization to the more immediate task of economic stabilization, the latter sought to fit their special demands into a larger framework of national welfare. The period of recovery confirmed the decline of the Conservatives, only twenty years earlier the most powerful force on the political scene. Even more symbolic was the fact that Socialist-Agrarian cooperation set an end to a period of Liberal predominance. Sweden in 1933 was entering the third phase of the cycle from inherited status to individualism to pluralism—a cycle which she had entered later but was completing more rapidly than other Western countries. Gradually the Liberals and the Conservatives were converted to the new conception of a social welfare state.

Swedish democracy weathered the storm of economic depression without undue strain. After years of a tenuous parliamentary balance between right and left, periodically adjusted in the committee room, the government once again was restored to its leading role within the legislative process. In sharp contrast to the situation abroad the transition was achieved without resort to executive emergency powers. The success of the depression policies halted the temporary upsurge of totalitarian movements long before these could assume menacing proportions. The effective and smooth operation of democratic institutions in time of stress seems the more remarkable when it is recalled that Sweden became a full-fledged democracy only in the wake of the First World War. The period of the mid-thirties thus marks the full maturation of that most fundamental yet most elusive quality of Swedish politics—the harmonious interplay of rival forces, the tradition of government by discussion and compromise.

Although the roots of that tradition go as far back as Swedish history itself, its continuous growth can be traced in the course of Swedish politics since the social and economic transformation of the latter part of the nineteenth century. The most notable political innovation of this period was the replacement in 1866–1867 of the traditional four estates by an elective bicameral parliament. The first three chapters of this study will examine the origins of the major political movements during the oligarchic regime of the last third of the nineteenth century, their vigorous yet fruitful interaction in the struggle for political participation by the entire community, and their organizational and ideological metamorphosis in response to the successive foreign, internal, and economic crises of the last seventy to eighty years. The remaining chapters will give a somewhat more systematic account of the role played in recent decades by the four groups that are the chief partners in the Swedish scheme of representative government—electorate, parties, legislature, and cabinet.

It remains, in this brief introduction, to point to some of the main factors—social, economic, and historical—that have made possible the Swedish version of democratic government and have cast it in the particular mold of the politics of compromise.

The Swedish environment offers many conditions favorable to the growth of a system of government by discussion. A small population of remarkable ethnic and religious homogeneity occupies a small territory endowed with adequate if not lavish natural resources. Its geographical position has given the country relative security from foreign invasion and interference. The people are heirs to a common and distinct historical tradition and have developed high standards of education and material welfare.

The area of Sweden (about 170,000 square miles) is a little larger than that of California, her population (the 1953 estimate was 7.2 million) a little smaller. All but a handful of her citizens speak Swedish as their mother tongue, and nearly all belong, at least nominally, to the Lutheran state church. The political unity of the various regions dates back to the early Middle Ages; since the mid-seventeenth century the country's external boundaries (disregarding former outlying possessions) have been unchanged.

Although Sweden's latitude corresponds to that of Alaska, with the northern part extending well into the Arctic zone, the Gulf Stream ensures a moderate climate. More than half of the land surface is covered with forest—wood, pulp, and paper have traditionally been among Sweden's most lucrative exports. Her iron ore deposits are among the richest in the world and Sweden alone accounts today for about one twelfth of total

4

world production. Less than one tenth of the entire land area is arable although the soil in Skåne, the most southerly region, is very fertile. For most of her coal and some of her food the country depends upon imports. Industrial products of high quality supplement ore and forest products among her exports: Swedish electrical apparatus, ball bearings, and furniture enjoy a world-wide reputation. The diversity of the economy has been sufficient to cushion some of the impact of price fluctuations in the international market.

The same pattern of moderate diversity is repeated in the three sections into which the country is historically divided. Götaland in the south is the most densely populated area. It includes the richest agricultural regions, such as Skåne at the tip of the Scandinavian peninsula and Västergötland between the two great lakes (Väner and Vätter); but some large industrial centers, such as the port cities of Göteborg and Malmö and the textile towns of Norrköping and Borås, are also located here. The central section, Svealand, includes the highly industrialized provinces of Västmanland and Örebro, the ancient mining region of Dalarna, the wooded province of Värmland, and an area of intensive truck and dairy farming interspersed with industry near the country's capital, Stockholm. Norrland, finally, which comprises the northern three fifths of the country, is largely covered with forest. Its many parallel rivers secure a convenient supply of timber for the string of sawmill towns along the Gulf of Bothnia. The largest iron mines are near Kiruna in the extreme north; there is some industry in southern Norrland and some scattered farming throughout.

Roughly two fifths of the Swedish population is engaged in mining, manufacturing, and construction work and about one fifth in farming, fishing, and forestry. Just under one half of the population lives in districts administratively classified as "urban"; yet only about 35 per cent lives in cities with a population of over 25,000 and only one Swede in ten lives in the capital. The size both of farm holdings and of industry is small. The average farm measures about 22 acres and over half the arable land is taken up by farms of less than 50 acres. Similarly the average industrial enterprise employs only about 48 workers with a majority of wage earners employed by concerns with fewer than 200 workers. Nearly half of the industrial population lives in rural rather than urban communities and much of the remaining half in small towns.

Her natural resources combined with the industry and skill of her inhabitants have enabled Sweden to build up what is probably the highest living standard in Europe. She exceeds all other European countries in the number of automobiles, telephones, and radio sets per inhabitant. Ninety-four per cent of her homes have electricity (as against 92.9 in Denmark and 89.8 in the United States), and there are 85 movie seats per 1,000 inhabitants (compared with 87 in Britain, 77 in the United States, and 142 in New Zealand). Although Sweden lacks the aggressive egalitarianism—as well as the material opportunities—of such frontier countries as the United States, Canada, Australia, and New Zealand there probably is as great a degree of social mobility as in any other European country. Educational standards are similarly high. Compulsory schooling was introduced over 100 years ago and literacy is nearly universal. In addition to the public school system there is an extensive adult education movement sponsored by trade unions, religious groups, and political parties and subsidized from government funds. Great social prestige attaches to learning and especially to the higher forms of academic training. To the extent that a distinction between upper and lower class continues to be felt today it is perhaps symbolized more by the *studentmössa* than by anything else—the colorful visored cap that graduates of the gymnasium, or junior college, are entitled to wear. It is not surprising in view of these data that Sweden has the highest per capita newsprint consumption of any European country. In 1952 the number of active voters (3.8 million) exceeded the total *weekday* circulation of newspapers (3.5 million) only slightly. Although nearly all the newspapers directly support one of the political parties they have extensive coverage and maintain high standards of detached judgment. It is customary, for instance, for newspapers to devote one or more columns on their editorial page to excerpts from the lead articles of other papers, including the opposition press.

None of the characteristics just listed are peculiar to Sweden. Small size, unity of language, religion, and historical tradition, moderate diversity of the economy, and a high standard of living and education—these are to be found elsewhere in the

Western world. But few countries offer all of them in combination. A number of other factors that have given Swedish politics some of its distinctive flavor will be discussed in greater detail in the following chapters. A few of them may be mentioned at this point.

First there is the individualist tradition rooted in Protestant Christianity with its emphasis on justification by faith and on the direct relationship between the individual believer and the deity. The Swedish state church combined these beliefs with Luther's passive doctrine of unquestioned obedience to constituted authority. Yet the dissenting sects which sprang up in the nineteenth century gave Protestantism a far more activist interpretation and as a result have exerted an influence on society and politics far beyond their numbers. The individualist spirit also pervades the secular utilitarianism and belief in progress which probably constitute the creed of the great mass of those who only nominally adhere to the Lutheran church.

A universal inclination to form societies in the pursuit of impersonal objectives provides a salutary complement to individualism. Swedish society is *genomorganiserad*—saturated with voluntary associations.[9] Almost the entire working population is organized according to its function in the productive process —the wage earners in trade unions, white collar workers in associations of salaried employees, farmers in agricultural marketing societies, and industrialists in employers' associations. One million four hundred thousand voters are card-holding members of the several political parties and their affiliates, 1,000,000 consumers belong to the cooperative movement, 800,000 sports fans to the National Alliance of Sports Federations, more than a quarter million Protestant dissenters to the various low-church sects, and 300,000 teetotallers to the many temperance societies—not to mention academic, philanthropic, philatelic, convivial, and innumerable more casual societies.

This informal yet intensive training in the arts of orderly debate and group decision provides a solid foundation for Swedish democracy. The governmental superstructure is imbued with an atmosphere of intimacy which forms a valuable heritage from a not too distant oligarchic past. Members of

---

[9] See Gunnar Heckscher, *Staten och organisationerna*, 2d edn., Stockholm: KF, 1951, p. 22 and passim.

parliament and high government officials follow rules of procedure and social customs developed at a time when government was the prerogative of a small elite which harbored no fundamental differences of interest or opinion and whose members were closely related by ties of ancestry, marriage, and friendship.

An equally important legacy of the past is the traditional, at times perhaps overmeticulous, regard for law and legal procedure. Medieval documents such as the mid-fourteenth century code of Magnus Eriksson regulated in detail the rights and duties of the monarch, the noblemen, and the commoners. The continuity of written law was not even interrupted by brief periods of royal absolutism or by successful *coups d'état*; autocrats and revolutionaries alike paid their respects to legal tradition by their prompt enactment of new codes. The word *lagom*—literally, "according to the laws"—has come to mean "suitable, appropriate, sufficient, just right."

All the foregoing factors have come to full fruition in a long period of peace, uninterrupted since 1815. It is true that Sweden from the sixteenth to the eighteenth century had actively participated in the game of European power politics, had won and lost a Baltic empire, and had only twice been at peace for as long as twenty years (1678 to 1700 and 1720 to 1741).[10] Yet once the advent of modern mass armies during the French revolutionary wars relegated her to the status of a second-rate power her relatively isolated geographical position made possible a gradual withdrawal from foreign entanglements. Even during the Second World War good fortune enabled Sweden to adhere to a policy of neutrality which by then had become a national tradition. The loss of most of her outlying possessions in the eighteenth century made political talents, developed on the scale of a Baltic empire, available for the elaboration of parliamentary and administrative institutions in a smaller territory. While the Swedes have retained what to the foreigner may seem like an intense concern about their reputation abroad, this reputation for over a century has been based not on military exploits but on solid accomplishments in science, technology, and democratic government.

[10] See the tabulations in Quincy Wright, *A Study of War*, Chicago: University of Chicago Press, 1942, I, 641 ff.

CHAPTER I

ORIGINS OF THE MODERN PARTIES

WHEREVER a group of equals seeks to arrive at a common decision it is likely to be divided. But only where decisions are weighty and frequent will division crystallize into competitive organization. Political parties, therefore, have generally emerged at two points in the history of modern states. First, as representative bodies secured a prominent share in the government, factions or parties arose in their midst. Later, as large masses of citizens sought and obtained the right to participate in the selection of these governing assemblies, national parties sprang up by the side of those in parliament. The English parliament in 1640 declared itself indissoluble, subdued the king by beheading his chief adviser— and was split into Roundheads and Cavaliers. The French revolutionary assemblies a century and a half later brought Louis XVI to Paris as a captive, forced him to approve a constitution, proclaimed a republic, at length executed him—and found themselves already engaged in the internecine battles of Feuillants, Girondists, Montagnards, and Thermidorians. The events of 1688–1689 in England confirmed not only parliament's right to determine the constitution but also its division into Whigs and Tories. The Reform Act of 1832 called into action the Chartists, the Anti-Corn-Law League, and other popular organizations; that of 1867 the Birmingham caucus. In the United States the unsuspecting constitutional fathers, by vesting the legislative power in a congress and the choice of a president in an electoral college, opened a wide field for partisan activity. National conventions took over the task of presidential nomination after 1832 when manhood suffrage was making rapid gains throughout the states.

Swedish political institutions down to the middle of the nineteenth century developed in relative freedom from foreign influence. Even so—or perhaps just for that reason—their history offers many parallels to that of French and especially of British institutions. Like Britain, and unlike France, Sweden

9

has a continuous tradition of monarchy and popular representation that dates back to the Middle Ages. Between 1718 and 1809 Sweden went through a cycle of absolute monarchy, parliamentary supremacy, royal restoration, and constitutional monarchy—as Britain did from 1640 to 1689 and France from 1789 to 1830. Each turning point was marked, as in France, by the adoption of a new written constitution; yet the later evolution of the modern cabinet system (after 1809) followed the British pattern of uncodified precedents. In all three countries, finally, parties first appeared during the second, or parliamentary, phase of the cycle.

The unique features of Swedish constitutional history are equally significant. While Sweden has had her *coups d'état*, tyrannicides, and peasant uprisings, there have been no social and political revolutions or civil wars like those of 1640, 1789, or 1870; nor has Sweden had any Bonapartes or Cromwells. The first Swedish parliamentary parties in the mid-eighteenth century therefore were not supported by any revolutionary wave, as in Britain and France; after a brief foaming they completely disappeared. The survival of medieval estates in Sweden proved a major obstacle to partisan organization, and only after the estates had been abolished (1866) did parties take firm root in a bicameral parliament. Above all, despite the long tradition of popular representation, the Swedish masses did not demand or receive the right of political participation until the turn of the present century, and national parties therefore emerged later than in most other European countries.

ESTATES AND FACTIONS

The Swedish riksdag, with a continuous tradition since 1435, is the second oldest parliament in the world.[1] From the beginning it rested on a broader basis than similar bodies elsewhere.

[1] See [Sweden, Riksdagen,] *Sveriges riksdag*, ed. Karl Hildebrand et al., 17 vols., Stockholm: Victor Petterson, 1931–1938. Standard treatments of Swedish history include Emil Hildebrand and Ludvig Stavenow, eds., *Sveriges historia till våra dagar*, 15 vols., Stockholm: Norstedt, 1919–1945; Ingvar Andersson, *Sveriges historia*, 2d edn., Stockholm: Norstedt, 1944; Andrew A. Stomberg, *A History of Sweden*, New York: Macmillan, 1931; Ragnar Svanström and Carl Fredrik Palmstierna, *A Short History of Sweden*, Oxford: Clarendon Press, 1934; and Carl Hallendorff and Adolf Schück, *History of Sweden*, 2d edn., Stockholm: C. E. Fritze,

In addition to representatives of the nobility, clergy, and burghers it included representatives for the peasantry, each estate meeting as a separate chamber. By the late sixteenth century the riksdag's right to share with the king and the council of the realm in the government of the country was well established. The estates considered requests for new taxes, regulated the royal succession when it was in doubt, and brought forth complaints and grievances. Even the erection of a regime of royal absolutism after 1680 did not seriously interrupt this estate tradition. Karl XII (1697–1718) was the first and only king of Sweden who began his rule without taking the traditional coronation oath or giving the royal pledge to the estates; yet twice while the king was in the field with the army during the Great Northern War (1700–1720) the council on its own initiative called the riksdag into session. That war constituted the most ambitious attempt ever undertaken by a Swedish monarch to enlarge and consolidate an empire which would have reduced the Baltic to a Swedish lake. The attempt ended in utter disaster. The war cost Sweden one tenth of her population, ruined the economy for decades, and entailed the loss of all her Baltic provinces except Finland. When Karl XII died in 1718 absolutism was hopelessly discredited; moreover, since he left no direct heirs, the riksdag had to choose a successor. It was a unique opportunity for the assertion of estate power.

Two successive constitutions, adopted by the estates in 1719 and 1720, required the monarch to sanction all laws passed by the estates, limited his power to that of casting two votes in the council, obliged him to fill vacancies on the council from lists submitted by the riksdag, and restricted his right to confer titles of nobility. Repeated interruptions in the line of succession in effect converted Sweden for a time into an elective monarchy. The fact that the choice fell first upon a woman and then upon two foreign princes was calculated to consolidate the position of the estates. A complete parliamentary regime thus had been established in the void left by the collapse of royal absolutism.

The following decades (1718–1772) are known in Swedish history as the Era of Liberty; and the factions that emerged in

1937. For the constitutional history see Nils Herlitz, *Grunddragen av det svenska statsskickets historia*, 4th edn., Stockholm: Norstedt, 1952.

the estates are strongly reminiscent of the parallel groupings of Whigs and Tories in eighteenth century Britain. The claim of a pretender; questions of an aggressive or conciliatory foreign policy, of alliance with France or Russia, of mercantilism or free trade; and the constitutional position of the monarch—all these provided fuel for partisanship. Any change in parliamentary majority entailed a complete turnover on the council of the realm with impeachment proceedings for the outgoing ministers. The chief contending factions were known as the Hats and the Caps, and the king at times tried to launch a separate royal party. The foreign powers, too, took a hand in Swedish affairs, and during the latter part of the Liberty Era France and Russia spent vast sums to bribe members of the administration, the estates, and even their electors. The humiliation of the king went far beyond anything known to Britain during this period. When he refused to sign state documents, the council applied a stamp of his signature. Sweden was a republic in all but name, and her hapless rulers were not even cutting very decorative figures. French philosophers like Voltaire and Mably hailed the Swedish constitution as the freest in Europe. The rule of the parties was tempered only by the principles of tenure within the administration and of freedom of the press, laid down in the royal promise of 1719[2] and a fundamental law of 1766 respectively.

The victory of the estates had been too complete to endure. Corruption, foreign influence, and defeat in two wars—against Russia in 1740–1741 and in the Seven Years' War of 1756–1763 —did much to discredit the parliamentary regime. Dissatisfaction among the lower orders with the predominant power of the nobility did the rest. In 1771 Gustaf III ascended the throne, the first native-born ruler since Karl XII and the first to succeed by hereditary right rather than election. When the new king at the head of the troops arrested the council of the realm (1772) he met no resistance. Gustaf's royal restoration by military coup succeeded where the more indirect attempts of George III failed in Britain. Meeting under armed guard, the riksdag approved a new constitution, restoring the king's legis-

[2] See *Konungaförsäkran* 1719, § 8; 1720, § 11, reprinted in Emil Hildebrand, ed., *Sveriges regeringsformer 1634–1809*, Stockholm: Norstedt, 1891, pp. 226, 238.

lative veto and his control over the administration. The riksdag retained its right to vote taxes and appropriations. Yet parliamentary "liberty" disappeared, and with it the early factions.

A period of moderate absolutism (1772–1809) came to an end following a war against Russia in which Sweden lost Finland and a coup in which Gustav IV lost his throne. Another constitution, drawn up by the estates and approved by King Karl XIII, embodied a series of checks and balances designed to prevent a recurrence of the former excesses of absolutism and estate rule. With many major and minor amendments it has remained in effect; it is thus the second oldest constitution in force in any country today. The constitution consisted of four separate fundamental laws, adopted in 1809 and 1810, and known respectively as the instrument of government, the parliament act, the act of succession, and the act of the freedom of the press.[3]

Constitutionalism emerged restored and strengthened. Yet despite the rebellious mood of the chamber of peasants nothing was done to remove the feudal burdens of which it complained. Nor was the base of representation broadened in any way. At a time when the ideas of liberty and equality were on their victorious course through Europe, Sweden's conservative palace revolution gave the medieval estates a new lease on life. For the half century during which the 1809 regime remained intact there was little prospect of a revival of organized partisanship.

[3] All four documents have been frequently and extensively amended; the last three in fact were completely rewritten in accordance with the amending procedures provided in the instrument of government—the succession act in 1810, that on the freedom of the press in 1812 and 1949, and the parliament act in 1866. The current version of these statutes will be found in Robert Malmgren's annotated edition of *Sveriges grundlagar*, 6th edn., Stockholm: Norstedt, 1951. Earlier versions are contained in C. A. Reuterskiöld, *Sveriges grundlagar*, 2d edn., 3 vols., Uppsala: Almqvist & Wiksell, 1934. For English translations see Amos J. Peaslee, *Constitutions of Nations*, Concord, N.H., 1950, III, 96 ff., and *The Constitution of Sweden*, tr. Sarah V. Thorelli, Stockholm: Royal Ministry for Foreign Affairs, 1954 (the latter gives the four organic laws as amended up to and including the year 1953).

Wherever provisions of the constitution are cited in this study the conventional Swedish abbreviations have been used. *RF* (*Regeringsformen*) stands for the instrument of government, *RO* (*Riksdagsordningen*) for the parliament act. The latest version is intended unless there is some indication to the contrary.

Rivalry between the king and the estates, to be sure, did not subside; and in the following decades a conservative and a liberal faction emerged as the champions on either side. These two groups, however, were hardly parties in the modern sense. Like the Hats and Caps they were linked by ties of family, personal friendship, and common ambition; yet the powerful party-forming incentive of the Era of Liberty—parliamentary control of the administration—was lacking. The two groups might display considerable activity when a major piece of legislation was being considered or when the perennial conflict between legislature and executive was coming to a head.[4] Soon they would relapse into their accustomed passivity. On most questions, moreover, the antagonism among the four chambers was so strong as to overshadow any alignments that might have cut across estate divisions. The role of the estates during this period, then, was similar to that later played by the parties in a bicameral riksdag. Both provided channels for the expression of diverse interests and opinions within the politically active population.

DECLINE OF THE ESTATES

Slowly the social foundations of the estate order were beginning to crumble. In the 100 years from 1766 to 1866 Sweden more than doubled her population—from 2.0 million to 4.1 million. During the same period the old village commons were divided and enclosed. The villagers, by successive exchanges of property, consolidated their scattered strips and moved to new homes on their several farms. Individual cultivation, which thus was replacing the age-old system of communal agriculture, encouraged initiative and made for more intensive production. Large tracts of forest and wasteland were brought under the plow for the first time. Even so there was not nearly enough land to absorb the rapidly growing population. An enormous increase in the number of landless rural proletarians fed the growing streams of internal migration and emigration abroad. During the early nineteenth century the timber and iron trades

[4] The outstanding example of such ephemeral partisan activity—the crisis of 1840–1841—is fully analysed in Gert Hornwall, *Regeringskris och riksdagspolitik 1840–1841*, Uppsala: Almqvist & Wiksell, 1951.

improved their equipment and expanded production to keep up with increased demand from industrializing countries, notably Britain. Soon the first steamboats and railways began to link the remote parts of the country. The new device of joint stock organization and the growth of private banking supplied capital for new and larger commercial and industrial ventures. The guild system, which had been the economic base of the power of the burghers, was in decay. Its last vestiges disappeared in 1864 when the government allowed complete freedom of occupation. Two years later the last estate session consented to the successive elimination of all import duties. Step by step the government relinquished its ancient ambition of fostering trade and manufacture, leaving instead the rising class of captains of industry and commerce to pursue their private gain and thereby, led by an unseen hand, to serve the public interest.[5]

Other policies carried into effect many of the humanitarian and political demands of nineteenth century liberalism. As early as 1842 schooling had been made compulsory throughout the country. The government about the same time renounced its right to confiscate oppositional newspapers. A new criminal code in 1864 reduced a bewildering array of retaliatory punishments to a uniform scale ranging from light fines to long prison terms and, in rare case, the death sentence. The new code also allowed complete freedom of assembly and association. Religious dissenters were now permitted to conduct their prayer meetings without fear of police molestation; if they wished they were free to secede from the Lutheran state church. Individualism was advancing on all fronts, giving rise to new social classes for which there was no place in the traditional status order. Increasingly the survival of the estates in the riksdag stood out as an anachronism in the minds of critical contemporaries.

Political attacks on the estate system of representation multiplied. The nobility traditionally had been the most powerful of the estates. The constitution of the Era of Liberty, for instance, entrusted most important parliamentary decisions to a "secret committee" of whom half were noblemen and the other half

[5] On the economic changes of this period see Eli F. Heckscher, *An Economic History of Sweden*, Cambridge: Harvard University Press, 1954, pp. 209ff.; on their social and political implications, B. J. Hovde, *The Scandinavian Countries, 1720–1865*, 2 vols., Boston: Chapman & Grimes, 1943.

clerics and burghers, with the peasantry entirely unrepresented. Within the nobility in turn the bureaucracy and the military predominated, for the absolute monarchs of the seventeenth century had broken the power of the feudal landlords. Gustaf III, following the royal restoration, had restricted the most valuable of the aristocracy's prerogatives—their exclusive title to tax-free lands and their monopoly on higher government offices—although the nobles continued to supply a majority of higher officials. The coup of 1809 set an end to the monarchy's tendency to play off the lower estates against the nobles, and the constitution makers of that year were quite successful in their attempt at erecting a structure that would be controlled by a "bureaucratic aristocracy."[6] Although the nobility now held an equal place with the other estates it had won a powerful ally in a monarch whose every act must be countersigned by ministers promoted from the ranks of officialdom. Criticism of this monarchic-bureaucratic system came from many quarters —landed noblemen jealous of the power of their cousins in the administration, a small but growing class of entrepreneurs chafing under the government's paternalistic tutelage, peasants weighed down by the feudal burdens on their land. All these were clamoring for the reform of a parliament whose cumbrous quadricameral organization enabled the king and his ministers to defy the articulate wishes of the public. From the eighteen-twenties proposals for a reorganization of the estates recurred at session after session; yet the sponsors could rarely agree on a common plan, and when they did the clergy and the solid phalanx of officeholders within the nobility could be relied upon to save the day for the regime.

The events of 1848 on the European continent convinced even the king and his ministers of the need for parliamentary reform. Yet the government's bill, in 1850, failed to secure approval. Once again the riksdag justified the hopes of the chief author of the 1809 constitution, showing itself "wisely slow in action, but quick and firm in resistance."[7] When the youthful minister of state for justice, Baron Louis De Geer, in 1861 drew

---

[6] The phrase is that of Hans Järta, secretary of the constitutional committee of 1809, quoted in Hovde, op.cit., II, 217.

[7] Hans Järta in the report of the constitutional committee to the 1809 riksdag.

up another plan to replace the estates with two elective chambers, he had little hope that his proposal would fare any better. But whatever the prospects he was determined to make at least an attempt.

De Geer's reform bill evoked a public response of unprecedented dimensions. A vigorous debate was carried on in the press, by pamphlet, and at last in the riksdag itself. The traditionalists denounced the baron as a traitor to his class. Many others enthusiastically rallied to the support of "the best of ministries." When the bill came before the estates for final action in 1865 it was assured of overwhelming support among the burghers and peasants, while the clergy bitterly denounced it. The decision was in the hands of the nobility. In one of the most dramatic debates in the riksdag's history, the two sides marshalled the familiar arguments for and against reform in a supreme effort. On the morning of the fourth day of debate the chamber of nobles set the final vote for 2 p.m., well ahead of the normal adjournment time, to permit members to reach their homes safely. A contingent of troops was standing by in case an adverse decision should incite a riot among the waiting crowds. The precaution turned out to be unnecessary: by a vote of 361 to 294 the bill was passed. The next day the clergy meekly joined in the decision of the other estates.

A majority of the nobles, no doubt, had become convinced that the abolition of the estates was only a matter of time. De Geer's bill, moreover, was far from being a radical scheme. It recast the form of representation but largely preserved its content—the existing distribution of political power. Nevertheless, the decision of the estates in 1865 remains one of the rare occasions in history when a time-honored and powerful institution left the stage voluntarily, giving way to persuasion rather than violence or threatened violence.

If De Geer had been far too diffident about the prospects of reform, he had been far too sanguine in predicting its effects. A major count in his indictment of the estates concerned their division "into two almost equally powerful factions [i.e. nobility and clergy against burghers and peasants] which, out of estate interest and estate animosity, turn everything into a party question." If only the bill were passed he was sure that Sweden would henceforth be spared this bitter factionalism. "For as soon as different interests are not separated off one against the other, a general opinion on the more important questions often emerges among the majority both of the wealthy and the less wealthy, of the more and the less educated."[8] De Geer's hopes were utterly disappointed. It was only a few weeks after the opening of the bicameral riksdag that the first full-fledged party arose in its midst; and the pitched battle that ensued between the chambers proved fully as paralyzing as had been the bickering among the estates.

Political parties, moreover, had come to stay. When the parliamentary battle temporarily abated, in the eighteen-eighties, the representative system of 1866 itself had already come under attack, and soon the contest resumed with re-doubled intensity both within the riksdag and among the citizenry at large. Despite the acrimony of partisan feelings, the devolution of the system of 1866—the transition from oligarchy to democracy—was achieved peacefully, rather than by violence as in many other Continental countries. A series of broad compromises laid the foundations for a progressive further reconciliation of interests and views. Although recent decades have brought a steady growth and consolidation of party activity there has thus lately developed a degree of unity, a "common opinion on the more important questions" unheard of in De Geer's own day—if of a very different nature from what he had anticipated. This dialectic movement toward antago-nism and from antagonism to unity will provide one of the underlying themes of this and the following two chapters.

THE BICAMERAL REFORM OF 1865–1866

De Geer's parliament act created a more favorable soil for party growth than had the old estate system. The riksdag now met in regular annual session—instead of every three to five years—the king retaining the right to call special sessions at any time. The number of chambers was reduced from four to two. Previously elections had been held only among the peasants,

[8] Louis De Geer, *Minnen*, Stockholm: Norstedt, 1892, I, 222f., quoting his memorandum to the king of July 1861. Here and throughout this study passages quoted from works in languages other than English have been translated by the present writer unless it is otherwise indicated.

the burghers, and the lower clergy. The higher clergy had held their seats by virtue of their offices, the nobility by heredity.[9] Now the entire membership of the riksdag was recruited by election. While these party-promoting features of Swedish bicameralism have remained in effect to this day, certain party-retarding features of the original scheme persisted until the two parliamentary reforms of 1907–1909 and 1918–1921. The act of 1866 failed to remove the latent rivalry between the houses of parliament. The new distinction between upper and lower chamber coincided even more closely with differences of economic interest than did the old one between the estates. Furthermore, while the clergy and burghers on many issues had been able to mediate between the two extremes posited by nobility and peasantry, all intermediate units now were removed, and the antagonists hence were prone to clash with undeflected force. Above all, De Geer's bill did nothing to broaden the narrow oligarchic base of the riksdag and thus provided little new incentive for constituency organization. The intention, as the late Professor Kjellén once put it, had merely been to "translate the existing occupation [i.e. estate] categories into the positive arithmetic idiom of a tax franchise."[10] There was some redistribution of power among the traditional groups of enfranchised citizens. The power of the clergy, of the déclassé elements within the nobility, and of the artisans diminished; that of the landed aristocracy, the merchants, and especially of the larger farmers was enhanced. The bureaucracy retained its former key position, whereas the lower middle class and the proletariat, whether industrial or rural, remained disfranchised. A small part of the text, as a matter of fact, was

[9] The three degrees of nobility in Sweden—counts, barons, and untitled—pass to all members of the family. In the house of nobles, however, each family held only one seat. A rule of 1762 specified that this seat should be held by the head of the oldest branch, who could designate another nobleman of his own or any other family to take his place. This practice led to a lively traffic in proxies. Louis De Geer, a younger son of a junior branch of the Barons De Geer af Finspång, attended his first riksdag by virtue of a proxy bought at 50 riksdaler in the open market. The next time he represented his own family. *ibid.*, I, 135 f., 153.

[10] Rudolf Kjellén, "1866 och 1909," in *Historiska studier tillägnade Professor Harald Hjärne*, Uppsala: Almqvist & Wiksell, 1908 [*sic*], p. 681; cf. De Geer's own comment cited by Georg Andrén, "Tvåkammarsystemets tillkomst och utveckling," in *Sveriges riksdag, op.cit.*, IX, 61.

lost in the translation: the new electorate comprised a slightly smaller segment of the population than did the estates.[11]

De Geer has generally been considered the outstanding representative of nineteenth century liberalism in Sweden (or of "old liberalism," as this tendency later came to be called). The economic, legal, and humanitarian reforms of his great ministry (1858–1870) certainly earned him that title. De Geer himself also characterized his parliamentary reform bill as a "liberal" proposal,[12] and to the ultraconservative defenders of estate privilege any suggestion of representation of persons rather than status groups carried an unmistakable flavor of individualism. But De Geer's views of representation were completely at variance with those of the utilitarian liberals in Britain, of the liberal revolutionaries of 1848 on the Continent, or even of the so-called New Liberals who were soon to step forward in his own country. At a time when the Tory Disraeli was preparing a bill that was nearly to double the electorate, and the Prussian Junker Bismarck was about to write the principle of equal manhood suffrage into the constitution of his North German Confederation,[13] De Geer constructed a franchise that left four fifths of the adult male population without a voice even in the more popular chamber.

The upper house, according to the parliament act of 1866, was to be chosen by the provincial and municipal assemblies created by De Geer's local government ordinance of 1862. Although the total electorate of these bodies was about twice the size of that for the lower chamber,[14] each local voter was

[11] In 1872, 21.9 per cent of all males over twenty-one could vote for the lower chamber (Andrén, *op.cit.*, p. 205), whereas the proportion of adult males in the four estate categories had amounted to 26.2 per cent in 1845 (calculated from figures given by Gunnar Heckscher, "Några drag ur representationsfrågans sociala bakgrund," in *Festskrift till Professor skytteanus Axel Brusewitz*, Uppsala: Almqvist & Wiksell, 1941, p. 37). Andrén's figures (*op.cit.*, p. 13) indicate that the size of the nobility and clergy in relation to the total population was about the same in 1862 as in 1845.

[12] De Geer, *op.cit.*, I, 226.

[13] Cf. Charles Seymour and Donald Paige Frary, *How the World Votes*, Springfield, Mass.: C.A. Nichols, 1918, I, 138 (Britain), and Karl Braunias, *Das parlamentarische Wahlrecht*, Berlin: De Gruyter, 1932, I, 81f. (Germany).

[14] Compare the figures in Andrén, *op.cit.*, pp. 213f., 205.

given a number of votes in strict proportion to his taxable wealth. Corporations also were represented on the same basis and held about one fifth of the voting power.[15] All in all, the ingenious device of multiple votes conferred majority control within the local electorate upon its wealthiest sixteenth—or little more than 2 per cent of the adult male population.[16] Indirect elections naturally accentuated this plutocratic bias, and the unequal division of voting power tended to discourage the poor from using what little power they had. In the Stockholm elections of 1872, for instance, only 1 voter out of every 1,000 in the lowest tax bracket appeared at the polls, whereas participation among the wealthiest group was as high as 26 per cent.[17] Wholesale abstention of the poorer voters in this case magnified the political inequality between voters at the two extremes of the scale from a mere 100:1, as provided by law, to a staggering 26,000:1.

The electoral order for the newly created Swedish senate in its plutocratic logic thus went far beyond that for the Danish senate (1866), or even that of the Prussian *octroyé* constitution (1850) with its well-known three-class franchise.[18] From the time when Burke likened society to a joint stock company where "all men have equal rights; but not to equal things,"[19] few if any legislators have come as close as Louis De Geer to converting that off-handed simile into stark reality.

In retaining the restrictive popular base of the riksdag while remodelling its structure De Geer's main motive was expedi-

[15] Statistical data are available only for 1892 and 1904; in the latter year the voting power of corporations in rural and urban districts amounted to between 17.0 and 22.5 per cent of the total. *ibid.*, pp. 218f.

[16] Once again the figure refers to 1904; see *Bidrag till Sveriges officiella statistik*, vol. XVII, Stockholm, 1907, p. xvii. Two changes, their effects largely cancelling one another, had occurred since 1867: (1) The relative number of voters in the upper brackets had steadily increased. (2) A ceiling had been set on the number of votes any one person could cast. Thus the ratio of voting strength between the richest and the poorest voters was fixed at 100:1 for the cities (1869) and 5,000:1 for rural areas (1901); also no urban voter could cast more than 1/50 and no rural voter more than 1/10 of his district's vote.

[17] Andrén, *op.cit.*, p. 220.

[18] On these two systems see Braunias, *op.cit.*, I, 45, 110.

[19] Edmund Burke, *Reflections on the Revolution in France* (1790), Everyman's edn., p. 56.

ency. If his bill was to have any chance of passing it had to
leave political power largely in the hands of those who already
held it. For all his professed eagerness to overcome the old
class animosities within the riksdag, De Geer's bicameral plan
embodied the very mistakes of which he had warned so eloquently: It "separated off different interests" and "set them
one against the other"; far from letting "both chambers ema-
nate from the people as a whole," it created two "different
electorates of such nature that the one represented the higher
and the other the lower [classes] in society." And the result, as
De Geer himself had predicted of such a system, was to be the
"outbreak of most dangerous internal conflicts within society,"
which were to "divide the people and sap its strength."[20] The
striking contrast between De Geer's avowed intentions and his
actual accomplishment has been called "one of the inexplicable
ironies of history."[21] It has also been suggested that De Geer
had "little awareness of the true implications" of the system he
was creating, since he formulated his proposals before the
reassessment of landed properties of 1861 and the local government act of 1862 had been tested in practice, and since these
two measures were to determine the political character of the
senate.[22] Perhaps, however, the irony of the reform of 1866 was
ultimately due to its author's ambivalence. In his autobiography De Geer reveals himself as a liberal by conviction and a
conservative by temperament—a combination of opposites that
he himself found "rather peculiar."[23] His memorandum of 1861
on parliamentary reform clearly indicates that he was of two
minds about the matter. He stresses, almost in the same breath,
both his desire to overcome the traditional estate jealousies and
the necessity (as he saw it) of "securing a voice to education and
property" and of "preventing one-sided and rash decisions"
by instituting an effective bicameral check.[24] While the memo-

[20] The quotations are from De Geer's memorandum of 1861, *op.cit.*, I,
222–224.
[21] Hovde, *op.cit.*, II, 537; cf. E. H. Thörnberg, *Samhällsklasser och
politiska partier i Sverige*, Stockholm: Bonnier, 1917, p. 128.
[22] Edvard Thermænius, *Lantmannapartiet*, Uppsala: Almqvist & Wiksell, 1928, p. 32; cf. pp. 39, 431f.
[23] The phrase occurs several times, e.g. in *op.cit.*, I, 42, 57.
[24] *ibid.*, I, 224.

randum was largely written by De Geer the liberal, the final
bill was written almost entirely by De Geer the conservative.

AN OLIGARCHIC SYSTEM OF REPRESENTATION

The parliament act of 1866 in effect drew three concentric
circles, dividing the population into four groups whose power
varied inversely with their size. The first circle represented the
lower house franchise; outside of it were some four fifths of the
(adult male) population. The second circle, comprising those
taxpayers who by their multiple votes controlled the composition of the senate, covered only one tenth of the area of the
first. The third and smallest circle represented the stringent
income and property qualifications for candidates to the senate.
In 1872, only 6,000 citizens were fortunate enough to meet
these; by 1885 their number had doubled, yet there still were
fewer than 100 potential candidates for each senate seat.[25]

A member of the 1867 senate aptly described it as a "new
chamber of nobles"[26]—except that the nobility it represented
was one of wealth and office rather than of birth alone. Its roll
read like a pocket-size government almanac combined with a
who's who of big business and real estate: supreme court judges,
provincial governors, heads of administrative agencies, large
landowners, merchants, civil servants, and army officers. The
first farmer, euphemistically masquerading as a "landowner,"
appeared in the senate in 1872;[27] manual workers were not
represented until the beginning of the present century.

[25] Edvard Thermænius, "Riksdagspartierna," in *Sveriges riksdag*,
op.cit., XVII, 77 (for 1872), and *Bidrag till Sveriges officiella statistik*, vol.
VII:2, Stockholm, 1885, p. xviii (for 1885). Because senators served
without pay their average income in 1867 was twice the minimum amount
prescribed by law.

[26] For an occupational classification of the senate in 1867 and later
years see Andrén, *op.cit.*, p. 228, and *Studier över den svenska riksdagens
sociala sammansättning*, Uppsala: Almqvist & Wiksell, 1936, pp. 101 ff.
The quotation, from an unnamed senator, is found in the latter, p. 105.

[27] Thermænius, *Lantmannapartiet, op.cit.*, p. 362. The Swedish language affords a long list of synonyms for "farmer" conveying a variety of
nuances. The term *godsägare*, somewhat inadequately rendered in this
study as "(large) landowner," refers to the social status of the owner—
his aristocratic or bourgeois origin—rather than to the size of his holdings. *Bonde*, which is the most commonly used term, and even more the

The lower chamber of 1867, by contrast, was a continuation, in diluted form, of the old chamber of peasants. The requirements for voters (ownership of land valued at 1,000 riksdaler or an annual taxable income of 800 riksdaler from sources other than land) were designed to accommodate all those formerly represented in the estates—and among these the farmers constituted an overwhelming majority. The electoral law, however, took away with one hand what it gave with the other: by assigning 1 representative to the towns and cities for every 10,000 and to the rural areas for every 40,000 inhabitants, it gave to the townspeople an influence in the lower chamber out of all proportion to their numbers within either the population or the electorate.[28] The pronounced cleavage between urban and farming interests, which had found periodic expression in conflicts between the chamber of peasants and the other three estates, thus persisted throughout the early bicameral period and, in attenuated form, until the reforms of 1907–1909. With equal districting the farmers would probably have occupied a majority of lower chamber seats after every election; as things stood they did so only once, in 1881. With 76 seats in a chamber of 190 the farmers in 1867 still furnished the largest single bloc, to which a contingent of 23 large landowners must be added. Most of the remaining seats went to public servants (including judges and university professors), to merchants and industrialists, and to a handful of professional persons. Once again the tenant farmers, farm laborers, and industrial workers were excluded altogether.[29]

collective noun *allmoge*, carry a connotation of lower class status; hence *bondeståndet* has been translated as "peasantry" or "chamber of peasants." *Hemmansägare* (homesteader) and *lantbrukare* or *jordbrukare* (agriculturist) are socially neutral terms. The first two today are used in the riksdag directory. A farmer with a university education, however, may call himself an *agronom*. *Lantman*, the term adopted by the Ruralist party, finally, connotes residence in the country rather than any particular occupation. Only two of the dozen or so farmer senators of the late nineteenth century called themselves *hemmansägare* (*ibid.*). The mere fact that they were courageous enough to do so heralded a social revolution.

[28] Andrén, *op.cit.*, pp. 46–130, gives a detailed analysis of the provisions concerning elections in the parliament act of 1866.

[29] The above list is based on *Studier över den svenska riksdagens sociala sammansättning, op.cit.*, p. 132; the same work gives comparable data for later years. An exact classification is complicated by, among other things,

The bureaucratic oligarchy of the eighteenth century, by virtue of the coup of 1809, had survived the impact of the French Revolution. De Geer's conservative reform brought oligarchy up to date by substituting property for status. It laid the foundations for an alliance between bureaucracy, landed wealth, and industry. The conservative order in Sweden now could rely for support on those upper middle class elements which earlier in England and France had spearheaded the advance of liberalism. De Geer's reform may be compared in its effects to Bismarck's conservative unification of Germany. Bismarck broke the back of the German liberal movement, converting its most numerous section to "National Liberalism." De Geer, facing a situation in which an organized liberal movement did not yet exist, postponed its advent by a generation.[30] Yet, despite some resemblances between late nineteenth century oligarchy in Sweden and the Hohenzollern Empire in Germany, the analogy does not carry too far. The vigorous opposition of the farmers in Sweden was to compensate in some measure for the absence of organized liberalism; and when a Liberal party did appear some decades later it recruited its followers chiefly from the lower middle classes and derived added strength from cooperation with the nascent socialist movement. The Swedish ruling class, long trained in the constitutional exercise of power, in the end was willing to renounce its position by degrees before an open clash became inevitable. Above all, in a country where industry has only recently displaced agriculture as the chief sustenance of the population, and where industrial units have remained small—a country without religious cleavages or memories of internal war—political conflict has at no point reached the degree of intensity and bitterness common in Germany and elsewhere.

---

the terminological problems touched upon in note 27 supra. Hence the figures vary from one work to another, and even within the same book; see, e.g., Andrén, *op.cit.*, p. 225, and Thermænius, *Lantmannapartiet*, *op.cit.*, pp. 440, 449.

[30] The failure of the New Liberal experiment of 1869 (see infra) clearly indicated that it was premature.

THE RURALIST PARTY

The first full-fledged parliamentary party was formed by the farmers in the lower house, and the relative disadvantage at which the electoral law put them may well have been an important factor in this turn of events. Neither the ruling oligarchy in the senate nor the handful of middle class representatives and farmers who from time to time strayed into that chamber were ready for party organization. Each group was united by ties of social status, economic interest, and political view; yet the oligarchy by its numbers was assured of control while the middle class representatives and farmers were so few as to be condemned to impotence. The farmers in the lower chamber, on the other hand, commanded just slightly less than a majority. If they held together and attracted some additional support they could hope to carry the decisive votes in the chamber.

Like many other parties the new group adopted a name invented by its opponents. On March 11, 1867 it presented itself to the public with a formal statement under the heading "The so-called 'Ruralist party' [*Lantmannapartiet*] in the lower chamber submits, as its adopted program, the following."[31] The very first points that followed contained, in pithy and circumspect language, the goals that were to guide Ruralist policy for decades to come: Reorganization of the country's defense, equalization of the tax burden, and strict economy with public funds.

The first two of these require some explanation. Both the organization of the armed forces and the collection of government revenue in Sweden were at the time based on an intricate pattern that dated back to the Middle Ages and had undergone little change since the late seventeenth century.[32] Its most notable feature was that it imposed liability to military service

[31] Reproduced in Thermænius, *Lantmannapartiet, op.cit.*, plate facing p. 447; cf. p. 173. The name *Lantmannapartiet* survived the split and reunification of the party (1888 and 1895) and even its final demise (1912). Its heirs, the lower chamber Conservatives, until 1935 officially called themselves *Lantmanna- och borgareparti*.

[32] For a systematic account of the military and fiscal systems and their devolution in the nineteenth century see Fredrik Lagerroth, *Indelnings- och grundskatteväsendets avveckling*, Lund: Gleerup, 1927.

and to a variety of taxes on the owners (or tenants) of certain categories of land. The so-called system of subdivisions (*indelningsverket*) was the main basis of military recruitment. The farms in most parts of the country were grouped into sectors of roughly equal size and productivity, and the farmers in each sector were required to furnish one soldier and to provide him in lieu of pay with enough land to sustain himself and his family. This military burden fell unevenly on the farmers in different provinces, and the scheme did not extend to some of the most fertile regions. Throughout the country, moreover, all land owned by the nobility was exempt from the subdivision system; in return noblemen traditionally supplied the bulk of the officer corps. Since in the course of time much land originally owned by the nobles had been leased or bought by commoners, this exemption further accentuated the existing inequalities. The subdivided soldiery until the end of the nineteenth century constituted the core of the Swedish army, whose ranks were supplemented by hired soldiers and conscripts. But since the conscription law provided for only a short training period (fixed at twelve days in 1812, and at thirty days in 1858), the conscripts accounted only for a fraction of the forces on active duty. The tax system was equally archaic. Traditionally most land taxes (including the rent for farms that were on the royal domains) had been payable in kind. Their conversion into money payments was not completed until 1869, and even after that many of these levies were not collected centrally by the state treasury. Instead they had been "permanently assigned" as salary to army officers and other government officials in the area where they were due.

Abolition of the military system of subdivisions and the fiscal system of tax assignment, both of which weighed heavily upon the farmers as a class and very unevenly upon individual farmers, remained the major demand of the Ruralist party throughout its undivided existence. Quite understandably, the party was also skeptical of the economic policies of the De Geer government which had liberated the merchants and manufacturers from fettering restrictions but had done little to emancipate the farmers. A group of former peasant estate representatives, led by Carl Ifvarsson, made up the nucleus of the party. But the Ruralists also became a natural rallying point for other opponents of the De Geer regime. Protectionist squires heartily approved of the party's cautious opposition to the cabinet's free-trade policies. Progressive liberals saw in it a movement that would work for political and social reforms on all fronts. Emil Key, a liberal journalist and landowner who was the chief author of the Ruralist program, was as ardent an advocate of improved public education as he was of the removal of the semifeudal burdens on farm land. The party's program also demanded the equalization of the local franchise, and August Blanche, the chief spokesman for the political radicals in the capital, was one of its early members. It was significant that Key tried to preempt for his movement the name of New Liberal party—which was subsequently adopted by a rival group. One of the Ruralist cofounders, finally, and, together with Ifvarsson and Key its most prominent leader in the eighteen-seventies, was Count Arvid Posse, who had been among the most determined ultraconservative opponents of the parliament act. His association with the Ruralists stemmed largely from personal ambition and the old aristocrat's personal hatred of Louis De Geer, whom he considered a tool of the victorious bourgeoisie.[33]

Despite these heterogeneities, the new party managed to preserve a degree of unity and discipline unequalled by any other group during the nineteenth century. "A name, a program, a group of energetic leaders, frequent meetings, ... the very fact that it dared to defy established prejudices ... by stepping forward publicly as a party—all these factors gave the Ruralist party a strength, a stability, and a continuity attained by no other party during this period."[34]

MINISTERIALS AND NEW LIBERALS

Although less successful in their organizational efforts, the Ruralists' rivals had not been idle. Anticipating the move of the opposition, supporters of the De Geer government had set up

---

[33] On the party's personnel see Thermænius, *Lantmannapartiet, op.cit.*, pp. 181 ff. On Key in particular see his memoirs, edited by his daughter, the well-known feminist author Ellen Key, *Minnen av och om Emil Key*, 3 vols., Stockholm: Bonnier, 1915–1917, and Erik Hedén, *Politiska essayer*, Stockholm: Tiden, 1927, pp. 119–142.

[34] Thermænius, "Riksdagspartierna," *op.cit.*, p. 44.

a rudimentary organization as soon as the first session of the new riksdag got under way in January 1867. One reason for quick action was the committee elections, scheduled for the first week of the session. The new parliament act had left intact the power of the traditional joint standing committees,[35] and since each chamber elected its committee members by simple majority, the stakes were high. Throughout the following decades the annual committee elections remained one of the chief incentives for party formation and party discipline in parliament. It soon became clear, however, that the Ministerials were even less homogeneous than the Ruralists. The large merchants, high officials, and aristocratic landowners supported both De Geer's extreme economic liberalism and his cautious political conservatism. But the party also included a few urban middle class members whose liberalism was primarily political and of a far more radical temper than De Geer's, and a large number of farmers who, appreciative as they were of the political gains that the new parliamentary regime had brought, were intent upon consolidating and expanding these. The party's chief weakness was lack of leadership. Louis De Geer, who dubbed this group "Ministerials *'quand même,'*"[36] was not available for that role; true to his personal ideals of political harmony and in deference to public notions of separation of powers and a government above the factions, he studiously avoided all direct contact with any of the political groupings in either chamber.

After only a year the urban radicals and some of the farmers split off from the Ministerials to found the New Liberal party (1868). Its program included such demands as manhood suffrage for the lower chamber, lifting of the tax qualifications for parliamentary candidates, and per diems for senators; strengthened parliamentary control over the administration; abolition of the multiple voting scale in local elections and greater local and provincial self-government; and increasing separation of church and state (specifically, secular education and civil instead of religious marriage).[37] The most prominent leader of the new group, Adolf Hedin, was a lifelong admirer of French liber-

---

[35] See chapter VI infra.
[36] *op.cit.*, II, 47.
[37] Thermænius, "Riksdagspartierna," *op.cit.*, pp. 46f.

alism, and all of the party's demands were frankly liberal-democratic in the Western European sense of those terms. Several months earlier Hedin, in a pamphlet entitled "What the People Expect of the New Representation," had elaborated on many of the same points. Pleading for the establishment of a "progressive" party, he had denounced the ruling "bureaucracy," as well as the prevailing "coercion of conscience and priestly power," and, in conclusion, ridiculed the monarchy itself: "... *la monarchie, c'est une affaire de la liste civile.* The only question is whether we can afford the expense of satisfying this romantic-poetic hankering."[38]

The Ruralists, because of their superior organization and the split within the Ministerial ranks, easily carried the committee elections of 1868. They were to retain their majority position for fully two decades. The conservative wing of the Ministerials now became known, in the facetious phrase of its antagonists, as "the Intelligence"; yet the resulting three-party system survived for only a few years. The New Liberals submitted their major program planks in a series of bills at the 1869 and 1870 sessions—among them one by Anders Wilhelm Uhr that would have extended the suffrage to all men over twenty-one years of age. In view of the composition of the chambers it was no surprise that all these were rejected—some without any debate or even a formal vote. A more serious setback was the party's failure in the 1869 elections to increase its representation in the lower chamber beyond the dozen or so mandates it previously held—and this despite attempts to set up branch organizations throughout the country and to conduct a systematic election campaign in the larger urban centers. Under the impact of the question of defense reorganization, which by 1871 became the overshadowing issue in Swedish politics, the New Liberal group dissolved altogether. Its leader, Hedin, favored a system of conscription as the only means of transforming the old royal army into a truly popular force. Despite his democratic premise, his conclusion on this concrete issue was, as we shall see, quite close to that of the conservatives. While Hedin took the logical step of joining the Intelligence, most of the

[38] The pamphlet is reprinted in Hedin's *Tal och skrifter*, ed. Valfrid Spångberg, 2 vols., Stockholm: Bonnier, 1904–1915, I, 1–57. For the quotations see pp. 4, 8, 20, and 57.

farmers in his party, and even some of his urban associates, put the abolition of the old feudal military system above the creation of a new popular one and hence aligned with the Ruralists.

BICAMERAL TENSION

Throughout the eighteen-seventies the lower chamber was thus divided into only two parties. The Ruralist majority now included all the farmers in the chamber, many of its large landowners, and a few urban radicals. The minority was more loosely organized, first as the Intelligence and after 1873 as the Center. Here was the political home of nearly all the urban and upper class representatives, from the most radical journalists to the most conservative bureaucrats, businessmen, and large landowners.[39] But the major antagonists in the defense question were not these two groups in the lower house, but rather its dominant Ruralist faction on the one hand and the solidly conservative senate on the other. The senators, who considered the existing subdivision system totally inadequate to the needs of the country's defense, could be counted upon to support the persistent efforts of the cabinet to supplement it with a larger contingent of conscripts. The Ruralists were not averse to conscription—this was, as a matter of fact, the solution they had proposed in their own program of 1867. But they balked at any extension of universal training that did not go hand in hand with a reduction—or better yet, total abolition—of the subdivision and land tax systems. It was between these two camps that the Center tried to mediate.

The Franco-Prussian War of 1870–1871 sharpened the conflict over military reorganization. To the conservatives it served as a vivid reminder of the extreme urgency of strengthening the defense system. The farmers tended to draw a contrary conclusion. Sweden by 1870 had been at peace for over half a century. She had been a neutral in the war of the Western powers against Russia (1854–1856), and Bismarck's three successive wars had left her untouched, even though the first had been directed against her immediate neighbor Denmark. All these considerations tended to reinforce the latent isolationism of the farmers. It became their "profound conviction...that

[39] Thermænius, "Riksdagspartierna," *op.cit.*, pp. 58 ff.

31

the long period of peace which our country had already enjoyed would continue indefinitely if only the Swedes kept quiet on their peninsula and did not meddle in affairs that were none of their business."[40] They were the less inclined to shoulder conscription as a third burden in addition to subdivision and land taxes.

Since any military reform required the consent of both the Ruralist lower house and the conservative senate a prolonged deadlock was inevitable. Louis De Geer (who in the meantime had resigned the premiership), together with a number of other moderate senators, persuaded his chamber to agree to a gradual liquidation both of the subdivision system and of the land taxes if the lower chamber majority would in return consent to a substantial extension of conscription.[41] But the resulting compromise (1873) merely stated the principles upon which a solution should be sought. When it came to translating it into specific legislation the chambers, each distrusting the other's intention, resumed their feud. A vacillating ministry, the absence of party organization in the senate, and lack of discipline among the Ruralists compounded the difficulty. The senate in 1874 caused the resignation of one prime minister by rejecting a subsidiary proposal connected with defense reform. When his successor the following year revised the bill in accordance with the senate's wishes, the latter reversed itself, and another cabinet crisis resulted. The riksdag rejected a government proposal for a conscript army with a 10½-month training period (1875). Nor did De Geer, back at the helm in 1875, succeed in breathing life into his own proposal. The Ruralists voted down a bill providing for only 62 days of training combined with a 10 per cent reduction in the obligations under the subdivision and land tax systems (1877). To prove their sincerity, the Ruralists took the unprecedented step of submitting a series of bills, signed by 102 private members, which contained their detailed counterproposals: a volunteer army to replace the old subdivisions, supplemented by conscripts whose training period would gradually be increased to 90 days; and a uniform real estate levy to replace the traditional land taxes. But the ministry was skeptical of the technical merits of these

---

[40] Thermænius, *Lantmannapartiet*, *op.cit.*, p. 241.
[41] For De Geer's own account see *op.cit.*, II, 141 ff.

bills and in any case was fearful lest the lower chamber should arrogate to itself the ministry's privilege of initiating major legislation. This cool reception from the ministry combined with outright hostility from the senate to thwart the Ruralists' plans (1878). Their own efforts disdained, the Ruralists in turn killed a conscription bill which De Geer submitted separately, thus causing his second (and final) resignation (1880).[42]

After fully a decade of attempts at solving the thorny defense and land tax questions, all of which had run head on into the irreconcilable opposition between senate and Ruralists, the king finally appointed Count Arvid Posse, the aristocratic cofounder of the Ruralists, to the premiership. Although only four of the eleven old ministers remained in office, Posse's ministry was composed, in the conventional manner, of aristocratic officials, army officers, and landowners, and hence was in no sense a Ruralist party cabinet. Nor did Posse succeed in carrying the Ruralists along in support of his own defense bill (1883). It was not until 1885 that his second successor, Robert Themptander, obtained the consent of both chambers to an extension of army training to 42 days, a transfer of 30 per cent of the costs of the subdivision system from the farmers to the state treasury, and a similar reduction of the land taxes.

THE NATURE OF THE EARLY PARTIES

Throughout the first period of party history in Sweden, partisan organization was confined to parliament and within parliament to the lower chamber. A plutocratic franchise still excluded the bulk of the population from any kind of political participation, and the electorate was as apathetic as it was diminutive. The early parties thus had no call for elaborate constituency organizations or systematic election campaigns: the few hundred active voters in the average district could easily be reached by more informal means. Under an optional clause of the electoral law, moreover, a majority of rural constituencies as late as 1875 chose their deputies by indirect vote—a method which discouraged participation among the primary voters and

[42] See Edvard Thermænius, "Ministärskiftet den 19 april 1880," in *Statsvetenskapliga studier*, Uppsala: Almqvist & Wiksell, 1944, pp. 571–606.

threw the ultimate selection of representatives into small bodies of only a few dozen secondary electors.[43] The major political contrast within the lower chamber electorate was that between urban and rural interests, and the strict separation of urban and rural districts therefore further reduced the need for political organization: the real antagonists did not meet on the hustings. Even in parliament, political alignments remained loose and shifting. The social and political distance between the squires, industrialists, and aristocratic officials in the senate, on the one hand, and the farmers and urban middle class representatives in the lower house, on the other, precluded any effective political cooperation between members of the two chambers. During the defense controversy in the eighteen-seventies the Ruralists tried to gain a foothold in the senate. But the absence of a salary for senators made it difficult to find suitable candidates even where a provincial assembly included a solid majority of farmers. The much-debated Ruralist "annex" in the upper chamber remained "fairly fictitious."[44] On the more important political questions, therefore, chamber stood against chamber, not party against party. The members of the ruling oligarchy in the senate occasionally formed *ad hoc* groups in the pursuit of specific legislative aims—e.g. for and against the compromise of 1873—but these combinations hardly deserved the name of political parties. The incoherence and instability of political groupings, together with the sharp cleavage between the chambers, also made any form of parliamentary cabinet government impossible. In all these respects the next phases of party development brought about incisive changes.

[43] The average number of *potential* voters per lower chamber mandate in 1872 was 1,500 for rural and 470 for urban districts; since participation in the rural areas was even lower than in the city, the average number of *actual* voters for either type of district was about 200 (calculated from figures in Andrén, *op.cit.*, pp. 205, 364). On the gradual transition from indirect to direct elections see *ibid.*, pp. 105 ff., 211. A sampling of twenty constituencies in the 1866 election where farmers ran against gentlemen — that is, of relatively hotly fought contests — shows that these were decided by electoral colleges consisting of from 17 to 53 persons. One representative owed his seat to only 7 electors. Thermænius, *Lantmannapartiet, op.cit.*, p. 438.

[44] Thermænius, *Lantmannapartiet, op.cit.*, p. 362.

THE TARIFF DISPUTE

The eighteen-seventies saw a continuous decline of prices on the world market, and the adoption of protective tariffs in Germany and other countries accelerated the downward trend. In Sweden agriculture felt the pinch of the depression most acutely. The wholesale price for wheat between 1881 and 1887 fell by 46 per cent, that for rye by 48 per cent.[45] The loudest cries for tariff protection, therefore, came from squires and large farmers who produced grain for the home market but could not compete with the flood of cheap foreign cereals. The Themptander government (1884–1888) firmly opposed these demands; yet the protectionists had hopes of winning the riksdag for their cause. Nor did they have to fear that traditional stumbling block to legislative action, intercameral disagreement. The parliament act of 1866 allowed the two chambers to settle questions of revenue and expenditure by a joint vote.[46] The shift of political attention to a financial question, such as the tariff, therefore had broad political implications. A minority in one chamber would no longer be without influence as long as it could join forces with a majority in the other. Since every vote in parliament counted, electoral campaigning promised to be far more rewarding than ever before. In 1885 protectionists from both chambers held the first of a series of joint caucuses to coordinate their strategy. That same year a protectionist league and a rival Association against a Tariff on Foodstuffs carried the dispute to the country at large. The battle was joined in the spring of 1887 when Premier Themptander dissolved the lower house to prevent an impending joint-vote victory for the tariff forces.[47]

Both the dissolution elections of April 1887 and the regular lower chamber elections the following September were fought with unprecedented intensity. In previous lower chamber elections only one out of every four or five potential voters had cast his ballot. The contest in the spring of 1887, on the other hand, brought nearly half the electorate to the polls—a level

---

[45] See [Stockholm, Högskolan, Socialvetenskapliga Institutet,] *Wages, Cost of Living and National Income in Sweden, 1860–1930*, London: P. S. King, 1933–1937, vol. III, part II, p. 53.

[46] See chapter VI, infra.

[47] Thermænius, "Riksdagspartierna," *op.cit.*, pp. 70 ff., and Torsten Petré, *Ministären Themptander*, Uppsala: Almqvist & Wiksell, 1945.

THE POLITICS OF COMPROMISE

of political interest not again reached until the height of the
suffrage controversy two decades later.[48] In both elections of
1887 the free-traders obtained a clear majority of the popular
vote, although the second time a legal freak turned their victory
into defeat. The city of Stockholm, one of the main strongholds
of free-trade sentiment, was entitled to twenty-two representatives, all of them elected at large by plurality. In September
1887 the free-trade list included one candidate who several
years earlier had been in arrears by a small amount with his
tax payments and hence was technically not eligible to run.
Similar irregularities had not been uncommon before but had
generally gone unnoticed.[49] This time, with partisan tempers
running high, the protectionists brought suit, the courts in-
validated all votes cast for the free-trade candidates, and the
slate of the minority faction was seated. It was this windfall of
twenty-two votes in the lower chamber that enabled the protectionists to pass a tariff bill in 1888. While the incident caused
bitter resentment among the liberals in the capital, it merely
precipitated a protectionist victory that would have come sooner
or later in any case. When the free-traders in 1890 recaptured
their lower chamber majority, the tariff supporters commanded
a wide enough margin in the senate to carry any joint votes.

The tariff dispute led to a complete realignment of forces
within the riksdag.[50] Although an import duty on cereals was
an agrarian demand, the Ruralist party was far from unanimous
on the question. Small farmers who did not produce a surplus
and larger landowners who specialized in animal products had
nothing to gain from the proposed tariff and were generally
opposed to it.[51] For several years the aging Carl Ifvarsson,
himself a free-trader, tried to keep peace in the party by having
it assume a position of complete neutrality. But as one of his
protectionist friends was quick to remind him, "a party . . .

[48] Participation, as usual, was higher in urban than in rural districts —
62.9 and 44.4 per cent respectively; the national average was 48.1 per cent.
See Andrén, *op.cit.*, p. 205; cf. the detailed examination of election
returns by Elis Håstad, "Tullstridens val och folkmeningen," in *Festskrift
till professor skytteanus Axel Brusewitz, op.cit.*, pp. 105–153.
[49] Hugo Hamilton, *Hågkomster*, Stockholm: Bonnier, 1928, pp. 202f.
[50] Thermænius, "Riksdagspartierna," *op.cit.*, pp. 96–130.
[51] G. A. Montgomery, *The Rise of Modern Industry in Sweden*, London:
P. S. King, 1939, pp. 145 ff.

36

cannot remain neutral in such a big and important question" as the tariff had become.[52] By 1888 the split among the Ruralists was beyond repair. The protectionist wing joined with a substantial contingent of landed squires and urban protectionists (including the twenty-two Stockholmers) to form a "New Ruralist party." There was no corresponding consolidation among the free-traders in the lower house: both the urban Center party and the free-trade wing of the Ruralists (now known as the "Old Ruralist party") retained their separate identities. But the senate at last gave up its cavalier disregard for the imperatives of political organization. For most of the past decade (1877–1887) the upper house had nominated its committee delegates by general agreement among the various factions and elected them by acclamation; now free-traders and protectionists each ran their own lists. The tariff forces in 1888 set up a regular party organization including a chairman, an executive committee, and a committee on committee nominations. The leadership enforced a certain amount of discipline and saw to it that members of the opposition and wavering party members lost their committee posts. Through its election committee, founded in 1890, the Protectionist party undertook a successful campaign within the provincial assemblies to insure the election of pro-tariff senators.[53] As a result, the party which had had in 1888 a margin of only 10 votes had rolled up by 1894 a crushing majority of 114 votes out of 148.

A CONSERVATIVE TRIUMPH

The protectionist victory of 1887–1888 for the first time created the possibility of a strong cabinet based on stable parliamentary support. At the very least the government would have to give up the isolation from the factions in the riksdag that it had maintained since De Geer's days. Themptander's free-trade ministry resigned in December 1887, but the king

[52] Nils Pettersson i Runtorp, cited by Thermænius, "Riksdagspartierna," op.cit., p. 97.

[53] See Arne Wåhlstrand, "Första kammarens valnämnd 1890–1910," in Statsvetenskapliga studier, op.cit., pp. 619–678; on the electoral activities of lower chamber protectionists during the same period see Harald Wigforss, "Fosterländska förbundet," Statsvetenskaplig tidskrift, 35:219–244 (1932).

refused to let the entire cabinet go at once. As on similar occasions, Oscar II (who ruled from 1872 to 1907) tenaciously
clung to the fiction of a strict separation of executive and
legislative powers. He could not keep his ministers in office in
the face of parliamentary adversity; but he resented any interference with his appointment power. At one time, when the
press carried rumors that Archbishop Anton Niklas Sundberg
had declined a commission to form a ministry, the king issued
an irate denial in the official gazette. Neither Sundberg, he declared, nor any one else for that matter, had ever been offered
such a commission; for any such procedure would be in clear
violation of the constitution. Sundberg, the king insisted, had
been offered the post of minister of state and had declined that
office only. Yet "The very fact that the king considered it necessary to issue such a statement goes to show to what extent the
position he asserted had actually been undermined."[54] Although
the king generally preferred to reconstitute his cabinets during
the parliamentary recess, the tariff crisis was serious enough to
rule out such delaying maneuvers. In February 1888 the king appointed a mixed ministry of protectionists and free-traders
headed by the veteran court official Baron Gillis Bildt. In the
fall of 1889 he replaced the remaining free-trade ministers with
protectionists and Bildt with the more vigorous Count Gustaf
Åkerhielm. Two years later the premiership went to Erik
Gustaf Boström, one of the founders of the New Ruralist party
and known as its most astute tactician.

When Boström took over the cabinet the Protectionists held
a firm majority in the senate, while the lower house was split
into three groups of almost equal strength—the New Ruralists
(composed of rural and urban protectionists), the Old Ruralists
(rural free-traders), and the Centrists (urban free-traders).
Boström's personal background fitted him admirably for the
task of multilateral mediation posed by this parliamentary
situation: his father had been a patrician in a provincial town,
from his mother he had inherited an aristocratic estate, and his
political convictions had made him a member of a party com-

[54] Gunnar Hesslén, *Den svenska parlamentarismens uppkomst*, Stockholm: Norstedt, 1940, p. 14. On Oscar II's policy with regard to cabinet
appointments cf. Leif Kihlberg, *Den svenska ministären under ståndsriksdag
och tvåkammarsystem*, Uppsala: Almqvist & Wiksell, 1922, pp. 492 ff.

posed predominantly of farmers. He was, above all, an ardent admirer of the Hohenzollern Empire and its Iron Chancellor.[55] Once in office Boström, like Bismarck, took care to make himself independent of the political groups in the legislature— including his own former associates—and proceeded to play off one against another. Again like Bismarck, he governed with the support of a solidly conservative upper chamber and a shifting combination of parties in the lower. It is for these reasons, no doubt, that a historian of Swedish cabinet government has characterized Boström's attitude toward the riksdag with a Bismarckian metaphor as that of an "honest broker."[56] The premier's diplomatic talents served him equally well in his contacts with Oscar II. Without in the least arousing the monarch's constitutional susceptibilities, he made himself sufficiently indispensable so that his wishes prevailed in the selection of ministers—and Boström's changing tactics made necessary personnel changes within the chancellery on an unprecedented scale.[57]

Several major pieces of legislation during the early part of Boström's premiership served to cement the recent alliance between upper class and agrarian interests. (1) With the support of the protectionist joint-vote majority (composed of the senate Majority party and the New Ruralists in the lower house) Boström increased the level of import duties on industrial products. The tariff of 1888 had provided for a number of such duties, but at that time a trade agreement with France, which had a few more years to run, stood in the way of further increases. When the treaty expired in 1892 the way was clear for more extensive tariff protection for industry. (2) At a special session of the riksdag that same year, Boström finally found a solution to the perennial questions of defense reorganization and tax reform. His proposals followed the lines of the compromises of 1873 and 1885, and they received some support

[55] See Hjalmar Haralds' biography, *E. G. Boström*, Stockholm: Bonnier, 1907, pp. 29, 53, and passim.

[56] Kihlberg, *op.cit.*, p. 497. Bismarck had used the phrase to describe Germany's role at the Congress of Berlin in 1878.

[57] Only one of his nine colleagues retained his portfolio throughout the nine years and two months of Boström's first premiership (1891–1900). During this same period five of the ministries had three, the finance ministry as many as four, different incumbents.

from all the major political groups in the legislature: conservative senators and urban free-traders interested in a strong army, and Ruralists (Old and New) eager to do away with the subdivision and land tax systems. Boström's bill extended the training period to 90 days and transferred from the farmers to the government the cost of recruiting and maintaining the subdivided soldiery. That portion of the land taxes which had remained in effect after the reduction of 1885 was to be reduced further by 10 per cent every other year, so that the old levies would disappear altogether at the end of twenty years. With this, the old dispute was finally laid to rest. Neither side had won a full victory, but the conservatives had obtained a strengthened army based mainly on conscription, and the farmers were at last relieved of their old burdens. (3) Agrarian representatives in both houses agreed to an amendment to the parliament act which put a ceiling on the relative strength of urban representation in the lower house. The act of 1866 had favored the cities, and as a result of the country's progressive urbanization their share of lower chamber seats had steadily increased since that time. The new apportionment rules (first adopted in 1892 and ratified in 1894) fixed the number of urban and rural seats at approximately the current ratio. While the cities lost nothing for the moment, this meant that their margin of overrepresentation would diminish as their share of the population increased.[58]

POLITICAL REPERCUSSIONS OF THE TARIFF

The tariff question, like the earlier defense and land tax issues, had given rise to a conflict between a higher and a lower social stratum; yet an important change of fronts had occurred. In the earlier struggle the farmers and the bureaucratic-agrarian-industrial oligarchy were the chief protagonists, the urban and rural working class mere bystanders. The tariff, on

[58] In 1866 the cities elected 28.9 per cent of the lower chamber, and in 1893, 36.4 per cent; their share in the population rose from 13.0 per cent in 1870 to 18.8 in 1890. The amendment limited the chamber to 230 representatives, 150 rural and 80 urban, so that the cities' share was frozen at 34.8 per cent. By the time these rules were superseded by the suffrage reform of 1909 the cities still were substantially overrepresented, for their population in 1910 amounted to only 24.8 per cent of the total.

the other hand, created a common bond of interest between some of the former enemies—notably the large farmers and the landed squires and industrialists. It also directly concerned the disfranchised and hitherto politically disinterested groups of the population. The events of this period therefore had far-reaching implications.

First, the political unity of the farmers as a class was irretrievably lost. The very victory they had won with the liquidation of the land tax and subdivision systems removed the common grievance upon which their solidarity had rested.[59] Neither the reunited Ruralists of 1895 nor the modern Agrarians were to recapture the undivided loyalty of the agricultural population.

Second, the tariff dispute brought to a close the first period of agrarian radicalism in Sweden and inaugurated a pattern of agrarian-conservative cooperation that was to persist until the depression of the early nineteen-thirties. The Ruralists of Key's and Ifvarsson's generation saw their fight for defense and tax reforms as part of a larger struggle against age-old injustices; the reunited Ruralists under Olof Jonsson were politically saturated and averse to major changes in the *status quo*. Even those farmers who later joined the Liberal party stood far to the right of the urban Liberals on such crucial issues as suffrage and social reform. The dwindling of the share of agriculture in the national economy may have been one of the underlying reasons for the adoption of a more defensive position. This conversion of the Ruralists differentiates Swedish party developments from those in Denmark and Norway, and thus accounts for the paradox that the liberal-agrarian movement of the nineteenth century became the lineal ancestor of the Conservatives in Sweden, the Agrarians in Denmark, and the Liberals in Norway.[60]

The third—and by far the most important—consequence of the tariff dispute was the political interest that it stimulated.

[59] Thörnberg, *op.cit.*, p. 9.

[60] See Dankwart A. Rustow, "Scandinavia," in Sigmund Neumann, ed., *Modern Political Parties*, Chicago: University of Chicago Press, 1956. On the relations between the Ruralists and the Danish and Norwegian Left see the concluding chapter in Thermænius, *Lantmannapartiet, op.cit.*

Surveying the Swedish panorama of the late nineteenth century, a prominent Swedish political scientist has noted that "the major impression [is] one of political stagnation. In no other country whose population had attained a comparable degree of education does there appear to have been so little interest in the major issues of national policy."[61] Toward the turn of the century Sweden was at last awakening from its hibernation. The parliamentary champions of free trade had the firm support of the disfranchised working class, for whom the tariff meant higher bread and meat prices. While the tariff had helped overcome the conflict within the bicameral system created by De Geer, it lent new urgency to the demand for suffrage reform which soon was to undermine that structure altogether. Politics no longer was the exclusive prerogative of the ruling oligarchy and the large farmers, and controversy was beginning to flow over from the lobbies and boudoirs into the market place.

[61] Herbert Tingsten, "Demokratiens seger och kris," in *Vår egen tids historia*, Stockholm: Bonnier, 1933, I, 574.

CHAPTER II

THE VICTORY OF DEMOCRACY

WITH the abolition of the estates one of the major obstacles to parliamentary party organization had been removed. National parties, however, were a by-product of the struggle for universal suffrage, and in Sweden this demand was asserted much later than in other European countries. There was an adequate niche within De Geer's parliamentary structure for the politically articulate groups—bureaucracy, landowners, industrialists, and farmers. Only the tariff dispute in the late eighteen-eighties aroused the lower middle classes into clamoring for admittance. Sweden thus is perhaps the only country where political liberalism and socialism emerged simultaneously. As an avowed political party the Socialists even predated the Liberals by almost a decade. Since in the fight for suffrage extension they were facing a common enemy, it was natural that they should make common cause.

The Liberal-Socialist alliance helped the democratic Socialists to maintain an ascendancy over the anarchist forces within their own ranks. Although a majority of the Liberals and individual conservatives were willing to seek a compromise on the suffrage question, the determined resistance of the upper chamber prevented an early settlement. As time went by the reform program of the rapidly growing popular movements broadened. Where first they had demanded a mere reduction of the income qualifications for lower chamber voters, they soon insisted on manhood suffrage, on the vote for women, and at length on a democratic senate and on parliamentary control of the cabinet. The protracted fight stirred the passions to an unprecedented degree, and on at least two occasions a violent clash seemed imminent. Yet both times the conservatives yielded at the eleventh hour. Earlier they had sacrificed the estates so as to preserve oligarchy. Now they endorsed manhood suffrage for the chamber (1907) to safeguard their position in the senate, and accepted a democratic senate and cabinet government

(1918) so as to preserve the monarchy. In the great compromise of 1907 they were able, moreover, to force the adoption of proportional representation, which appreciably slowed the parliamentary ascent of the Liberal and Socialist parties. Proportionalism also was fraught with lasting consequences for party structure and political alignments.

The intricate tactical moves in the transition from oligarchy to democracy between 1890 and 1920 merit detailed study because it was during this period that Swedish politics was cast in its present mold. The major parties of the contemporary epoch all emerged during these three decades. The demand for political participation called the Socialists and Liberals into the field, thus hastening the decay of older groupings. Universal suffrage and proportionalism led to a consolidation of conservative forces and to the rebirth of an Agrarian party. Although the process of constitutional transition was completed within a single generation, it was gradual enough to insure the survival of parliamentary attitudes and procedures from an earlier period. The principle of government by discussion emerged from the crisis more secure than ever before, for it had become the possession not just of a privileged few but of the nation as a whole.

SUFFRAGE DEMANDS AND POPULAR ORGANIZATION

Individual voices raised the demand for a wider franchise long before there was any organized mass movement to intonate it in chorus. In the wake of the 1848 revolutions on the Continent, a group of radicals had held several meetings in the city of Örebro to adopt resolutions in favor of manhood suffrage. There was little hope then that the riksdag would consider such proposals, and the scattered radicals therefore fully supported De Geer's plan when it was first announced in 1862. Conservative though the scheme was, individual representation seemed a step in the right direction—and very likely as long a stride as the estates were then prepared to make. Yet once adopted, the plutocratic franchise and the bicameral contrast turned out to be so many roadblocks in the way of further steps. The New Liberal party's suffrage motion in 1869 fell on a mere voice vote, and the next year the party itself disbanded. Attempts to reduce the income and property requirements for the lower chamber were as persistent as they were futile. The Ruralists proved lukewarm, so that for a decade the reform motions did not even pass the lower chamber. When the farmers, in a rebellious mood after the defeat of their tax and defense program (1878), threw their full weight behind demands for a moderate reform the senate remained adamant. By the time the senate agreed to join the house in asking the government to appoint a commission to study the matter (1884) and by the time the royal commission had gathered the pertinent data and prepared its voluminous report (1887)[1] the tariff question had markedly cooled the Ruralists' reformist zeal. The protectionist farmers had no more desire than their senate allies to open the electoral rolls to additional thousands of consumers of agricultural products. Suffrage reform was at best a secondary issue in parliament, and hence exposed to all the vagaries of maneuver. By 1890 it had run the full parliamentary cycle from high hopes to bicameral disagreement and on to dead center. Popular support alone could provide a new impetus.

The growth of democratic sentiment among the population reflected the changes that had occurred since 1866. The social transformation of the nineteenth century, while still largely in the stage of a commercial revolution, had precipitated the downfall of the estates. As it assumed the character of a full-fledged industrial revolution, it began to erode the oligarchic structure that had taken the place of the estates. In the early eighteen-nineties Sweden was mining four times the amount of iron ore and exporting ten times the amount of timber she had been fifty years earlier. Between 1867 and 1888 the number of industrial workers more than doubled—and by

[1] *Statistiska centralbyråns underdåniga redogörelse angående valrätt till riksdagens andra kammare år 1885*, 3 vols., Stockholm, 1887–1895. The commission's truly startling verdict was that the legislators could not have their cake and eat it. Any substantial extension of the lower house franchise would affect the social distribution of power. Specifically the commission found that even under the most moderate scheme then under discussion the farmers and landowners, who had a majority in 138 of 214 districts, would lose it in all but 87. The conclusion was partly vitiated by the faulty premise of equal voting participation in town and country — a condition which has not obtained even now after thirty years of universal suffrage; yet in view of the approaching storm over the tariff the argument was particularly well timed.

1902 it was to double once again. The booming metal factories of Gävle, Örebro, Eskilstuna, and Västerås, the textile mills of Borås and Norrköping were attracting hundreds of new workers every year. Stockholm, Göteborg, and Malmö with their bustling ports and diversified industries nearly doubled their population in the two decades from 1870 to 1890. Nor was industrial expansion confined to the cities. To this day some of Sweden's chief industries, notably mining, lumbering, and glass manufacture, consist of small enterprises and are located overwhelmingly in rural communities or small towns. Rapid as was this process of industrialization it did not at once relieve the population pressure from agrarian regions. Year after year thousands of peasants, sharecroppers, and farm laborers left the crowded parishes of southern and central Sweden to seek new homesteads in the fertile plains of the American Middle West. During the peak years of emigration (1881, 1882, 1887, and 1888) 1 Swede out of every 100 left his country. A steady stream of migrants from the older farming regions to the underdeveloped agricultural areas of Norrland completed this picture of a nation on the move. In 1890 almost one tenth of the rural and fully one third of the urban population consisted of persons born outside their province of residence.[2]

The spiritual and material needs of the hundreds of thousands who were torn loose from their social and geographical environment in a span of only one generation led to a rapid growth of new types of voluntary association. Freedom of association was guaranteed by a statute of 1864, and during the following decades Sweden was becoming what increasingly she has been since: the "Sweden of organizations."[3] Baptists,

[2] Detailed statistical data will be found in G. A. Montgomery, *The Rise of Modern Industry in Sweden*, London: P. S. King, 1939; Dorothy Swaine Thomas, *Social and Economic Aspects of Swedish Population Movements, 1750-1933*, New York: Macmillan, 1941; [Stockholm, Högskolan, Socialvetenskapliga Institutet,] *Wages, Cost of Living and National Income in Sweden, 1860-1930*, London: P. S. King, 1933-1937, esp. vol. II; Torsten Gårdlund, *Industrialismens samhälle*, Stockholm: Tiden, 1942; and *Statistik årsbok för Sverige*, Stockholm, annually.

[3] Gunnar Heckscher, *Staten och organisationerna*, 2d edn., Stockholm: KF, 1951, ch. II; cf. E. H. Thörnberg, *Folkrörelser och samhällsliv i Sverige*, Stockholm: Bonnier, 1943, and Hilding Johansson, *Folkrörelserna och det demokratiska samhället*, Karlstad: Gleerup, 1952. On the religious

46

Methodists, and other evangelical sects spread in the 'sixties and 'seventies; temperance societies and consumers' cooperatives multiplied; trade unions and political parties followed closely.

LIBERAL ORIGINS

The popular political movement of the late nineteenth century consisted of two main streams, one Liberal, one Socialist; and the Liberal stream in turn was fed by a number of distinct tributaries. As early as the eighteen-seventies petitions from workers' associations in the major cities had supported the New Liberal and Ruralist moves in the suffrage question. These societies still consisted predominantly of craftsmen rather than industrial workers, and their political sympathies well into the 'nineties were liberal rather than socialist. Suffrage was one of the topics of debate at the first Swedish workers' congress in 1879, and the fourth congress in 1886 formally endorsed universal suffrage and called for the election of liberal candidates to the riksdag. A few years earlier a student association named Verdandi had been formed in Uppsala (1882) in support of a bill for broader religious freedom then pending in the riksdag, and over the next decade the society became a focus for the discussion of public issues in Sweden. Many of the future leaders of the Liberal party—Karl Staaff, David Bergström, and Otto von Zweigbergk—were among the most active members of the society; Knut Wicksell, the founder of the Swedish school of marginalist economics, presented to it his hotly debated views on marriage, religion, and the social question. In the late eighteen-eighties radical intellectuals and liberal workers founded a network of regional suffrage societies, and in 1890 a dozen of these joined in the Universal Suffrage Association of Sweden. Julius Mankell, once a leader of the New Liberal party, and Bergström sat on the association's first executive committee. The demand for religious freedom with which Verdandi was identified soon

movements see Alarik Klefbeck, *Etiska idéer i svensk frikyrklig väckelsereligiosität*, Stockholm, 1928; on the early trade unions, Tage Lindbom, *Den svenska fackföreningsrörelsens uppkomst och tidigare historia 1872–1900*, Stockholm, 1938.

attracted to the nascent liberal movement another important source of support—that of the politically conscious members of the dissenting sects.[4] For the first time since the ill-fated New Liberal experiment of the late 'sixties Swedish liberalism had at its disposal a nation-wide organization and this time one that proved capable of conducting electoral campaigns and of recruiting the active support of the disfranchised masses throughout the country. In these efforts the suffrage associations received the vigorous assistance of another movement, far smaller in numbers but even more tenacious in its pursuit of the common goal, the Social Democratic party.

THE SOCIALIST PARTY AND ITS TACTICS

In 1881 August Palm had founded the first Swedish Social Democratic Association, in Malmö. Palm was a tailor who during his travels as a journeyman had become familiar with the political ideas of the Social Democratic movement in Germany and Denmark.[5] Back in Sweden he travelled up and down the country, giving lectures under the auspices of local trade union committees, expounding his socialist doctrine in debates with liberal labor leaders, founding newspapers, and organizing Social Democratic clubs. His journalistic ventures rarely prospered, and he periodically fell out with his financial sponsors and with the officers of the clubs he had helped organize. But the new ferment spread. A vigorous campaign of legal prosecutions for lèse-majesté, blasphemy, and similar outdated verbal crimes, which for a short time filled the jails

[4] On the early history of Swedish liberalism see Hans-Krister Rönnblom, Frisinnade landsföreningen, 1902–1927, Stockholm: Saxon & Lindström, 1929, pp. 11–62.

[5] Half a century earlier another itinerant tailor, Wilhelm Weitling, had helped transplant socialism from France to Germany; see Carl Wittke, The Utopian Communist, Baton Rouge: Louisiana State University Press, 1950. On Palm see his autobiographical sketch Ur en agitators lif, Stockholm: Björck & Börjesson, 1904. On the early history of Swedish socialism see John Lindgren, Det socialdemokratiska arbetarpartiets uppkomst i Sverige, 1881–1889, Stockholm: Tiden, 1927; G. Henriksson-Holmberg, "Die Entstehungsgeschichte der Arbeiterbewegung in Schweden," Archiv für die Geschichte des Sozialismus und der Arbeiterbewegung, 6:32–83 (1916); and Rudolf Heberle, Zur Geschichte der Arbeiterbewegung in Schweden, Jena: G. Fischer, 1925.

with Socialist editors, only served to weld the movement more closely together. In 1889 a congress of delegates from some sixty trade unions and Social Democratic clubs which "stood on the ground of the class struggle" convened upon Palm's initiative to found the Social Democratic Workers' party of Sweden.[6]

The congress did not attempt to write a formal program for the new party. It was content to endorse the aims of the international socialist movement as they had been laid down in the Gotha program of the German Social Democratic party in 1875. (Palm as early as 1882 had rendered a Danish version of that document into Swedish.) The ultimate goal thus was the establishment of a classless society through the socialization of the means of production. But there was considerable disagreement, both at the founding congress and at subsequent meetings, over the more immediate goals. Some of the trade union delegates would have subordinated all party activity to the fight for better working conditions in industry. Other members insisted that the most urgent task ahead was the adoption of universal suffrage, in which they saw an essential precondition for any future socialist policy. A third group, led by Hinke Bergegren, denounced all this as so much "parliamentary humbug" and called for immediate violent action. The second, or moderate, group in turn was divided between those who wanted to cooperate with the Liberals in the common struggle for democratic reforms and others who, like Axel Danielsson, professed to see no difference between the Liberals and other "burgeois reactionaries" and considered suffrage agitation only as a vehicle for the propagation of purely socialist ideas.

In a series of pronouncements on specific issues, the opening congress tried to steer a middle course between these various positions. The party maintained close contact with its union affiliates while dedicating itself wholeheartedly to political activity. It counted on a popular revolution at some indefinite point in the future but forswore any violent intentions in the meantime. The opening congress endorsed a resolution passed earlier at a socialist rally in Stockholm which urged party

[6] G. Hilding Nordström, *Sveriges socialdemokratiska arbetareparti under genombrottsåren, 1889–1894*, Stockholm: KF, 1938, p. 97.

members to work for universal suffrage as "the only way to a peaceful solution of the social question," but in a preamble the congress warned that "class oppression can exist in countries both with and without universal suffrage" and disclaimed for the party "any illusions concerning the immediate consequences of [its] introduction."[7] The pronouncement on suffrage thus was little more than a juxtaposition of contradictions which appeased both sides without satisfying either. The resolution on the "question of violence," on the other hand, was the succinct statement of a well-reasoned political position and clearly foreshadowed the strategy that the party was to follow in the next thirty years:

"The congress declares that the Social Democratic party of Sweden, in its endeavor to organize the Swedish working class for the conquest of political power, intends to use only such means as correspond to the natural sense of justice of the people. The program of immediate demands that we have adopted and are working for is the best proof that we for our part are in no way seeking a violent revolution. The Congress repudiates emphatically the foolhardy plans sometimes attributed to us by our enemies that we should wish to jeopardize the whole labor movement by attempting a violent coup of one sort or another without sufficient popular support. The party, on the contrary, will continue as heretofore to use its influence to prevent rash and violent eruptions of popular dissatisfaction that cannot be supported with sufficient power.

"Revolutions can never be 'made'; but if the blindness and selfishness of the ruling circles should provoke a violent revolution as an act of desperate self-defense our place is assigned and we shall stand ready to do everything to obtain and secure for the people as valuable fruits of the struggle as possible, so that its sacrifices shall not have been in vain."[8]

The implications of the document were clear. The party did not repudiate violence as a means of attaining political power: the time might come when it would take a leading part in a

---

[7] Reprinted in Lindgren, *op.cit.*, p. 348.

[8] Reprinted in *ibid.*, p. 349. Herbert Tingsten in his work *Den svenska socialdemokratiens idéutveckling*, Stockholm: Tiden, 1941, II, 21–23, gives an interpretation of the document and stresses that some of the apparent inconsistencies are "well thought out and intentional" (p. 23).

political revolt. But the party would not take such a step without the spontaneous support of the masses. Three distinct arguments were set forth to justify this caution. The first was an estimate of the probable consequences of premature action such as would commend itself to any revolutionary sincerely interested in the success of his revolution. The second asserted that revolutions are not "made" — or at any rate not made by the revolutionaries. This accorded well with Marx's belief that the "fall [of the bourgeoisie] and the victory of the proletariat are equally inevitable"[9] but gave no hint of the revolutionary activism with which Marx at times and Lenin consistently overbalanced this fatalist notion. The third made reference to a "natural sense of justice" attributed to the people. Though nothing was said about the possible manifestations of such a sense, the party clearly acknowledged it as a higher norm than even the conquest of power itself. Here the reasoning was based on ethical considerations, not prudence, and was likely to entail not just a reinterpretation of Marxism but a complete repudiation. The position, indeed, was one enunciated just ten years earlier by the British idealist philosopher Thomas Hill Green, who asserted that "the members of a state ... have no right to disobey the law unless it be for the interest of the state. And even then only if the law violates some interest which is *implicitly acknowledged* by the conscience of the community."[10]

The author of the resolution on the "question of violence," which the congress adopted unanimously, was Hjalmar Branting, a young man who had recently exchanged a promising career as a scientist for journalism in the service of the labor movement. The party, torn by petty squabbles as well as serious disagreements over principles and tactics, did not see its way clear to selecting a chairman until nearly two decades after its founding. Yet Branting's acute perception of political realities, combined with a seething indignation at social injustice, profound sincerity, and a remarkable ability to keep all personal animosity out of the sharpest political debate, soon secured

[9] *Communist Manifesto*, part I, in fine.
[10] Thomas Hill Green, *Lectures on the Principles of Political Obligation*, summary of sections 142–143, reprint ed. A. D. Lindsay, London: Longmans, Green, 1941, p. xxxi; italics in the original.

him a position of unquestioned authority. Under Branting's guidance the party resolutely pursued the suffrage policy endorsed by the founding congress — a policy which Branting had already sketched in the first statement of his socialist creed in 1886: "If the upper class wishes to respect the will of the people even when they demand the abolition of its own privileges, then the Socialists will not wantonly appeal to violence.. .. Universal suffrage, then, is the price for which the bourgeoisie may purchase its liquidation by way of reorganization rather than by bankruptcy proceedings conducted before the tribunal of revolution."[11]

Swedish Socialists joined delegates from eighteen other European countries in founding the Second International, whose first congress was held in Paris in 1889 only a few months after the founding of the Swedish party. In many other countries, such as France, Germany, and Italy, Socialism already was a mass movement and thus forced to square its revolutionary ideology with the need of securing specific benefits for its supporters. This was the dilemma which gave rise to the prolonged controversy within the International between "revisionists" and "radicals." The former openly renounced revolution so as to work for improved social conditions for the workers within the existing liberal-capitalist regime. The "radicals," on the other hand, who constituted the dominant faction within the International, rejected this piecemeal approach. They cherished the Marxian revolutionary ideology but did nothing to prepare a revolution. Rather, they pursued a "policy of unflinching obstructionism"[12] and in the meantime (as one critic put it) relied on "the powerful authority of the middle-class State [to protect them] from the consequences of [their] own 'revolutionary' speeches."[13]

In Sweden the nascent Socialist movement faced a situation which contained apparently contradictory elements. Industrialization had set in late and was largely confined to light industry.

[11] Hjalmar Branting, *Tal och skrifter*, Stockholm: Tiden, 1927–1930, I, 115. On Branting see Zeth Höglund, *Hjalmar Branting och hans livsgärning*, 3d edn., Stockholm: Tiden, 1939.

[12] Arthur Rosenberg, "Socialist Parties," in *Encyclopaedia of the Social Sciences*, New York: Macmillan, 1930–1935, XIV, 215.

[13] Arthur Rosenberg, *A History of Bolshevism*, London: Oxford University Press, 1934, p. 66.

The party and the trade unions developed under complete
freedom of association, so that the Swedish movement was
spared bitter memories of systematic persecution (think of the
Paris Commune or Bismarck's anti-Socialist laws) such as
haunted the parties elsewhere on the Continent. The liberal
free-traders and suffragists, moreover, welcomed the support
of the labor movement. All these factors might have inclined
Swedish Socialism toward a moderate, "revisionist" course.
Yet social reforms could not be attained unless the suffrage
first was won, and there was no assurance that legal means
alone would be sufficient for that purpose. By using the threat
of revolution as a reserve weapon in the legal struggle for
political participation, Swedish Social Democracy thus resolved
the "revisionist-radical" dilemma. From the beginning its
aims, unlike those of the "revisionists," were political as well
as economic. And its talk of revolution, unlike that of the
"radicals," served a pragmatic purpose. It was this synthesis
which enabled Swedish Socialism to avoid what has been
called "the basic weakness of European labor...the lack of
real political participation and constructive thinking on basic
social problems."[14]

The simultaneous emergence of Liberalism and Socialism
and their opportunity for cooperation in the suffrage question
was one of the most important factors in fostering a moderate
and pragmatic spirit within the Swedish Social Democratic
movement. A comparison with Norway and Britain illustrates
this point. In Norway a strong Liberal party had achieved its
major political demands—parliamentary government in 1884
and manhood suffrage in 1898—singlehandedly, before the
labor movement represented a force in politics. The development of hydroelectric power in the years before the First
World War, moreover, led to a far more rapid growth of the
working class than had occurred in Sweden. Thus at a time
when the Swedish Socialists were forming their first cabinets,
together with the Liberals and by themselves, the Norwegian
Labor party temporarily joined the Third International (1919
to 1923).[15] The British Labour party, like its Swedish counter-

[14] Adolf Sturmthal, *The Tragedy of European Labor*, New York: Co-
lumbia University Press, 1943, p. 4.
[15] Cf. Edvard Bull, "Die Entwicklung der Arbeiterbewegung in den

part, entered the political stage when close cooperation with the Liberals was a practical necessity. The major suffrage reforms, of course, were far behind, and the Liberal party was strongly entrenched. Just then, however, it was embarking upon its program of social reform (1906–1913), and the Labour party "could not help abandoning its opposition to a Liberal Government which year after year put some reform measure on the Statute Book."[16] Nevertheless, while British Labour underwent a gradual process of radicalization, the Swedish Socialists pursued their increasingly moderate course. The very synthesis between revolution and reform just referred to inverted the Marxian scheme, in which a working class revolt was to be the end product of, rather than the prelude to, political democracy. Since revolutionary action to obtain the suffrage proved unnecessary, it was no coincidence that the Swedish Socialists became the first party of the Second International to attain cabinet office by legal means and also the first to serve under a crowned head of state.

THE PEOPLE'S PARLIAMENTS

The Socialists' first major initiative in the suffrage question came in 1891 in the form of a scheme for a "people's parliament" which was to confront the official parliament with its demands for political reform. If these demands were ignored, a general strike would be called, followed by the assembling of another people's parliament "so all-inclusive and imposing that there can be no thought of further resistance on the part of the 'loyalists.'" To lend substance to these vague threats, the party urged all workers to enlist in voluntary rifle associations.[17] The 7,000-odd members of the infant Social Democratic party were hardly in a position to carry out such an

drei skandinavischen Ländern," *Archiv für die Geschichte des Sozialismus und der Arbeiterbewegung*, 10:329–361 (1921–1922), and Dankwart A. Rustow, "Scandinavia," in Sigmund Neumann, ed., *Modern Political Parties*, Chicago: University of Chicago Press, 1956.

[16] M. Beer, *A History of British Socialism*, London: G. Allen & Unwin, 1948, II, 377.

[17] The manifesto, issued by the second Socialist congress in Norrköping, is reprinted in Nordström, *op.cit.*, p. 336. On its implications cf. Tingsten, *op.cit.*, II, 40f.

ambitious project, and the Universal Suffrage Association—
then numbering some 50,000 registered followers[18]—was afraid
to compromise its cause by close cooperation with the Socialists. While steering clear of any plans for organized popular
pressure on the ruling classes, the association reluctantly agreed
to issue the call for a people's parliament, provided its followers approved such a step in a nation-wide poll.

The results of the vote were overwhelmingly favorable, and
the people's parliament met in Stockholm in the spring of
1893—the first assembly in Sweden ever to be elected on the
basis of manhood suffrage. But when it adjourned a few months
later it could not point to any concrete accomplishments.[19] King
Oscar had listened to its respectful petition without promising
to consider it. The party leaders in the lower house also had
listened but would not go beyond supporting a moderate
reduction of the tax qualification. The senators and the prime
minister had not even received the deputation, and Boström
had remarked trenchantly that he did not know "any representatives of the Swedish people selected in a manner other than
that which our basic laws prescribe."[20] The Socialists had urged
the people's parliament to consider ways and means of applying
further pressure, such as a general strike, a concerted refusal
to serve in the army and to pay taxes, or the formation of large-
scale rifle associations. The overwhelming Liberal majority,
however, refused to discuss these suggestions and merely agreed
to call another people's parliament for 1896.[21] The Liberals'
fears that Socialist propaganda would turn the moderate groups

[18] For membership figures for the two groups see Socialdemokratiska
partistyrelsen, *Berättelse för år 1948*, Stockholm, 1949, p. 173, and Edvard
Thermænius, "Riksdagspartierna," in [Sweden, Riksdagen,] *Sveriges
riksdag*, ed. Karl Hildebrand et al., Stockholm: Victor Petterson, 1931–
1938, XVII, 19.

[19] Cf. Rolf Fridholm, "Folkriksdagarna 1893 och 1896," *Statsvetenskaplig tidskrift*, 30:411–440 (1927).

[20] See the manifesto of the first people's parliament in Branting, *op.cit.*,
III, 90–95.

[21] Following the defeat of the original Socialist motion the congress
adopted a compromise proposal drawn up by Branting and instructed him
to compose its manifesto. Both facts were eloquent testimony to Branting's political realism and to the wide respect he had come to enjoy even
outside his own party.

in parliament against reform proved to have been justified.[22] Even the free-trading Old Ruralists, in their 1893 election manifesto, would not go below a 500 kronor income limit, and at the 1895 session the lower house, for the first time in five years, turned down all reform proposals. The second people's parliament, which lacked the novelty appeal of the first, thus came as something of an anticlimax. It also led to an open break among the sponsors. The Liberals once again rejected the Socialists' proposals for a general strike. The latter dissociated themselves from the "submissive tactics" of the Liberals which called for another peaceful demonstration in the form of a giant suffrage petition.

Despite this complete lack of immediate tangible results, the popular demonstrations of the eighteen-nineties substantially furthered the suffrage cause. Some 150,000 citizens had voted for the delegates to the first people's parliament—more than had ever gone to the polls in a regular lower house election.[23] As many as 205,000 had responded to the preliminary referendum called by the suffrage society. The liberal suffrage petition, which was presented to the king early in 1899, contained an imposing 364,000 signatures and this despite the Socialist boycott of this last move. For all their protestations that they would not be bullied into extending the franchise the Ruralists and Centrists in the lower and the conservatives in the upper chamber could no longer simply ignore a demand that, by 1899, had won the active support of one fifth of the adult male population, including about half the normally active lower chamber electorate.

PARTY ALIGNMENTS OF THE SUFFRAGE CONTEST

The party groupings of the tariff dispute had clearly become obsolete. The Old Ruralist party's chairman, Olof Jonsson i Hof, in a skillfully executed maneuver early in 1895, induced the New Ruralists to a merger under his leadership. The Center party, which since its inception in 1873 had undergone a series

[22] Branting himself acknowledged this. *ibid.*, III, 131.
[23] Only the hotly contested dissolution election of 1887 had brought a comparable turnout. On the support of the various suffrage demonstrations see Rönnblom, *op.cit.*, pp. 62, 72, 80.

of splits and fusions and now was hopelessly divided over the suffrage question, soon dissolved altogether. Its extreme left, consisting of radical city representatives, in 1895 formed the People's party, and this new group also became a refuge for left-wing Old Ruralists who were disaffected by the merger with the protectionists.[24] For the first time since the early 'seventies the democratic forces disposed of a parliamentary party, backed up this time by solid cadres of the Universal Suffrage Association in the constituencies.

Even the break between the Liberals and the Socialists at the second people's parliament promoted the crystallization of reform sentiment. The People's party, founded by such outspoken suffragists as David Bergström and Fridtjuv Berg, did its best to increase its rural following. Unencumbered by tactical regard for the Socialists, it adopted a program of gradual suffrage extension (the key phrase—increasing recognition of the "personality" principle—could mean many things to many men), temperance legislation, economy in public expenditure, and stricter parliamentary control over the ministry.[25] Its suffrage policy during the following years veered even more sharply to the right. In 1896 the Populists campaigned for a reduction of the income qualification from 800 to 500 kronor as a "minimal demand," and in 1899 they rallied around a compromise proposal that would have enfranchised all local voters over twenty-five. (The local electorate, it will be remembered, was only about twice the size of that for the lower chamber.) The first fruit of this self-imposed moderation was an election victory in 1899 which increased the membership of the People's party in the chamber from 30 to 43. More significant was the formation in 1900 of a Liberal Union party, in which the People's party joined with an equal number of moderate independents.[26] The chairman of the new group, Sixten von Friesen, was an ex-Centrist; the first executive committee of seven included only two former members of the People's party—and those from its rural wing; and the

[24] On the People's party see *ibid.*, pp. 76 ff.; on other realignments, Thermænius, *op.cit.*, pp. 131–156.

[25] *ibid.*, pp. 142 f.

[26] Cf. Hugo Hamilton, *Hågkomster*, Stockholm: Bonnier, 1928, pp. 253 ff.

Liberal suffrage plank was a reaffirmation of the 1899 compromise. Modest as was the party's program it had a far better chance of success than earlier, radical ones.

The left wing of the reform movement also registered some notable advances. In 1896 Branting had been elected to the lower chamber with Liberal support in Stockholm, the first member of a steadily growing Socialist delegation.[27] In 1902 a Liberal electoral organization (*Frisinnade Landsföreningen*) officially replaced the older suffrage society.[28] From the start it stood to the left of the parliamentary group; its leading force was Karl Staaff, a prominent criminal lawyer who had been a founder of the Verdandi society. In the 1902 elections the reorganized Liberals displaced the Ruralists as the largest lower house party, winning 106 of the 230 seats. The next few years were to show whether the Liberal movement would consolidate itself and, if so, whether it would be led by radicals such as Staaff and Bergström or moderates such as von Friesen and the farmers.

At the other end of the spectrum the senate too had abandoned its original uncompromising position. In 1892 it voted to extend the suffrage to certain categories of leaseholders, but this proposal won by only 14 votes over another that had passed the lower house and would have reduced the income qualification to 500 kronor. If electoral laws, like the tariff, had been subject to joint votes, the lower chamber electorate would thus, one year before the first people's parliament, have been increased by nearly one half. Even as things stood some impetus from the government might have helped overcome the deadlock. A steady increase in money wages had bolstered the number of workers on the electoral rolls,[29] and the more far-sighted members of the ruling oligarchy were realizing that the question was no longer whether the suffrage should be extended, but how soon, how far, and on whose terms the inevitable extension would come. A nationalist

[27] Cf. Ragnar Edenman, "Brantings första riksdagsår (1897–1902)," in *Statsvetenskapliga studier*, Uppsala: Almqvist & Wiksell, 1944, pp. 179–213.

[28] Rönnblom, *op.cit.*, pp. 97 ff.

[29] Georg Andrén, "Tvåkammarsystemets tillkomst och utveckling," in *Sveriges riksdag, op.cit.*, IX, 206f.

historian, Harald Hjärne, was advocating the simultaneous introduction of universal military service and universal suffrage. This program of democratic militarism, except for an inversion of premise and conclusion, was a revival of Hedin's plea of 1868 for a democracy in arms. Bishop Gottfrid Billing, one of the most perceptive and independent members of the senate Protectionist party, urged the adoption of a wider suffrage combined with "guarantees" that would "forestall or mitigate the dangers of an extension."[30] In plain language these dangers reduced themselves to a single one—the sudden displacement of the traditional elite by a parliamentary working class majority—and the "guarantees" that Billing had in mind included a scale of multiple votes (up to five) according to income, military service as a precondition for voting, a higher voting age, cancellation of per-diems for lower house members, and proportional representation. Billing knew that time was running short for such a program of tory democracy; hence he would rather have "stronger guarantees and a further extension of the suffrage than weaker guarantees and a lesser extension." Increasingly he considered proportionalism both the most hopeful and, from a conservative point of view, the most effective solution; for the old ruling class would become a minority and PR offered the best guarantee against "oppression of the minority or any semblance thereof."[31]

By 1896 the government saw its way clear to submitting its first reform bill—a timid proposal that would have lowered the income barrier from 800 to 600 kronor but at the same time disqualified all voters who had not paid their taxes in full for two years prior to the election; by substituting PR for plurality elections in the large cities only, it would, moreover, have cut heavily into the urban representation of Liberals and Socialists. Premier Boström's attempt at a "homeopathic suffrage reform"[32] found favor with no one, a majority of the conservatives remaining unconvinced of any need for reform

[30] Gottfrid Billing, *Anteckningar fran riksdagar och kyrkomöten, 1893 to 1906*, ed. Carl Hallendorff, Stockholm: Norstedt, 1928, p. 45. On Hjärne's position cf. Ragnar Andersson, *Svenska dagbladet och det politiska livet*, Uppsala: Almqvist & Wiksell, 1952, pp. 95 ff.

[31] Quoted by Andrén, *op.cit.*, pp. 309, 305.

[32] *ibid.*, p. 315.

and the Liberals complaining that it threw out as many voters through the back door as it admitted at the front. The government suffered a resounding defeat.

ATTEMPTS AT COMPROMISE

While the riksdag was taking its first steps along the tortuous road of compromise between two extreme positions, the radicals were seeing to it that the issue of reform remained in the forefront of public attention. The Socialists did not make good on their vague threats of sabotaging tax collection and military recruitment or of arming their followers; but they were seriously considering a general strike. Their membership by 1899 had reached 44,000 and the year before their affiliated trade unions had formed the Swedish Federation of Labor with a total enrollment of close to 60,000 workers.[33] Organized labor had become a power factor to reckon with. The parties in the riksdag now frankly faced the reform question, but they had little help from the bureaucratic cabinet, headed since 1900 by a superannuated admiral, Fredrik Wilhelm von Otter. Over the next few years, moreover, the reform issue became entangled with other political questions, some of which hampered and some of which furthered its final disposition.

The defense compromise of 1892 had supplemented the old subdivision system by introducing a ninety-day training period for recruits. Nevertheless, an ominous policy of Russification in Finland and the increasing importance of the ore deposits in the extreme north of Sweden underlined the need for stronger defense. Hedin's and Hjärne's proposals for a popular army within a popular system of government thus gained new significance. The poet Verner von Heidenstam, in his "Citizen's Song," first published in 1899, lent his powerful voice to the plea for political equality in the name of patriotism.

> *As sure as we have a fatherland*
> *We are heirs to it one with another,*
> *By common right and in equal band*
> *The rich and his needy brother.*

[33] Socialdemokratiska partistyrelsen, *op.cit.*, p. 133, and Jörgen Westerståhl, *Svensk fackföreningsrörelse*, Stockholm: Tiden, 1945, p. 31.

Let each have his voice as we did of old
When a shield was the freeman's measure,
And not be weighed like sacks of gold
By a merchant counting his treasure.

We fought for our homes together when
Our coast by the foeman was blighted.
It was not alone the gentlemen
Drew sword when the beacons were lighted.
Not only the gentlemen sank to the ground;
The serfs, too, gave their lives in the struggle.
'Tis a stain on our flag that by penny and pound
The citizen's right we juggle.[34]

The conservatives were not averse to granting other reforms—
such as a progressive tax—in return for an increased training
period of about eight months. At one point Sixten von Friesen
and Count Hugo Hamilton, two of the right-wing founders
of the Liberal Union party, had hopes of obtaining their party's
consent to the defense bill in return for some major concession
on the suffrage question.[35] At the last moment however, the
radicals and sectarian pacifists within the party refused to
sanction the deal. While von Frisen was content to follow his
party where he could not lead it, Hedin, Hamilton, and others
came out for the defense bill pure and simple. Even Branting
was willing to endorse a plan for a truly popular army outright,
since he was confident that the suffrage would soon be won in
any case.[36] The defense bill thus was passed without bringing
the suffrage question closer to a solution.[37]

[34] No translation can fully capture the vigorous rhythm of the original.
The first twelve lines are quoted from Charles Wharton Stork's *Anthology
of Swedish Lyrics from 1750 to 1915*, New York: American-Scandinavian
Foundation, 1917, p. 167. In the last four lines I have tried to adhere more
closely to the Swedish text (see Verner von Heidenstam, *Nya dikter*,
Stockholm: Bonnier, 1915, pp. 10f.). The poem first appeared in the
(then) moderate liberal newspaper *Svenska Dagbladet*, Stockholm,
September 22, 1899; see Ragnar Andersson, *op.cit.*, p. 99.

[35] Hamilton, *op.cit.*, pp. 242 ff.

[36] His article, significantly, was entitled "Suffrage and Conscription:
Some Scattered Heretical Thoughts." Branting, *op.cit.*, v, 111–116.

[37] A limitation on the number of votes that any person could cast in
local elections in rural areas (see chapter 1, note 16) was the only reform
adopted in 1901.

At several points during the next few years an agreement between the chambers again seemed imminent. But the longer the senate hesitated to surrender all the old oligarchic privileges, the more impatient the reformers in the lower house became. A government bill in 1902, combining the Liberal program of 1900 with various "guarantees," offered too little too late. Karl Staaff found the bill unacceptable; Branting, joined by Carl Lindhagen of the Liberals, demanded universal and equal suffrage for men and women; even the conservatives were at best lukewarm. A Liberal called the bill "a document chiefly of antiquarian interest," and the riksdag treated—or rather disregarded—it accordingly. The Socialists this time had called a general strike, and while parliament debated the bill 100,000 workers were idle. To what extent this demonstration influenced decisions is of course difficult to assess.[38] At any rate both chambers agreed to instruct the government to prepare another bill based on universal suffrage and proportional representation.[39] A first major step toward reform had been taken, and at the end of three days of parliamentary debate the workers were back on their jobs.

Proportional representation thus had become a major issue in the reform controversy. Its conservative advocates reasoned, quite realistically, that universal suffrage, if combined with the existing plurality system of elections, would give the Liberal-Socialist forces an overwhelming majority in the popular house as well as a deciding voice in joint votes on financial questions. If the conservatives, on the other hand, succeeded in preserving the plutocratic basis of the senate and in forcing the adoption of proportionalism for the lower house, the left-wing majority in the latter would be substantially reduced and the conservatives could hope to maintain their traditional control of the purse. Among the Liberals and Socialists there was at first little objection to the proportional principle. Both

[38] The number of strikers was the more impressive since membership in the Swedish Federation of Labor then numbered only 66,000 (Westerståhl, *op.cit.*, p. 31). On the strike cf. *ibid.*, p. 224; on its effects cf. the conflicting judgments of a Conservative and a Socialist author: Andrén, *op.cit.*, p. 342, and Tingsten, *op.cit.*, II, 50.

[39] Only the senate's insistence on additional guarantees unacceptable to the lower chamber, e.g. a plural voting scale, prevented agreement on a more detailed joint resolution.

Branting and Staaff conceded what they considered its inherent justice.[40] Von Friesen, who was one of the Liberal
representatives on the royal commission appointed to study
the matter, even was ready to support proportional representation for the lower chamber alone.[41] The Liberal electoral
organization, on the other hand, insisted that proportionalism
would be acceptable only if applied to *both* chambers or if the
existing powers of the senate were substantially curtailed.[42]
Once again the party's chairman was out of step with the rank
and file, and this time von Friesen's role as leader was at an end.
On second thought the Liberals rejected proportionalism
altogether. Staaff and other radicals became increasingly convinced that the majority of the people would not be able to reap
the benefits of the vote if the cabinet was allowed to play its
traditional role of an arbiter between two opposing chambers,
one popular, one oligarchic. In trying to supplement universal
suffrage with parliamentary cabinet government based mainly
or exclusively on the lower chamber, the Liberals had no desire
to strengthen the senate by rendering it more representative.
Above all they feared that proportional representation, by
permitting the growth of a multitude of small parties, would
erode the solid majority support in the lower chamber that
a future parliamentary cabinet would require.[43]

[40] For Staaff's position (in 1902) see Rönnblom, *op.cit.*, p. 122. For
Branting see his parliamentary motions of 1899 for equal suffrage with
PR in local elections and of 1902 for a revision of lower chamber districts.
op.cit., III, 186ff., 217ff. In the former he assured the conservatives that
his party, though long exposed to the "unjust rule of a majority which
arrogates to itself even those seats to which the minorities are indisputably
entitled," did not "desire any reprisals" (p. 187).

[41] The commission's report, published without formal dissent, stressed
the democratic arguments in favor of proportionalism. "A truly universal
suffrage requires that this right be extended to the minorities as well. This
end is attained by the proportional method of elections. In principle that
method must therefore be considered an integral part of the program of
universal suffrage." *Betänkande med förslag till proportionellt valsätt vid
val till riksdagens andra kammare*, Stockholm: Hægerström, 1903, p. 69.
On the speciousness of this argument in most situations where universal
suffrage is combined with parliamentary government see, e.g., Dankwart
A. Rustow, "Some Observations on Proportional Representation,"
Journal of Politics, 12:107–127 (1950), esp. p. 116.

[42] See the resolution of November 1903. Rönnblom, *op.cit.*, pp. 128f.

[43] On this shift in emphasis in the reform debate from suffrage to

The riksdag's treatment of the third and fourth reform bills (submitted by the second Boström cabinet, which after the 1902 defeat had replaced von Otter's cabinet) indicated the rapid shift in party sentiment that had taken place. The senate now agreed that Billing's tory program represented the best hope of a conservative solution. "If we wish to get universal suffrage with guarantees," a leading Protectionist warned his colleagues, "we must get it now—if we tarry, make no mistake about it, we shall assuredly get it without guarantees."[44] In 1904 the government's proposal for manhood suffrage combined with proportional representation passed the senate, but the lower house instead adopted a Liberal amendment that would have reduced the voting age further (from twenty-five to twenty-four years) and eliminated proportionalism. Another government bill, similar to the previous one, produced the same deadlock in 1905, except that the lower house this time was unable to agree on any counterproposal.

Both conservatives and Liberals had moved to the left, and the party picture once again was in flux. The Ruralists in the 1902 elections had lost the majority position that they had held since 1868, and the following election in 1905 reduced them to half their former size. From 1903 to 1905 the chamber also included a tory group, known as the Moderate Reformers, whose most prominent member was Harald Hjärne. In 1906 another group, the National Progressive party under Hans Andersson i Nöbbelöf and Alfred Petersson i Påboda, split off from the Ruralists. In the senate the two-party division of the tariff dispute persisted, save that the free-traders after 1905 called themselves the Moderate party and the Protectionists after 1908 the United Party of the Right. More important

parliamentary government see Brita Skottsberg, "Den svenska diskussionen om parlamentarismen i samband med rösträttsfrågan 1904–1907," *Statsvetenskaplig tidskrift*, 37:1–16, 130–152 (1934). An independent conservative, Johan Widén, voiced a different objection—that proportionalism would "lock into place the majorities and minorities" (remark in the lower chamber in 1905, quoted by Andrén, *op.cit.*, p. 429). This observation seems to have been ignored at the time; how perceptive it was has recently become apparent after three to four decades of experience with PR (see chapter VII infra).

[44] Gustaf Axel Berg in the senate (1902), quoted by Andrén, *op.cit.*, p. 346. On the changes in the cabinet see Arne Wåhlstrand, *Regeringsskiftena 1900 och 1902*, Uppsala: Almqvist & Wiksell, 1947.

than these splits and rechristenings was the formation in 1904 of the General Voters' Alliance (*Allmänna valmansför-bundet*), which endeavored to meet the challenge of the Liberal constituency organizations by coordinating the campaigns of the various conservative groups.[45] The association was to become the lineal ancestor of the consolidated Conservative party of the present period. Despite these efforts the left won another victory in the 1905 elections. In the 1906 riksdag the combined Liberal and Socialist forces for the first time commanded a slim margin over their conservative opponents in the lower chamber.

CONFLICT OVER CABINET GOVERNMENT

In the summer of 1905 an acute crisis of foreign policy gave Sweden the first cabinet which truly represented the parties in the riksdag. In 1814 Norway had been forced into a personal union with Sweden under the House of Bernadotte, but from the middle of the nineteenth century onward the dominant Liberal-Agrarian party in Norway had systematically tried to reduce Swedish influence in Norwegian affairs. The constitutional ties between the two countries were severed one by one, though not quickly enough, by any means, to satisfy the advocates of Norwegian independence. When the Swedish government refused to grant a demand for separate consular services for the two countries, the Norwegians insisted upon complete dissolution of the union. Boström's policy had come under fire from the parliaments of both countries, and after a short interim under Premier Ramstedt (April to July 1905) the Swedish crown prince, acting on behalf of his ailing father, decided to give the riksdag an opportunity to negotiate directly with the other side. The new cabinet (appointed early in August) was headed by Christian Lundeberg, chairman of the senate Protectionists. The foreign, justice, and navy portfolios went to the same party, and Karl Staaff and Elof Biesèrt represented the Liberals. Individual party men, even leaders, had sat in the cabinet before; but invariably, as with Arvid Posse and Gustaf Boström, both the ministers and the parties from

[45] See Arne Wåhlstrand, *Allmänna valmansförbundets tillkomst*, Uppsala: Almqvist & Wiksell, 1946.

which they were drawn had been careful to maintain their complete political independence. This time, at a moment of national emergency when nationalist hotheads were demanding military action, the ministry acted as an executive committee of the major groups in the riksdag. The most notable appointment from a historical perspective was perhaps that of the Ruralist Alfred Petersson i Påboda as minister of agriculture. Cabinet positions so far had been the exclusive prerogative of higher officials, large landowners, and industrialists. Conversely, any farmer who accepted even a minor government appointment would a few decades earlier have been considered a traitor to his class. The presence of "the first peasant in the king's council" foreshadowed the doom of the old oligarchic order more palpably than any parliamentary resolutions.[46]

Lundeberg's coalition resigned in November 1905 after concluding an agreement with the Norwegians by which the union was peaceably dissolved. Government and riksdag once again could turn to the burning internal questions. In view of the left wing election victory in September, the next cabinet, formed by Karl Staaff, included four Liberal lower chamber members, three other Liberals, and four nonpartisans. It was thus the first Swedish ministry with a clear party coloring.[47] Staaff's reform bill, submitted to parliament in 1906, was based on the Liberal program of 1904: suffrage for all men over twenty-four provided they had performed their military service and paid their taxes to both state and commune, and elections in single-member districts. In the lower house the bill was assured of passage with Liberal and Socialist support:

[46] Noting the elevation to the cabinet of another person with the same simple "peasant name" ending in *-son* (Albert Petersson, a schoolteacher's son and career civil servant), a contemporary cartoonist depicted two liveried ushers outside the cabinet room in the following epitomizing scene. First usher, sneezing, to his colleague: "Petersson, for shame! And two at that!" The other's reply: "Now we won't have to wait long for the revolution." The cartoon is reproduced in Åke Thulstrup, *När demokratin bröt igenom*, Stockholm: Bonnier, 1937, p. 27; cf. the comment by Sten Carlsson, *Svensk ståndscirkulation 1680–1950*, Uppsala: J. A. Lindblad, 1950, p. 130. On the cabinet changes of 1905 see Arne Wåhlstrand, *1905 års ministärkriser*, Uppsala: Almqvist & Wiksell, 1941.

[47] On Staaff's first cabinet see Arne Wåhlstrand, "Kring tillkomsten av Karl Staaffs första ministär," *Statsvetenskaplig tidskrift*, 37:285–322 (1934), and Ivar Öman, *Karl Staaffs första ministär*, Norrköping, 1923.

all depended therefore on the senate's attitude. To meet the most potent argument of the proportionalists—that the traditional plurality method would lead to the election of minority candidates—Staaff now proposed majority elections. If no candidate obtained more than half of a district's vote, there would be a second ballot and only then would a mere plurality decide. Apparently he was not aware that such a system easily leads to a more extreme party splintering than even proportional representation—so that all the Liberal arguments against the latter applied a fortiori.[48] Although Staaff had made an important concession to the Conservatives, his bill was sure to have rough going in the senate, where the Liberals did not have a single follower. But the brusque manner in which he demanded its support clinched his defeat. It was the function of the lower chamber, he told the startled senators, "to see to it that the clock is going," that of the senate "to see what the clock has struck."[49] Not that the senate was impervious to pressure: under the impact of popular demonstrations in favor of the suffrage it had in a span of fifteen years completely reversed its negative attitude. The Liberals under Staaff's leadership were now taking a far more radical position than they had in 1900 or even the People's party had in 1895. But since 1893 and 1896 they had solemnly forsworn all forms of extralegal pressure. Staaff himself, earlier in 1906, had obtained the riksdag's consent for a drastic sharpening of penalties for incitement to crime and riot and for antimilitarist propaganda. In view of this record his veiled ultimatum to the senate produced all the irritation, but lacked the effectiveness, of a real threat. The senate this time rallied around an amendment that would have extended proportional elections to *both* chambers. (This line of "double proportionalism" had been tentative-

---

[48] There were to be no restrictions on candidacies on the second ballot. The system, then, was that in force throughout most of the French Third Republic, rather than a runoff between two leading candidates as applied, e.g., in Imperial Germany. Professor Hermens has convincingly demonstrated that the French system converted the first ballot into a "trial shooting" and that the net result was a "no-party system." See Ferdinand Aloys Hermens, *Demokratie und Wahlrecht*, Paderborn: Schöningh, 1933; cf. Maurice Duverger, *Les partis politiques*, Paris: A. Colin, 1951, pp. 269–275.

[49] Upper chamber, May 14, 1906.

ly followed by the Liberal electoral association in 1903; in 1905 it had been taken up in a motion by Påboda endorsed by the National Progressives and Ruralists.) Staaff's bill, which had passed the lower house with at least a dozen Conservative votes in addition to those of the left, was overwhelmingly defeated in the senate.

In order to break the deadlock between the chambers Staaff advised the king to dissolve the lower house. He was confident that the electorate would return an imposing Liberal majority and seems to have assumed that, with the solid support of the lower house, he would be able to force the upper into accepting his suffrage program. Only three and a half years later, in January 1910, a Liberal government in Britain obtained a dissolution of the house of commons after having been defeated in the house of lords. But the British upper house could ultimately be forced into submission by the threat to create new peers—as the crisis of 1832 had demonstrated—and prior to a second dissolution, in December 1910, the British government secured the king's promise to that effect.[50] No similar weapon was at King Oscar's—let alone Staaff's—disposal. It is doubtful, therefore, whether the Swedish senate would have yielded to a mere Liberal victory in a lower chamber election. Dissolution, in any event, presupposed the cooperation of the king, and once again Staaff's provocative formulations ("Shall royal power with lordly power or royal power with popular power govern in the Swedish realm?")[51] were hardly designed to make converts for his cause. The king flatly refused, indicating that he saw no valid reason for dissolving a chamber that had just carried a government bill; the cabinet resigned at once. King Oscar's statement seemed to imply that if any chamber were to be dissolved it should be the senate. Actually the constitution left dissolutions of either chamber entirely within the king's discretion, and the king and everyone else were well aware that a senate dissolution would not have helped resolve the issue; for the local assemblies (themselves indissoluble) would have been sure to return an equally conservative body. The only constitutional point that the exchange between

[50] W. Ivor Jennings, *Cabinet Government*, 2d edn., Cambridge: University Press, 1951, pp. 395 ff.
[51] Lower chamber, May 15, 1906.

the monarch and his premier settled, for the time being, was
that the king, like the senate, was unwilling to accept Staaff's
ideal of parliamentary government based on the confidence of
the lower chamber alone. The whole episode confirms the
judgment of a Socialist critic that "Staaff, who was so enam-
ored of tactics, actually was not a tactician at all. A tactician
must appear to give when really taking. Staaff surrendered real
values for illusory gains. He made a great number of concessions to the Conservatives, but irritated them tremendously
with his speeches. To some extent the same applies to his
relations with the king."[52] It is significant that Branting, whose
sense of political realities rarely failed him, thought Staaff's
request for a dissolution badly timed.

THE GREAT COMPROMISE

Staaff, like his conservative predecessors (Boström in 1896
and 1904 and von Otter in 1902) had been unable to bring the
chambers together on the reform question. The only untried
program with some prospect of success was that of the tories
of Billing's type. The next premier, Arvid Lindman, was an
industrialist of boundless energy and a moderate member of
the senate Protectionists; his cabinet has aptly been described
as one of "proportionalist rally."[53] It included Petersson i
Påboda, the main spokesman for a double-proportionalist compromise; another National Progressive; a member of the senate
Moderate party; an ex-Liberal who favored proportional representation; and a number of career officials, among them
two who had just served under Staaff. Since the change in
leadership from von Friesen to Staaff, discipline in the Liberal
party had shown signs of strain, and in submitting his proposals
to the 1907 session of the riksdag Lindman was clearly wagering
on sizable defections from that quarter. He not only accepted
Staaff's program of a lower house franchise for men over
twenty-four but also offered a limitation of the multiple votes

[52] Erik Hedén, *Politiska essayer*, Stockholm: Tiden, 1927, p. 220. On
Branting's position see the editor's note in Branting, *op.cit.*, III, 305. On
dissolutions in Sweden cf. chapter VII infra.
[53] Elis Håstad, "Konungen och regeringsbildningen," *Svensk tidskrift*,
34:367-373 (1947), at p. 369.

in local elections to a maximum of forty per person. The distinctive feature of Lindman's plan was of course proportional representation; this time, however, it was to be applied not only to the lower house but to the senate and to its electoral colleges as well.[54] For the first time a leading Conservative had attacked the plutocratic basis of the senate—the juggling of representation according to penny and pound which Heidenstam had satirized but which even the Liberals had hitherto left untouched. Although the senate had not immediately yielded to Staaff's attack the year before, the encounter clearly had left its imprint. It was too late now to fight a last-ditch battle for a future Conservative joint-vote majority: if the senate was to carry any weight as a counterpoise against a democratic lower chamber of the future, it must itself be recruited on a popular basis.

Although Staaff and his radical followers would have preferred to let the senate wilt unreformed, a leader of the rural Liberals, Daniel Persson i Tällberg, announced his support for Lindman's plan, provided the government agreed also to reduce the existing income qualifications for senate candidates and to grant a salary for senators. Lindman now knew the terms upon which he might get sufficient support from right wing Liberals to carry his bill in the lower house, yet he was in danger of losing the backing of the senate. But he had already met the Liberals more than halfway and would not jeopardize the entire scheme by refusing a small additional adjustment. By taking the unusual step of threatening to resign if the senate adopted his original bill rather than the amended version sponsored by Tällberg, he finally secured passage in both houses.

The new suffrage provisions were embodied partly in a new electoral law and partly in a series of constitutional amendments which required confirmation by a second riksdag following a general election to the lower chamber. The last election on the old system, in 1908, brought a substantial gain for the Socialists and slight losses for the three other parties (Liberals, Moderate

[54] On Lindman's suffrage policy see Erik Timelin, *Ministären Lindman och representationsreformen 1907–1909*, Karlskrona, 1928; cf. Axel Brusewitz, *Kungamakt, herremakt, folkmakt*, Stockholm: Tiden, 1951, pp. 15–44.

Progressives, and Ruralists). Only the Socialists and a small number of left wing Liberals in the lower chamber, and an equally small group of die-hards in the senate opposed ratification, which came in 1909. The reform, though by no means a full victory for democracy, constituted a first long step toward it.

Four major political groups could be discerned amid the shifting alignments of the suffrage struggle of the eighteen-nineties and early nineteen-hundreds. Each took a variety of positions over the years and through their dynamic interplay each made an essential contribution to the settlement of 1907–1909. The Socialist workers fought most resolutely for the introduction of democracy and, in the early stages of the controversy, were inclined to use revolutionary means to that end. At the opposite pole the conservative representatives of the ruling classes at first opposed any change whatever. A third major group, the radical elements of the middle class, was thoroughly identified with the demand for universal suffrage but followed a vacillating course. Nevertheless, if an open clash between the extremes was averted this was largely due to the very waverings of the Liberals. For some years they co-operated with the Social Democrats—long enough to help set that party upon the path of peaceful agitation for democracy. Later, by dissolving their alliance with the Socialists and diluting their own program, they gave encouragement to those Conservatives (or tories) who were becoming convinced of the futility of stubborn resistance to all reform. Only after the Conservatives too were firmly committed to a policy of negotiation did the Liberals once again swing to the left. A fourth group, the farmers (first united in the Ruralist party, later divided among this party, the National Progressives, and the right wing Liberals), for many years remained aloof from the entire controversy. In the final stages, however, their spokesmen took a prominent part in formulating the details of the great compromise[55]—a formula that combined the Liberal

[55] The contributions of Petersson i Påboda and Persson i Tällberg have been mentioned. Another farmer, the Liberal Per Olsson i Fläsbro, proposed in 1904 that the suffrage be made conditional upon full payment not only of state but also of local taxes. Although Staaff at the time only reluctantly endorsed this proviso, it reappeared in his bill in 1906 and

demand for a more democratic franchise with the tory guarantees of proportional representation and bicameralism.

PARTY REORGANIZATION

Any thoroughgoing redistribution of voting power within
a population is likely to change the character of the existing
party system. Both the history of British parties after 1832,
1867, and 1884 and that of American parties during the mid-
nineteenth century confirm this generalization, and the
Swedish electoral reform of 1907–1909 proved to be no exception. The lifting of income qualifications for lower house
voters at a single stroke doubled the electorate. Proportionalism, moreover, made necessary a complete redrawing of
constituency boundaries. Whereas single-member districts had
been the rule everywhere but in the largest cities, each of the
new districts included an average of four representatives.
Anyone running for the lower chamber thus found himself
confronted with a constituency about eight times its former
size. The days were past when a politician could announce his
candidacy to an informal gathering at a country-town tavern,
win his election with little or no outside support, and proceed
to join the parliamentary group of his choice or, if he preferred,
remain an independent. In order to win the votes of the new inclusive electorate the candidate had to appear at mass meetings
in the towns, make extensive trips by rail or road to the outlying
rural areas, and have his name put on a party list. In short he
required the financial and political backing of a large-scale
party organization. Proportional representation, nevertheless,
allowed rival political groups to thrive within the same area.
Previously the Conservatives had conducted only token cam-

in Lindman's in 1907. That year the motions upon which the chambers
adopted Lindman's proposals as modified by Tällberg were sponsored by
the Moderate Olof Jonsson i Hof, the former Ruralist leader, in the
senate, and by the National Progressive Hans Andersson i Nöbbelöf in the
chamber. The two motions differed on a single minor point, concerning
the income qualification for senators, which the chambers at last settled
by splitting the difference. The role of the farmers in the suffrage conflict,
therefore, was that which E. Pendleton Herring assigns to the passive
voter who, activated at a time of crisis, resolves the controversy (see his
Politics of Democracy, New York: Norton, 1940, p. 32f.).

paigns in many of the large cities, and the Liberals and Socialists had conceded to the Conservatives the old Ruralist strongholds in the southern and central portions of the country. The new provisions for minority representation strengthened the urban element among the Conservatives and the rural element within the left wing parties. For the same reason proportionalism in some cases encouraged the formation of new parties and the secession of dissident groups from old ones. The extended franchise combined with PR thus at one and the same time contributed (1) to a consolidation of party organization, (2) to a regrouping of forces within each major party, and (3) to an increase in the number of parties.[56]

The Liberals and Socialists, with their large mass organizations, were well equipped to meet the challenge of an expanded electorate. Many Conservatives, on the other hand, had always tended to consider intensive campaigning as slightly beneath a gentleman's dignity. "The left is well organized," Lundeberg had complained as late as 1906; "the right superior and indolent."[57] In the 1911 elections, however, the General Voters' Alliance coordinated the campaigns of the four Conservative groups in parliament; and Arvid Lindman, who became its chairman in 1912, devoted his energies to making the organization fully competitive with its rivals. Despite these efforts the enfranchisement of thousands of lower class persons was bound to reduce Conservative strength in parliament. As early as 1909, with the first application of proportionalism within the senate electoral colleges, the Conservatives had lost their virtual monopoly there. Following the first local elections according to the forty-vote scale in 1910 and a senate dissolution in 1911 the combined strength of the United Rightists and Moderates dropped from 133 to 86. In the lower house the manhood suffrage elections of 1911 similarly decimated the ranks of the Ruralists and National Progressives. To forestall further losses a merger was clearly indicated. Early in 1912 the two senate groups formed the "Nationalist party," and those in the lower

[56] That this last tendency was less pronounced in Sweden than in many other PR countries was largely due to the smaller size of Swedish constituencies and to the absence of provisions by which the parties' unused remainders could have been pooled among the constituencies; see chapter v infra.

[57] In a letter to Gottfrid Billing. Billing, *op.cit.*, p. 320.

house the "Rural and Urban party." The two new groups in many respects acted as the branches of a single party: they held joint caucuses on major policy questions; on the relatively infrequent occasions when a Conservative member of one chamber was reelected to the other he would automatically join the parallel group; both groups entrusted their campaigns to the General Voters' Alliance; and all three organizations were popularly known as *Högern*—literally "the Right" but here translated as "Conservatives." Arvid Lindman, who after 1913 combined the chairmanship of the lower chamber group with that of the national organization, more than any other person symbolized and guaranteed the unity of the Conservative movement; yet personal rivalry between him and Professor Ernst Trygger, the Conservative leader in the senate, prevented a complete amalgamation for more than two decades.

The fusion of 1912 was a logical outgrowth of the Ruralist–upper chamber alliance concluded during the tariff conflict. Swedish Conservatism, nevertheless, had undergone a profound if gradual transformation since Boström's day. The landed aristocracy continued to support the party, but the Åkerhielms, Tamms, and Sparres no longer occupied the front ranks. A majority of Conservative voters still lived in rural areas, and farmers continued to fill high places in the official hierarchy (e.g. those of vice-chairmen in the lower chamber group and the national organization). But the party already was polling larger percentages in the cities than in the country, and its most prominent leaders were recruited from the managerial class and the higher civil service (including university professors). Under Conservative aegis Sweden had taken a first long step toward democracy—a step that naturally enhanced the influence of those who supported the change in principle and not merely for the sake of expediency. The outstanding intellectual figure from whom the younger Conservatives increasingly took their bearings was Professor Rudolf Kjellén, best known outside of Sweden as one of the founders of the school of geopolitics. Kjellén's political program, like Hjärne's two decades earlier, combined conservative and reformist elements. In his "national democracy" there was to be no room for women voters; yet he supported universal suffrage for men, party government, and even compulsory voting. Although

74

a champion of the state church he wished to see it strengthened through cooperation with dissenting sects. While insisting on government protection for strikebreakers and a wider use of corporal punishment in state prisons, he called for an extensive system of government old age and disability insurance. One of his most urgent pleas was that for a strong army, and in the following years this point increasingly became the major concern of the Conservative movement as a whole. Yet the popularity which Kjellén's slogans "the People's Home" and "National Rally" have recently enjoyed among leading Social Democrats indicates that his influence was by no means restricted to his own party.[58]

With the disappearance of the Ruralists, the farmers for the first time in recent Swedish history had lost their distinct party representation in the riksdag. Soon the demand for a separate Agrarian party was heard, and in 1913 and 1915 two such organizations were founded. The older of these, called *Bondeförbundet* or Peasant's Union, drew its main strength from the smallholders in the western and northern parts of the country and competed chiefly with the Liberals; the other, called *Jordbrukarnas Riksförbund* or National Farmers' Association, appealed chiefly to the larger farmers in Skåne and Östergötland and attracted a number of former Conservatives. Wartime control measures, such as the imposition of price ceilings on agricultural products, aroused the opposition of the farming population, and in 1917 the two parties succeeded in electing a total of fourteen parliamentary candidates. Proportional representation, whose introduction Liberal and Conservative farmers had sped along, now made possible the resurrection of the political farmers' movement in a new form. In 1921 the two organizations merged in a single Agrarian party (*Bondeförbundet*).

One of the immediate effects of the electoral reform, as mentioned earlier, was a strengthening of the rural elements within the Liberal party. During the suffrage controversy these had generally pursued a more moderate course than Karl Staaff and other urban leaders, and in 1907 some of them had

[58] Kjellén's political program is laid down in his books *Nationell samling*, Stockholm: Geber, 1906, and *Ett program: nationella samlingslinjer*, Stockholm: Geber, 1908.

deserted the party in the decisive fight against Lindman's bill. The party, however, quickly buried this internal feud,[59] and Staaff, who remained its leader until his death in 1915, did his best to preserve harmony. The Liberal campaign platform of 1911 was designed to please townspeople and farmers alike. The first of its three points—parliamentary cabinet government—constituted the chief unfulfilled demand of the urban radicals, whereas the other two—reduced defense spending and local option — reflected the pacifism and prohibitionism of rural sectarians. As yet the line between the two groups was blurred and their difference chiefly one of emphasis. However, changes in the political situation were to lead soon to a minor split on the defense question and about a decade later to a major one on prohibition.

The Social Democrats, too, were beset by internal conflicts which in their case dated back to the party's infancy. The 1889 congress, as we have seen, had followed Branting in assigning priority to the fight for universal suffrage and subordinating all revolutionary propaganda to that end. The struggle for the franchise lasted longer than the Socialists had anticipated, and in twenty long years committed the party "to a peaceful, reformist line much more surely than any debates or resolutions."[60] The party, during the same period, became a mass movement including not only industrial workers but also farm hands, tenants, and smallholders, as well as a growing number of middle class intellectuals.[61] A vast majority of its new followers were more interested in continuing the work for specific political, social, and economic reforms which the party had so successfully begun than in translating into reality the vague revolutionary slogans which were inscribed in its program and which con-

[59] Persson i Tällberg, whose defection had cost him his seat on the parliamentary executive committee of the Liberal party, was reinstated after only one year. And when Petersson i Påboda resigned from Lindman's cabinet in 1909 to join the Liberals he was quickly admitted into the leading circle.

[60] Tingsten, op.cit., II, 42; cf. II, 63.

[61] Between 1909 and 1911 a number of prominent left wing Liberals and nonpartisans joined the party. The former group included Carl Lindhagen, later a leader of the Left Socialist party, and Baron Erik Palmstierna, who was soon to become one of Branting's most trusted assistants; the latter included the well-known sociologist Gustaf Steffen, excluded from the party in 1915, and the psychiatrist Alfred Petrén.

tinued to inspire much of its oratory. The only means of organized pressure, moreover, which the party had been willing to use in the fight for the suffrage had in the meantime lost much of its usefulness. The three-day strike of 1902 served to impress upon businessmen the need for an organization to counter similar threats in the future.[62] The Swedish Employers' Association, founded later in 1902, had grown at an even quicker rate than the unions, and in 1909 a series of smaller labor conflicts led to a major test of strength in the form of a mass lockout and general strike. After several weeks the conflict was gradually confined to a smaller and smaller portion of those originally involved, until peace was at last restored. Although the employers had been unable to force its dissolution, the Swedish Federation of Labor emerged from the struggle impoverished and badly decimated. The Social Democratic party as a result of the strike lost nearly half of its dues-paying members and for the better part of a decade was hard at work repairing the damage. Although the 1909 strike was a purely economic and organizational conflict, its outcome made a repetition of the political experiment of 1902 unlikely.

While the vast majority of Socialists thus supported Branting in his cautious policy, a small but vocal minority continued the earlier, revolutionary tradition. Palm, who in 1891 had broken with the dominant group in the party, urged the creation of a secret conspiratorial organization. The chief agitator for the extreme left was Hinke Bergegren, whose frame of mind may be inferred from a speech to the 1891 congress in which he advocated a campaign of random assassinations designed to produce a degree of hate "such that we would be ripe for violence of any kind." Although he did not altogether disdain such comparatively tame measures as a general strike, he held that to waste them on universal suffrage "would be just about as clever as firing a cannon to get permission to fire a rifle."[63] In the Socialist Youth Association, founded in 1897, Bergegren found a suitable instrument for his anarcho-syndicalist propaganda. Although a moderate minority in 1903 seceded from that group to form a Social Democratic Youth Association, the

[62] See Carl Hallendorff, *Svenska arbetsgivareföreningen 1902–1927*, Stockholm: Norstedt, 1927, pp. 19f.
[63] Tingsten, *op.cit.*, II, 35, 32; cf. Nordström, *op.cit.*, p. 331.

party delayed taking sides in the dispute. Only in 1908 did it see its way clear to excluding Bergegren, whose Socialist Youth movement thereafter rapidly sank into insignificance.

Even the members of the new youth group, their professions of loyalty to the party notwithstanding, stood far to the left of Branting and the other leaders. They demanded the abolition rather than the democratization of the army, saw in parliamentary activity a platform for radical propaganda rather than an avenue for gradual reform, and tended to be sharply critical of cooperation with the Liberals.[64] As early as 1912 the youthful opponents had created a factional organization of their own within the party, and a bitter struggle for control of the party's machinery and press soon exacerbated the theoretical and tactical differences between the two groups. The breaking point came when Zeth Höglund and other leftists in 1916 called a congress to prepare a general strike that would thwart alleged plans to involve Sweden in the World War. Early in 1917, in face of an ultimatum from the party, the opposition seceded to form the Left Social Democratic party.

ADOPTION OF CABINET GOVERNMENT

In the years immediately before and during the First World War, matters of defense expenditure, wartime shortages, and neutrality were in the foreground of public attention; yet the internal contests of this period also provided an answer to the constitutional question that Staaff had raised in 1906—that of the relative positions of the cabinet, the monarch, and the two chambers. The history of cabinet formation since 1905—and even since 1866—had clearly illustrated the difficulty of making a cabinet responsible to two houses of parliament equal in power but radically different in political complexion. Ironically, Staaff's failure and Lindman's success in the suffrage question indicated that, the parliamentary situation

[64] On the (second) youth movement see Tage Lindbom, *Den social-demokratiska ungdomsrörelsen i Sverige*, Stockholm: Tiden, 1945, and John Lindgren, *Per Albin Hansson i svensk demokrati*, vol. 1, Stockholm: Tiden, 1950. On its offspring, the Left Socialist party, see Helge Stålberg, "Sveriges socialdemokratiska vänsterparti," *Statsvetenskaplig tidskrift*, 39:38-55, 99-132 (1936).

being what it was, the opponents of parliamentary cabinet government came closer to realizing that principle than did its theoretical supporters.

There are only three ways in which cabinet responsibility can be engrafted upon a bicameral system with two equal but sharply dissonant chambers: (1) The dissonance may be preserved while the power of one house is drastically curtailed, or voluntarily limited, so that the cabinet will in effect be responsible to the other house only. (2) The equality of the houses may be maintained while the difference in their political complexion is reduced to such an extent that their majorities can be expected to coincide on major political questions. (3) Both the dissonance and bicameral equality may be maintained; in that case only a diluted form of cabinet responsibility is possible—for not even the nimblest of politicians can honestly serve two masters unless the two agree. The first solution was adopted by Britian in 1832, 1911, and 1949; by France in 1946; and by Germany in 1919 and 1948. It also was the solution envisaged by Karl Staaff.[65] Swedish practice prior to the senate reform of 1918 followed the third solution—if solution it was—and since that time has followed the second.

The Liberals and Socialists won a clear victory in the 1908 lower chamber elections, and with the ratification of parliamentary reform in 1909 and the resignation that year of Påboda and other middle-of-the-road ministers Lindman found himself at the head of a purely Conservative cabinet. He stayed in office in defiance of repeated expressions of lack of confidence in the lower chamber until a second electoral defeat in 1911. When he finally resigned he stressed that "Cases may arise where it would be a cabinet's duty to remain at its post even under similar conditions. But," he added, "there would have

[65] For Staaff's constitutional ideas see his posthumous work *Det demokratiska statsskicket*, 2 vols., Stockholm: Wahlström & Widstrand, 1917 — a comparative study of government in Britain, France, the United States, and Switzerland; cf. Brusewitz, *op.cit.*, pp. 135–140. The Third French Republic on the whole followed the third solution, though the French chambers were neither as equal nor as dissonant as the Swedish chambers before 1918. Except for the absence of stable party alignments, responsibility probably would not have been diluted as much as it was in oligarchic Sweden. Cf. Herman Finer, *Theory and Practice of Modern Government*, New York: Holt, 1949, pp. 422 ff., 628 f.

to be an emergency such as in our opinion does not exist at the present time."[66] Despite this disclaimer he was setting a two-fold precedent. The tariff elections of September 1887 had brought about only a partial cabinet change, which the king, moreover, succeeded in delaying for several months; and Lundeberg, who withdrew promptly after the 1905 elections, had only held a temporary mandate to begin with. Lindman thus was the first premier to resign with his entire ministry in deference to the electorate's wishes—and from 1917 to 1936 every lower chamber election was to produce a similar result. Also future premiers, like Lindman, resigned right after the election, thus allowing their successors to prepare the budget and other major bills in time for the opening of the riksdag in January.[67]

The king in 1911 once again turned to Staaff, whose second cabinet consisted of ten Liberals and only one nonpartisan official. The premier for the first time combined his office with the chairmanship of a parliamentary party group, and the appointment of two civilians to the army and navy portfolios constituted another important break with tradition. As in 1906 Staaff had the support of the plurality party in the lower house; this time, however, his party was flanked by an equal number of Conservatives and Socialists, and following a senate dissolution in October 1911 the Liberals and Socialists held a joint-vote majority. The Socialists had turned down Staaff's invitation to enter the cabinet but had promised to cooperate informally. Realizing that a cabinet can be fully responsible to parliament (and through parliament to the electorate) only if it receives support from a stable majority, Staaff was determined not to fall back upon Boström's and Lindman's device of playing off one parliamentary group against the other. Yet this position proved untenable, and serveral of his bills were passed with Conservative support over Socialist objections. The experience

[66] The statement is reprinted in Gunnar Hesslén, *Den svenska parlamentarismens uppkomst*, Stockholm: Norstedt, 1940, p. 46.

[67] In Britain it was Disraeli who set the second precedent in 1868; see Jennings, *op.cit.*, p. 455. In Norway, on the other hand, the prevailing notion of parliamentary supremacy requires the cabinet to return its mandate into the hands of the incoming storting; see Arne Björnberg, *Parlamentarismens utveckling i Norge efter 1905*, Uppsala: Almqvist & Wiksell, 1939, passim.

of Staaff's second cabinet in many ways presaged developments during the nineteen-twenties and 'thirties: the absence of a party with a majority in both houses, the difficulty of forming a coalition, and the see-saw policy of the center party in alternately aligning itself with the right and the left—all these constitute points of similarity.

Although the Staaff government and the parties of the left in 1911 were ready for parliamentary government (as they may have been as early as 1905), the king and the Conservatives again demonstrated that they were not. One of Staaff's first actions was to delay the building of a new type of cruiser which had been authorized by the previous riksdag. King Gustaf V acquiesced under protest, and a Conservative drive which secured the necessary funds by private contributions further embarrassed the cabinet. Staaff was willing to consider an extension of the period of active service for recruits, such as the Conservatives had been proposing for some time, but in view of his election pledge of 1911 and of widespread resistance in his own party he decided to await the next regular lower chamber election in September 1914. Once again a popular demonstration and the king's action forced the issue, and this time an open break resulted. In February 1914 a procession of 30,000 farmers called on the king to assure him of their willingness to serve their monarch and their country. In thanking them the king stated that he disagreed with those who would delay a decision in the defense question, assuring them that he favored immediate action. The cabinet, which had no advance notice of the statement, took it as a clear repudiation of its announced policies. When the king refused to refrain from making similar statements without the cabinet's knowledge in the future, Staaff and his colleagues resigned in protest.

Public reaction was sharply divided. The Socialists and many Liberals saw in the king's action an attempt to resurrect the autocratic regime of the early nineteenth century. The Conservatives, together with a number of right wing Liberals who formed themselves into an association of Liberal Defense Supporters, denied that there was a constitutional conflict, and instead stressed the concrete issue which in view of the threatening international situation did not allow for any delay. There is no indication that Gustaf V in disavowing his premier had any ulterior motives beyond forcing a cabinet change. He was, it would seem, quite willing to leave political decisions to the cabinet and the riksdag, provided these decisions did not weaken the country's defensive strength—which, in his conviction, it was a monarch's duty to uphold at all cost. It happened that King Gustaf's conception of his royal duty made him a partisan in one of the most hotly debated questions of the day and involved him in a conflict in which he was aligned against his cabinet as well as majorities of the lower chamber, the two houses taken together, and the electorate. His conduct thus clearly implied rejection of a parliamentary cabinet system of government, such as the parties of the left were pledged to introduce in Sweden.[68]

Following Staaff's resignation the king called to his council Baron Louis De Geer, son of the sponsor of bicameralism and now a member of the dissident Liberal "Defense Supporters." When De Geer failed in his attempt to form a cabinet the commission went to Professor Hjalmar Hammarskjöld, a recognized authority on international law and a man of Conservative leanings but without official party connections. Hammarskjöld's ministry (February 1914–March 1917) included four Conservatives and several officials without party ties. The new cabinet, which was determined to take up the king's fight in the defense question, met with a hostile reception in parliament and immediately dissolved the lower chamber. The dissolution election of May 1914 resulted in a Liberal defeat, with substantial gains for the Conservatives and smaller gains for the Socialists. Nevertheless, the Conservatives, who were the only supporters of the Hammarskjöld government, were far from having a majority in either the lower house or the two houses together. Only seven or eight Liberal deputies, including De Geer, had gone over to the Conservative camp. With improved party discipline resulting from proportional representation, and with the recent sharpening of political antagonism, it seemed extremely unlikely that the Conservatives would make any more converts or that Hammarskjöld would be able to

[68] It is noteworthy that even a monarch with such notoriously autocratic leanings as Kaiser Wilhelm II promised a few years earlier, after a similar incident (the *Daily Telegraph* affair of 1907–1908), to refrain from making public political statements without consulting his ministers.

repeat Lindman's tour de force of splitting the major parties and rallying the dissidents around his banner. However, following the outbreak of the First World War (August 1914) Staaff and a majority of the Liberal party decided to give up their opposition to the government's defense program and to support its policy of neutrality. It was largely Staaff's sense of patriotic responsibility in a time of war which spared the government a prolonged and acrimonious fight with the lower chamber majority.[69]

The wave of national sentiment which at the beginning of the war had rallied the parties around the government gradually subsided, and even among the Conservatives complaints were heard that the cabinet was not giving parliament enough of a voice in the conduct of Swedish internal and external affairs. In the spring of 1927 the riksdag, condemning the government's high-handed attitude, defeated a naval appropriation that the cabinet had pronounced essential, and refused to renew a set of emergency powers. Hammarskjöld resigned, and there followed a brief interlude with a government headed by Conservative leaders from both chambers, including Carl Swartz as premier and Arvid Lindman as foreign minister. The 1917 elections resulted in a major left wing victory, which caused Swartz to resign.

In October 1917 the king made an attempt to bring about a national government of Conservatives, Liberals, and Socialists, under the leadership of a moderate Liberal, Speaker Johan Widén. Plans for a broad coalition broke down, however, when the parties of the left insisted on immediate adoption of the demands on which they had won the electoral campaign. These included abolition of the remaining suffrage restrictions for the lower chamber, adoption of woman suffrage, and universal and equal suffrage for the senatorial electoral colleges. Finally the king appointed a Liberal-Socialist coalition cabinet under Professor Nils Edén, who had become Liberal leader after Staaff's death in 1915. The new government's demand for

[69] Their patriotic *volte face* cost the Liberals another fourteen seats, lost to the Socialists in the September 1914 elections. All in all their tergiversations in the defense question reduced the Liberals in less than a year from the largest to the smallest of the three parliamentary parties (102 seats in January 1914 and only 57 the following January).

immediate constitutional reform still met with determined resistance from the Conservative senate majority. The senators realized that if the Liberal-Socialist proposals were adopted the Conservative party would lose its last citadel within the government, one which Lindman and other Conservatives had so valiantly fought to preserve only ten years earlier. The Conservatives would be reduced to a minority in both houses. At the same time it seemed almost certain that the principle of a "balance of powers" within the government (which to many Conservatives was the very cornerstone of the constitution and the ultimate guarantee of individual liberty) would be destroyed: for once both chambers were elected by a completely democratic franchise the senate would no longer provide a check against "rash action" by the majority. With the victory of universal suffrage, the king would be forced to yield once and for all to the pressures of parliamentary cabinet government—and parliamentary government in the foreseeable future would very likely mean government by the parties of the left. The only hope for continued "balance" within the government would lie in the long-range effects of proportional representation—the Conservative "guarantee" against radical majorities. In spite of grave misgivings the senate did not reject the government's proposals outright; rather it played for time by asking for further investigation and appointment of a royal commission.

The deadlock was not broken until the late fall of 1918. In November the German Empire, in whose single-handed struggle against a democratic world anguished Swedish Conservatives had found solace, was finally defeated. There were ominous rumblings among the working class at home. The young firebrands in the newly formed Left Socialist party spoke vociferously of general strike and revolution, and even some of the moderate Socialists thought that the time was ripe for forcing the introduction of a republic.[70] Eleven years earlier the Conservatives had accepted a widened franchise in order to save the senate; now it would be difficult to save the

---

[70] See a letter by Karl Schlyter, a jurist and civil servant and later minister of justice and presiding judge of a circuit court, to Per Albin Hansson, reproduced in Lindgren, *Per Albin Hansson i svensk demokrati, op.cit.*, I, 400.

oligarchic structure of the senate without risking the continued existence of the monarchy itself. Edén lost no time in resubmitting his constitutional reform program to a special session of parliament. The Conservatives surrendered, and, with only some insignificant concessions to the Conservatives, universal male and female suffrage for both chambers was adopted. (Because of the constitutional requirement that amendments may not be passed at a special session, only the provisions concerning the local franchise were definitely adopted in 1918. The parties, nevertheless, came to an agreement on the entire reform program, and those parts requiring constitutional amendment were passed in 1919 and ratified in 1921.)[71]

Conservative authors have minimized the importance of foreign events in bringing about their party's change of heart in 1918. Yet Edén's tactics were predicated on the assumption that the fall of Germany had prepared the Conservatives for capitulation, and his success seemed to bear out the assumption.[72] It is to the credit of the Swedish Conservatives that once they became convinced of the futility of further resistance they yielded gracefully and henceforth played the democratic game in good faith according to the rules.

CONSOLIDATION OF THE FOUR-PARTY SYSTEM

The constitutional reform of 1918–1921 marks the beginning of the most recent period of Swedish party development. Universal suffrage and parliamentary government had become the cornerstones of the political system, and all the present major parties had entered the arena. The effect of the second democratic reform was to consolidate the changes in party organization, in both legislature and constituency, that resulted from the reform of 1907–1909. For five years (1912–1917) the riksdag included only Conservatives, Liberals, and Socialists. The Liberal split of 1914 did not affect this situation, for the

[71] For the details of the new electoral system see chapter IV infra.

[72] Cf. Edén's own account in his book *Den svenska riksdagen under femhundra år*, Stockholm: Norstedt, 1935, pp. 302 ff.; Gunnar Gerdner, *Det svenska regeringsproblemet 1917–1920*, Uppsala: Almqvist & Wiksell, 1946; and Gunnar Gerdner, "Ministären Edén och författningsrevisionen 1918," in *Statsvetenskapliga studier*, Uppsala: Almqvist & Wiksell, 1944, pp. 256–296.

dissidents soon joined the Conservatives. But with the secession of the Left Socialists in February 1917 and the election later that year of the first representatives for the two newly formed Agrarian groups, the three-party system was clearly doomed. Although the riksdag since the early 'twenties has at times included as many as seven distinct parties,[73] only four of these have been represented continuously—the Social Democrats, Liberals, Agrarians (united in 1921), and Conservatives. In the next three decades these four major parties were to poll between 88.5 and 95.8 per cent of the popular vote, to occupy 93.5 to 98.7 per cent of the lower chamber seats, and to elect 96.7 to 100 per cent of the senators.[74] Sweden thus has had a four-party system, and there have been no signs of any basic change in this situation.

Splits and mergers of parties have with one or two exceptions been limited to the extremist fringes of the right and left, and none of these recent changes can compare with the momentous realignments of the period from 1888 to 1912.

First, the negative outcome of a consultative referendum on prohibition of liquor in 1922 led to a split within the Liberal party the following year. There had long been considerable distrust between the urban and rural groups by whose merger the Liberal movement had been founded in 1895–1902. The former supported democracy and parliamentarism on secular, rationalist grounds, tended to favor larger defense expenditures, and considered the consumption of liquor, like religion, a purely private matter. The latter were steeped in the ardent faith of the Protestant nonconformist sects, and to them liberty, equality, pacifism, and temperance were so many

[73] The number of parties in the lower chamber varied between seven (1921, 1925, 1933–1936), six (1922–1924, 1926–1932, 1937–1940), and five (after 1941); that in the senate declined from seven (1921) to six (1922–1934), five (1933–1937), and four (1938), and was back at five in 1939. See table 6. There has been a similar decrease in the number of members unaffiliated with any party group; after 1939 there remained only one of these, Speaker Johan Nilsson of the senate.

[74] In 1924 fourteen senators formed a fifth (urban Liberal) group. All of these, however, had been elected on tickets of the undivided Liberal party, and only four of them were reelected under the new party label in the course of the next eight years. Although the minor parties thus have occupied up to 9.3 per cent of the senate, they have never elected more than 3.3 per cent of the incumbents.

corollaries of principles of Christian ethics. The partnership of these urban and rural groups in the fight for constitutional reform and Staaff's circumspect leadership had allowed the groups to postpone their fundamental differences. As a result of the events of 1918–1921, however, universal suffrage and parliamentary government, which had once been the cornerstone of the Liberal program, beame the common possession of the major parties. As in the case of the Ruralists three decades earlier, the party's victory weakened the very unity by which victory had been won. In the end a seemingly trivial incident—the prohibition referendum—was enough to cause an open break. The leadership, supported by a majority of the party's 1923 convention, decided to call off further prohibitionist agitation; the prohibitionist faction, supported by the majority of the rank and file, seceded. For over a decade (1923–1934) the Liberal Prohibitionists (*Frisinnade folkpartiet*), led by Carl Gustaf Ekman, and the urban minority group (*Sveriges Liberala parti*), under Eliel Löfgren, continued their separate existence. In the decade preceding the split the Liberal party had lost over three fifths of its following to the Socialists and Agrarians, and its separate branches continued to decline in election after election. Only after a change in the leadership of both parties was a remerger effected in 1934. Since then the Liberal party (once again adopting the name of the original Liberal group of 1895, *Folkpartiet*) has made a remarkable comeback.

Second, the radical dissidents from the Social Democrats who in 1917 had formed the Left Socialist party underwent a series of splits and re-groupings. Like many new parties, the Left Socialists at first showed a pronounced distaste for formalized organization. In their case the impulse for rigid control was to come from the outside—the leadership of the Communist International in Moscow. A majority of the party, in 1921, accepted the twenty-one conditions (the so-called Moscow theses) that the International had laid down for affiliation. Under the leadership of Zeth Höglund and Karl Kilbom it adopted the name "Swedish Communist party (Section of the Communist International)," whereas a dissident minority, led by Carl Lindhagen and Ivar Vennerström, retained the appellation Left Socialists. As a result of periodic shifts in the strategy of the International new conflicts ensued; yet the fact that the

Swedish party at this time was the only Communist movement financially independent of Moscow considerably strengthened the hand of its leaders.[75] In 1924 Höglund and Kilbom parted ways, the latter receiving the backing of Moscow. Five years later Kilbom repudiated the International while retaining control of the party's press and local apparatus, forcing the Stalinists, under Hugo Sillén, to build up a new organization. The Kilbom Communists in 1934 joined with a number of dissident Social Democrats in a so-called Socialist party, but a new split, between Kilbom[76] and Nils Flyg, ensued in 1938. Under Flyg's leadership the Socialist party adopted an intransigent nationalist attitude well-nigh indistinguishable from that of the National Socialists; after losing its last parliamentary seats in 1940, the Flyg group sank into complete insignificance. The recurrent factional disputes within the Communist movement during the nineteen-twenties sapped its strength. "Animals of the lower orders propagate by fission" was Höglund's cynical comment in retrospect.[77] All the original leaders of the Left Socialist–Communist movement eventually returned to the Social Democratic fold: Lindhagen and Vennerström in 1923, Höglund in 1926, and Kilbom in 1938.

Third, the Conservatives in 1934–1935 overhauled their party structure. In 1934 the party's youth movement (*Nationella Ungdomsförbundet*) declared its independence and adopted the name Nationalist party. The break was largely due to the refusal of the youth leader, Elmo Lindholm, to take an unequivocal stand against the German Nazi regime. Earlier in 1934 a tactful suggestion from his followers had caused the Conservative senate leader Ernst Trygger to retire at the age of seventy-six. This cleared the way, in 1935, for the long-expected formal merger of the Conservative groups in the two houses. The united parliamentary party officially adopted the name *Högern* (the Right), by which its two branches had been known popularly for many decades. A new youth organization loyal to the party and its democratic principles was established

---

[75] Franz Borkenau, *World Communism, A History of the Communist International*, New York: Norton, 1939, p. 347.

[76] On Kilbom's varied career see his autobiography *Ur mitt livs äventyr*, 2d edn., Stockholm: Tiden, 1953.

[77] *op.cit.*, p. 541.

in 1934. For several years (1934–1936) three ex-Conservatives represented the Nationalist party in parliament; yet neither this group nor two National Socialist factions that contested various elections between 1932 and 1944 ever managed to elect any candidates on their tickets. The same holds true for various Liberal and Socialist splinters that emerged from time to time during the nineteen-thirties and 'forties.

The relative stability of formal party organization in the last three decades must not be allowed to obscure the changes in party policies that the prospect of peace and menace of war, prosperity and depression, changes in social structure, and the internal dynamics of the four-party system have brought about. The continual readjustments of the parties to their environment and to one another as expressed in their policies will be the subject of the next chapter.

CHAPTER III

THE FOUR-PARTY SYSTEM: SWEDISH
POLITICS SINCE 1920

BY 1920 the Swedish party system had attained its full maturity. The parliamentary parties of the late nineteenth century had represented the interests of the agrarian, bureaucratic, and industrial oligarchy. Under the impact of dynamic popular movements embodied in the Liberal and Socialist parties, the heirs of the traditionally privileged groups had joined forces. The new Conservative party had accepted the need for organized popular support. An Agrarian party was about to take its place next to the Conservatives, Liberals, and Socialists as the fourth major party. During the following decades several minor parties were to appear on the scene. Yet only those which split off from one of these four managed to secure a place in parliament. None of the splinters has threatened the four-party system; only the Communists in their various incarnations have attained any degree of permanence.

In the wake of the First World War a number of fundamental changes in the country's political structure had reached their culmination and fulfillment—changes which had accompanied the growth of the modern party system as both cause and effect. The suffrage had been extended to the adult citizenry on equal terms. The political contrast between the houses of parliament had been reduced to insignificant dimensions. The king had yielded the exercise of his legislative and executive powers to cabinet and riksdag. The riksdag had accepted ministerial leadership and the cabinet had submitted to parliamentary responsibility. In sum, the nineteenth century constitutional monarchy, with its tenuously balanced structure rising upon a narrow oligarchic base, had given way to parliamentary cabinet government and democracy. Aristocratic defenders of privilege and proletarian champions of revolution had met on a middle ground of liberal constitutionalism. Popular support for the Liberals declined in proportion as their demands approached fulfillment; yet for a time the party continued to make on the parliamentary swings what it lost on the electoral roundabouts.

Two phases may be distinguished within the modern period, with the depression year of 1932 as a dividing point. During the first phase, governments of the left, right, and center formed in quick succession, yet no group could rule without Liberal support. Time after time, therefore, demands for a strong army by the Conservatives and for an active welfare policy by the Socialists were whittled down until they met the Liberals' criteria of economy. During the second phase the Social Democrats replaced the Liberals as the dominant force. In alliance with the Agrarians they developed their antidepression program. In alliance with the three other democratic parties they followed a precarious course of neutrality during the Second World War. Under Socialist and Socialist-Agrarian leadership Sweden has been working to preserve prosperity at home and peace with her neighbors in a turbulant postwar era.

SHIFTING ALIGNMENTS (1920–1932)

Within less than two years after its accession the Liberal-Socialist coalition under Nils Edén had accomplished one of the greatest constitutional reforms since the abolition of the estates in 1866. It had obtained the extension of the suffrage for both houses to all adult men and women and the harmonization of the political character of the houses themselves. In persuading the Conservatives to agree to the democratization of the senate it had won over its most resolute opponents to the cause of democracy and parliamentary government. Late in 1919 the Conservative electoral organization drafted a new program and new bylaws with a view to "adapting [its] composition and organization to the new features which were recently introduced into the governmental system."[1] Point Two of the program included a demand for "popular self-government"—a term that in official Conservative parlance frequently replaces the foreign- and radical-sounding word "democracy." It was unlikely that the king without Conservative support would attempt to resist the new political order. Following the senate dissolution

[1] Yearly report of *Allmänna valmansförbundet*, 1919, quoted by Edvard Thermænius, *Sveriges politiska partier*, Stockholm: Geber, 1933, p. 27.

of 1919 the Edén government had the support of a majority in
that house as well. It was thus the first cabinet since Lundeberg's national coalition of 1905 that had the unquestioned
confidence of the two branches of the legislature jointly and
separately. Its policy, moreover, was based on a well-defined
program that, unlike Lundeberg's, had been endorsed by a
majority of the voters at the polls. The Liberal-Socialist alliance,
however, broke up in the very wake of victory, and Edén's
cabinet was to remain for some sixteen years the only one that
had fully met the requirements of parliamentary cabinet
government. During the constitutional conflict of 1917–1918
the parties of the left had temporarily put aside many disagreements on social and economic questions. The last major
achievement of the coalition was the passage in 1919 of a law
limiting working hours in industry to eight a day and forty-
eight a week. In the spring of 1920 the Liberal ministers declared that they were unable to endorse a plan for a reform of
the local tax system which the Socialist minister of finance,
Fredrik Thorsson, had worked out. As a result the entire
cabinet resigned.[2]

The rules of parliamentary cabinet government require that
the task of forming a new cabinet be entrusted to the party or
the combination of parties that has a majority in parliament. In
the spring of 1920—and for two decades after that—no single
party had a majority in either house. Of the two potential
majority combinations one, that of Liberals and Conservatives,
hardly seemed a realistic possibility. The bitter feud between
Liberals and Conservatives that had recently come to an end
(1918) was still fresh in everyone's mind. Since the second
possible combination had just broken up, a minority government seemed inevitable—unless and until the elections of
September 1920 brought a change in the parliamentary situation. When the Liberals declined to form a government by
themselves, the king asked Hjalmar Branting to form a purely
Socialist cabinet. The Socialists, who were the largest party in
the riksdag, saw no way of refusing without endangering the
newly established parliamentary regime.[3] The new cabinet

[2] See Gunnar Gerdner, *Det svenska regeringsproblemet 1917–1920*,
Uppsala: Almqvist & Wiksell, 1946.

[3] Herbert Tingsten, *Den svenska socialdemokratiens idéutveckling*, Stockholm: Tiden, 1941, II, 107.

declared that, in the absence of a Socialist majority and pending the forthcoming elections, it would not attempt to carry out any of the specifically Socialist demands of the party's program. Although the government appointed a royal commission to study the question of socialization it did not contemplate any immediate legislative measures.[4] Meanwhile the government continued its work on the major piece of unfinished business left by the coalition government, the revision of the local tax structure. In accordance with its announced policy the cabinet submitted a proposal that made some concessions to the other parties. Although the government version of the bill was defeated in the riksdag, which instead adopted a Liberal amendment, the cabinet stayed until after the elections.

In the elections of 1920 the Socialists suffered a slight setback, the first electoral reversal in that party's history.[5] The government resigned shortly afterward. The parliamentary situation, however, remained as confused as it had been. The Social Democrats, though still the largest party, seemed further removed from the goal of a parliamentary majority, and the Liberals refused to reenter into a coalition with the Socialists. The king therefore appointed a cabinet of high officials without pronounced political connections, headed by Baron Louis De Geer (the younger). The new cabinet was unique in that it did not include a single member of the riksdag.[6] The premier announced that the ministry would carry on day-to-day business as long as the party situation in the riksdag did not warrant a parliamentary cabinet. At the same time he proposed that general elections to both chambers be held in the fall of 1921

[4] The commission continued its work for sixteen years—a record even for the methodical Swedish royal commissions. The only result was a dissertation on the "problem of socialization" from the pen of Rickard Sandler which contained no legislative recommendations. Tingsten remarks caustically that there was a tendency to consider "the socialization commission... a permanent institution for the protection of the mysteries of socialization" (*ibid.*, 1, 331).

[5] The loss of fifteen seats in 1917 had been due to the splitting off of the Left Socialists.

[6] De Geer, a senator from 1901 to 1914, had left the Liberal party during the defense conflict. Cf. his reminiscences *Politiska hågkomster från åren 1901–1921*, Stockholm: Norstedt, 1926. The defense minister, General Carl-Gustaf Hammarskjöld, served as a Conservative member of parliament both before and after, but not during, his cabinet tenure.

so that the new constitutional provisions of 1919 (which were to
be ratified at the beginning of the 1921 session) could be put
into effect at once. The government would resign immediately
afterward. The De Geer government has gone down in Swedish
history as the Caretaker Government (*expeditionsministären*).
Ironically this most unparliamentary government was the first
one to make in its initial policy declaration any explicit reference
to the principle of parliamentary government.[7] De Geer's
premiership did not even last for the modest span of one year
that he had in advance allotted to it. A conflict between the
cabinet and the legislature soon led to his resignation. In
February 1921 the two houses rejected a government proposal
for an import duty on coffee. The finance minister, Henric
Tamm, who had borne the brunt of the attack, felt that De
Geer had not given him sufficient support during the debate
and left the cabinet in protest. Since the other ministers refused to continue serving under De Geer the whole cabinet
resigned.

The king's appointment of the De Geer cabinet had been
severely criticized. Edén, during his audience with the king,
had insisted that the monarch appoint a Conservative cabinet,
and the Liberal press later insinuated that the outgoing
ministry had suggested the selection of the interim government
so as to cover up the Social Democratic defeat at the polls. Before attempting to replace De Geer the king therefore metic-
ulously complied with all the rules of etiquette. After conferring
with the speakers of both houses the king offered the premiership to the leaders of the three major parties in the order of
party size (Socialists, Conservatives, Liberals); only after he had
received a refusal from each did he proceed to reconstruct the
Caretaker Government under a new premier (Oscar von Sydow)
and with a new finance minister. Before the end of the 1921
riksdag session another minister—General Carl-Gustaf Hammarskjöld—left the cabinet under parliamentary fire. The re-
vamped Caretaker Government resigned, as originally intended,
after the 1921 elections.

Any hopes that the first elections under the new suffrage
provisions would result in a parliamentary majority for one

[7] The irony is pointed out by Axel Brusewitz, "Vad menas med parlamentarism?" *Statsvetenskaplig tidskrift*, 32:333 (1929).

party proved entirely unfounded. Actually a new system of larger electoral districts, which had been adopted together with the new suffrage provisions for the purpose of greater proportionality,[8] made it even less likely that any party would gain a majority in the future. Shortly before the 1921 elections the two agrarian parties had merged, but a few months earlier the Communists had split off from the Left Socialists, so that the total number of parties remained at six. (In 1923 a merger between the Left Socialists and the Social Democrats and a split within the Liberal party again left the number of parties unchanged). The Socialist vote in 1921 had resumed its upward trend, but the party still did not have a majority in either chamber. All three non-Socialist parties had suffered losses, so that it now took a combination of Conservatives, Agrarians, and Liberals (instead of only Conservatives and Liberals) to form a "bourgeois" majority in the lower house.[9] The parliamentary alignment remained equally inconclusive for over a decade (1922–1933): no party had a majority and neither the three bourgeois parties nor the two parties of the left (Liberals and Socialists) managed to overcome their differences to the point of forming a government coalition. The experience with the De Geer–von Sydow cabinet had convinced political leaders that a nonpartisan caretaker government was likely to receive less support in parliament than even a ministry formed by a minority party. The next years therefore brought a succession of minority cabinets—Socialist, Conservative, and Liberal.

Following von Sydow's resignation Branting formed a second Socialist ministry. During the winter of 1921–1922, unemployment reached an all-time high in Sweden,[10] and the government was therefore eager to liberalize existing provisions regarding unemployment assistance. Specifically the government proposed to change a regulation according to which any

[8] On the revision of districts in 1921 and its significance for party development see chapter IV infra.

[9] The term "bourgeois" in the sense of "nonsocialist," though of Marxist origin, is used in Sweden without any pejorative connotation by Socialists and nonsocialists alike.

[10] See, e.g., Harrison Clark, *Swedish Unemployment Policy—1914 to 1940*, Washington: American Council on Public Affairs, 1941, pp. 28 ff., and Gunnar Dahlberg and Herbert Tingsten, *Svensk politisk uppslagsbok*, Stockholm: A.B. Svensk Litteratur, 1937, pp. 26 ff.

workers who refused to take work in a struck plant were ineligible
for unemployment benefits for the duration of the strike.
Invariably, however, Branting's proposals in the unemployment
question met solid resistance from the three non-Socialist
parties. When the senate in 1923 defeated the cabinet on a vote
of confidence in the same matter, he resigned. The Conservative leader in the senate, Ernst Trygger, thereupon attempted
to bring together a bourgeois coalition and, failing that, formed
a Conservative cabinet. It fell to the new government's lot to
work out the details of a program for the reduction of defense
expenditures which a royal commission appointed by a previous
ministry had outlined. Since traditionally one of the main Conservative program points was the maintenance of the country's
defensive strength, Trygger submitted a proposal that would
have effected some economies without substantially reducing
the strength of the armed forces. All the other parties insisted
on further cuts in the defense budget, the amounts proposed
forming a continuous scale from right to left. The Conservatives favored the highest sum; the Agrarians, Löfgren Liberals,
Prohibitionist (Ekman) Liberals, and Socialists came out for
progressively smaller amounts; the Communists, finally, proposed immediate and complete disarmament.[11] On the decisive
vote in the riksdag the senate endorsed the original government
bill while the lower chamber backed the Socialist amendment.
In spite of this defeat on a major question the Trygger cabinet
stayed until after the 1924 elections. (These resulted in slight
gains for the Conservatives and Agrarians and somewhat
greater gains for the Socialists—all at the expense of the rapidly
dwindling Liberal party). When the Socialists and Liberals
announced publicly that they saw no possibility for a solution
of the defense question under Conservative aegis, the cabinet
finally resigned.

Branting formed a third Socialist cabinet in October 1924;
but when a serious illness (which proved to be fatal) forced the
veteran leader to resign a few months later, his place was taken
by a Socialist intellectual of the younger generation, Rickard
Sandler. Together with the Liberals the Branting-Sandler

[11] Herbert Tingsten, *The Debate on the Foreign Policy of Sweden 1918–
1939*, tr. Joan Bulman, New York: Oxford University Press, 1950, pp.
155 ff., summarizes partisan views on defense during this period.

cabinet worked out a compromise on the defense question that both houses accepted. The cabinet resigned in 1926 when a bourgeois alignment defeated it on the same question that had caused the resignation of the second Socialist government—that of the benefits of unemployed workers who refused to help break a strike.

The prevailing parliamentary constellation largely explains the successive government defeats and government crises of the early 'twenties. The relative strengths of the parties were such that the Liberal party held the balance between the Socialists on the one hand and the Conservatives and Agrarians (who during this period generally followed the Conservative lead) on the other. While the main concern of the Conservatives was the strengthening of national defense and that of the Socialists the strengthening of social services, the Liberal program during this period may roughly be described as one of economy in both these areas. In Carl Gustaf Ekman the larger (Prohibitionist) wing of the party found a shrewd and determined parliamentary leader who made skillful use of the party's strategic position at the center in pursuing this program. By aligning themselves with the Conservatives in the local tax and unemployment questions the Liberals had defeated three Socialist governments—in 1920, 1923, and 1926—and by joining with the Socialists on the defense issue they had outvoted the Conservatives in 1924. On the last three of these occasions Ekman had personally marshalled the anti-government forces in the parliamentary committee handling the bill, and each time the cabinet was eventually forced to resign. It looked as though Carl Ekman almost singlehandedly had converted Swedish cabinet government into its caricature—committee rule. The only way out of recurrent crises and back to a system of cabinet government seemed to be to make Ekman himself the next premier.

When offered the premiership in 1926, Ekman formed a cabinet which included only representatives of the Löfgren group and of his own Prohibitionist party. Although the direct parliamentary support of the cabinet was smaller than that of any of its predecessors (the Liberals controlled only 14 per cent of the lower chamber vote and 23 per cent of the senate) its legislative efforts were much more successful. With Socialist support the Ekman government passed a major school reform act, and with the support of the Conservatives and Agrarians it passed two far-reaching laws in the field of labor relations, a collective contracts act and a labor court act.[12] The Liberals began to develop a theory of "gravitational parliamentarism" (*tyngdpunktsparlamentarism*), according to which, whenever there was no majority party, the party at the "center of gravity" was to take over the government. The Ekman cabinet stayed in office until after the 1928 elections. Although the Prohibitionists maintained their strength and the Löfgren group lost but one seat, the election led to a brawl within the coalition and eventually to its resignation. Eliel Löfgren, leader of the smaller of the two Liberal parties and foreign minister in the Ekman cabinet, had been crossed off his own party's list by a rebellious faction within his Stockholm constituency. While Löfgren was thus forced to run as an independent, the prime minister announced his candidacy at the head of the Prohibitionist list in the same constituency. When the vote was counted it developed that Ekman had been elected and Löfgren defeated. Löfgren and his two party friends in the cabinet resigned—suspecting, rightly or wrongly, that Ekman had run in Stockholm for the sole purpose of defeating the rival Liberal leader. Since the king insisted that the entire cabinet withdraw, a full-fledged crisis resulted.

Ekman's first government was by many standards the most successful of all cabinets since Edén's coalition: it attained a longer life-span than any of the preceding minority cabinets, it was the only one that did not suffer any major legislative reversals, and it was the only one whose resignation was due to difficulties outside the riksdag. Thus the record seemed to justify the theory of "gravitational parliamentarism" on which the Liberals based their claim to political leadership. On the other hand neither the Conservatives nor the Socialists were willing to concede this claim. To them it seemed absurd that the government should be entrusted to a party with a bare handful of supporters—a party that had lost votes at every election but one since 1911. Did not the democra-

[12] See James J. Robbins, *The Government of Labor Relations in Sweden*, Chapel Hill: University of North Carolina Press, 1942, pp. 108 ff., and Jörgen Westerståhl, *Svensk fackföreningsrörelse*, Stockholm: Tiden, 1945, pp. 366 ff.

tic principle demand that the party with the largest popular support should carry on the government? Ekman's adversaries could point to the fact that the Conservatives had twice, and the Socialists three times, as many supporters both among the voters and in the riksdag as did Ekman's tiny cohort. Why should one Liberal vote outweigh five votes of the parties of the right and left when it came to cabinet formation? Yet it was the very size of the Conservative and Socialist parties that enabled Ekman to control Swedish politics with the support of only the diminutive Prohibitionist group. The Conservatives and Socialists might inveigh against Ekman's "shifting majorities" (*hoppande majoriteter*—literally "jumping majorities"),[13] yet as long as the parliamentary situation remained essentially unchanged they were caught in the seemingly inescapable logic that made Ekman the "balancer" (*vågmästare*) of Swedish politics.

Since the Conservatives had made the greatest single gain in the lower chamber elections of 1928, the task of forming a new cabinet fell upon their leader in the lower house, ex-premier Arvid Lindman. Lindman, with umistakable reference to his predecessor's tactics, announced that his government would attempt to pursue a policy designed "to bring about cooperation on the broadest possible basis for the best [interests] of our people."[14] To receive majority support, however, he had to find a basis broad enough to ensure the cooperation at least of the Agrarians and Liberals, and Ekman soon made it clear that he for one would continue to cooperate with the right or with the left as he pleased. At the 1929 session a Liberal-Socialist majority defeated three major government proposals —one to introduce a protective tariff on sugar, one to reduce

[13] A cartoon published in 1930 in *Dagens Nyheter*—a Liberal paper of Löfgrenite persuasion—conveys the feeling of frustration that Socialists and Conservatives alike experienced. Under the caption "Why till the political soil?" it depicts the two party leaders, Per Albin Hansson and Arvid Lindman, each plowing his field, the former from left to right, the latter from right to left, both with sweat pouring from their brows. Right behind them in the two fresh furrows an ugly weed grows in long rows, its flower bearing the unmistakable profile of Carl Gustaf Ekman. The cartoon is reproduced in *Per Albin Hansson, ett minnesalbum*, Stockholm: Tiden, 1946, no pagination.

[14] Quoted in Georg Andrén et al., *Sveriges styrelse*, 2d edn., Stockholm: Victor Petterson, 1945, p. 122.

income and property taxes, and one to increase military expenditures in order to strengthen the artillery. Further reversals followed. Two ministers in the Lindman cabinet were singled out for criticism by the constitutional committee. In its 1929 report on its examination of the cabinet minutes, the committee included a sharp attack on the finance minister, Professor Nils Wohlin. In the report for 1930 the foreign minister, Ernst Trygger, was criticized for his failure to consult with the riksdag on foreign policy decisions. Both times the lower chamber took what by this time had become an extraordinary step in endorsing the committee's criticism by a formal vote; the parliamentary storm against the finance minister became so violent that Wohlin saw himself forced to resign.[15] The government's legislative program for 1930 fared even worse. Agricultural prices had been rising steadily since about 1925,[16] and the Lindman government therefore submitted a twofold program designed to stabilize internal prices for Swedish wheat and rye. The government proposed on the one hand a higher tariff on cereal imports and on the other hand a regulation according to which all Swedish flour mills would be required to use a certain minimum percentage of Swedish grain. While the Socialists rose to the defense of consumer interests and condemned the entire program, the Liberals rejected the tariff but endorsed the second part of the government proposal. Ekman, once again presiding over committee deliberations, succeeded in getting the special committee that was handling the bill to go along with the Liberal plan. During the floor debate the government remained adamant and made acceptance of the whole program a question of confidence. At this point a large group within the government's own party, fearful lest the entire program be defeated, voted for the committee proposal, which thus carried a majority.

After the resignation of Lindman's cabinet, Ekman once again assumed the reins. In view of the unpleasant memories of

---

[15] On the constitutional committee's scrutiny of the cabinet minutes and the chamber's occasional practice of endorsing the findings see chapter VII infra. On the votes of 1929 and 1930 see Axel Brusewitz, "Statsrådets ansvarighet," in [Sweden, Riksdagen,] *Sveriges riksdag,* Stockholm: Victor Petterson, 1931–1938, XV, 453.

[16] See Dahlberg and Tingsten, *op.cit.,* pp. 172 ff.

1928 the Löfgren group this time refused to join the ministry. Composed only of Prohibitionist Liberals, the second Ekman cabinet therefore marks an all-time low for parliamentary support of the government (there were twenty-eight Prohibitionists in the lower chamber and, following the partial senate elections in 1931, twenty-two in the senate). Nevertheless, Ekman's second cabinet, like the first one, survived two entire riksdag sessions without a major defeat, and the premier's resignation again was the result of complications unrelated to the parliamentary situation. In the spring of 1932 the suicide of a well-known Swedish financier, Ivar Kreuger, and sensational investigations into his bankrupt financial empire made the international headlines. The investigators soon discovered that Prime Minister Ekman in the previous year had accepted a campaign contribution of 50,000 crowns from Kreuger. The premier paid back this sum to Kreuger's receivers but persistently denied rumors that he had accepted any further contributions. When another check for 50,000 crowns with Ekman's endorsement was discovered among Kreuger's papers he went so far as to deny his own signature. Finally, when the receivers threatened a lawsuit, Ekman paid back the second sum. At this point his public position had become untenable, and both the monarch and Ekman's colleagues in the cabinet insisted on his immediate resignation. For a few weeks (August to September in 1932) Felix Hamrin took over the premiership, but after a major Socialist victory in the September elections the entire cabinet resigned. Ekman's political career had come to an abrupt and ignominious end.

SOCIALIST PREDOMINANCE (SINCE 1932)

The nineteen-twenties in Sweden were on the whole a period of relative prosperity and peaceful foreign relations. Toward the beginning of the period a conflict with Finland over the possession of the Åland archipelago brought some temporary foreign tension,[17] and in 1921–1922 there was a temporary peak in unemployment. Yet these passing disturbances cannot compare

[17] See Eric Cyril Bellquist, "Some Aspects of the Recent Foreign Policy of Sweden," in *University of California Publications in International Relations*, 1:284 ff. (1929).

with the internal and external stresses that resulted from the Great Depression of the early 'thirties and later during the Second World War. On the other hand the machinery of government during the nineteen-twenties was undergoing what to many Swedish observers has seemed like a single great crisis, while the 'thirties and 'forties brought a period of singular governmental stability. This combination of opposite trends may explain in part why Sweden managed to preserve constitutional and democratic processes at a time when these processes broke down in many countries on the European continent. With some oversimplification it might be said that during the last generation the Swedish governmental system was weakest when the nation was enjoying peace and prosperity, and that when grave internal and external problems beset the nation the government had recovered enough strength to cope with them successfully.

In the history of Swedish parliamentary cabinet government, therefore, the years from 1920 to 1932 and from 1932 to the present stand out as two clearly distinct periods. During the former period the life expectancy of cabinets was considerably shorter than at any time before or after; during the later period cabinets have attained a considerable age and there has been more continuity in cabinet membership than at any time since the nineteenth century. During the nineteen-twenties governments of the left, right, and center followed one another in fairly rapid succession, yet the Liberal party at all times was in a position to dictate the most important parliamentary decisions. Since 1932, on the other hand, the Social Democrats have been predominant and have continuously sat in the cabinet (either by themselves or as senior partners in a coalition) except for a brief interlude in 1936. The ministries of the 'twenties were minority cabinets; those since the 'thirties nearly always have been able to rely on majority support. The new developments in Swedish cabinet government during the last two decades were made possible, at first, by cooperation between the Socialists and Agrarians, and later by the majority or near-majority position that the Socialists held after 1936.

The 1932 elections came at a time of economic crisis. Sweden had begun to feel the effects of the Great Depression in the winter of 1931–1932. Unemployment had climbed back to the

1921–1922 level and by the end of 1932 surpassed it. In 1933 nearly 8 per cent of all industrial workers were out of work. The price index for agricultural products early in 1933 dropped to about 70 per cent of its 1929 level. Unemployment in agriculture, although not as widespread as in industry, also assumed major proportions.[18] It is probably no coincidence that the 1932 elections brought a major victory to the parties that represented the two groups of the population hardest hit by the crisis, the Socialists and the Agrarians. Social Democratic gains reduced the bourgeois majority in the lower house to a scant margin of six votes (118 : 112). The Agrarians replaced the Liberals as the second largest non-Socialist party; the Conservatives, in spite of heavy losses, remained the largest bourgeois group, while the Liberals took third place.

When the Hamrin government resigned immediately after the 1932 election, various attempts to form a majority coalition were made. Since neither a bourgeois coalition nor a Liberal-Socialist combination proved feasible, the Socialist leader, Per Albin Hansson, at length formed another minority cabinet. In a policy proclamation the government stated that its major objective would be to "find a way of helping the victims of the crisis."[19] It proposed to combat unemployment with extensive public works; it also recognized the need for bringing agricultural prices up to a higher level and preventing farm indebtedness. All of the major parties in parliament, from Socialists to Conservatives, recognized a need for far-reaching antidepression measures; yet the Conservatives and many Agrarians and Liberals were anxious to limit expenditures on public works, which they feared might hamper industrial recovery. Disagreements with non-Socialist majorities in parliament over measures to combat unemployment had been the traditional stumbling block of Socialist cabinets. Would the crisis program of the Hansson government also be defeated by a bourgeois bloc under Liberal leadership? For a while a common bourgeois front against the cabinet seemed a definite possibility; soon,

[18] For detailed figures see Dahlberg and Tingsten, *op.cit.*, pp. 24 ff., 172 ff., and Mauritz Bonow, *Staten och jordbrukskrisen*, 2d edn., Stockholm: KF, 1935, p. 129.

[19] *Socialdemokratiska partistyrelsens berättelse för år 1932*, Stockholm: Tiden, 1933, pp. 49 f.

however, it became apparent that an important change in the tactical situation had occurred.

From 1919 to 1932, only two party combinations had been assured of a majority in both houses: the old leftist combination of Liberals and Socialists and the more recent bourgeois alignment of Liberals and Conservatives (or Liberals, Conservatives, and Agrarians). It was this constellation that had enabled Ekman to control legislation by cooperating now with the Conservatives and Agrarians and now with the Socialists. Following the 1932 elections, however, a third combination of parties appeared on the list of possible majority blocs—namely, that of Socialists and Agrarians.[20] This meant that the Agrarians, if they managed to cut themselves loose from their exclusive association with the other two bourgeois parties and to overcome any psychological barriers to an understanding with the Socialists, would be able to challenge the "balancing" position of the Liberals. Yet a balance with two "balancers" is a contradiction in terms: a see-saw can have but one pivot. The only way in which the center parties could maintain the see-saw system of legislation was by agreeing on a joint policy and common tactics.[21] If they allowed themselves to be divided, control over legislation would slip into the hands of one of the outer parties—or, more specifically, into the hands of the Socialists. For the Socialists were in a position to gain majority support for their measures by striking a bargain with *either* of the center parties, whereas the Conservatives had to form a common front with *both* of them in order to gain a majority. It would be entirely wrong to suppose that tactical considerations were the impelling motive behind the political realignments that took shape in Sweden during the middle 'thirties. The men who helped formulate Swedish policy during this period were honestly concerned to save their nation from the devastating effects of the depression. The breakdown of the Weimar regime early in 1933 in the midst of an economic crisis further im-

---

[20] A Socialist-Agrarian combination would have commanded a lower house majority as early as 1924, yet only after a slight Socialist gain in 1932 did the combination have a majority in the senate as well. See tables 6 and 8, appendix.

[21] Cf. Georg Andrén, "Tvåkammarsystemets tillkomst och utveckling," in *Sveriges riksdag, op.cit.*, IX, 624 ff.

pressed on Swedish leaders the need for quick and decisive action. Yet no political leader is free to disregard the tactical situation—i.e. the pursuit of power as such—in the service of a high cause, unless he is willing to imperil his own leadership and the very cause he is trying to serve. The most prominent political figures of this period, and above all the new Socialist premier, Per Albin Hansson, combined a deep concern about the issues at stake with a keen sense of political realities. While tactical considerations in no way determined the course of political events, they defined the range of possibilities.

The major disagreement between the Hansson government and the three non-Socialist parties in the riksdag revolved around the question whether the depression was to be overcome by an expansionist or a deflationist economic policy. The leaders of the Conservative, Agrarian, and Prohibitionist parties all advocated stringent limitations on public expenditures, while the government proposed to overcome the crisis by reflationist measures. Early in May 1933 the non-Socialist representatives on the committee that was considering the government's public works program agreed on a common policy, and it seemed certain that the major government bills would be rewritten in accordance with opposition demands. Meanwhile, however, the cabinet, sidestepping the committee and the party leaders, had contacted individual members of the Agrarian and Liberal parties. The government thus discovered that large segments of these two parties did not share the point of view of their leaders and would be willing to go along with most of the government's unemployment policy, provided the reflationist measures were extended to agriculture. The new program which emerged from these negotiations was finally accepted in the riksdag with the support of the Socialists, a majority of the Agrarians, and a small group of Prohibitionists.[22]

[22] On the political negotiations leading up to the passage of the anti-depression program see two works by Olle Nyman: *Krisuppgörelsen mellan socialdemokraterna och bondeförbundet*, Uppsala: Almqvist & Wiksell, 1944, and *Svensk parlamentarism, 1932–1936*, Uppsala: Almqvist & Wiksell, 1947, esp. pp. 89–164. Dr. Nyman's account is supplemented by the reminiscences of Ernst Wigforss, who, as Socialist minister of finance, was one of the principals in negotiations with the Agrarians. See Ernst Wigforss, *Minnen*, 3 vols., Stockholm: Tiden, 1951–1954, III, 30ff.

The adoption of what has been called the "Swedish New Deal"[23] constituted a spectacular victory for the Hansson government. At the same time it marks the actual point of transition from the first to the second phase in the history of Swedish cabinet government. Three major aspects of this transition can be distinguished. First, the Socialists at the last minute had managed to prevent the formation of a common bourgeois front. Second, the initiative in formimg a legislative majority for the first time since 1920 had come from one of the large, outer parties rather than from the small parties of the center. Third, the political initiative had returned from the committees to the cabinet. These developments were accompanied by important changes in the party situation. The circumstances under which the government's antidepression program was passed amounted to a palace revolution within the two center parties. The disgruntled leaders of the two parties, ex-Premier Hamrin of the Liberals and Olof Olsson i Kullenbergstorp of the Agrarians, joined in the chorus of those who denounced the government and the insurgent members of their parties as "horse traders." Changes in party leadership seemed inevitable. The two wings of the Prohibitionist party reached a compromise by which leadership was divided between Hamrin and the head of the insurgents, Ola Jeppsson. The provisional duumvirate continued until the merger between Prohibitionists and Löfgrenites late in 1934. The aged Olsson i Kullenbergstorp, on the other hand, had been thoroughly repudiated by the younger members of his party and actual leadership had entirely passed into the hands of the "horse traders," headed by Axel Pehrsson i Bramstorp and Professor Karl Gustaf Westman. Early in 1934 the Agrarians unanimously elected Bramstorp their official leader.[24]

The Agrarians under Bramstorp maintained their informal alliance with the Socialists, and during the 1934 session the two parties completed the antidepression program that they had embarked upon during the previous year. A small group of Liberals continued their support of the Socialist-Agrarian

[23] Bjarne Braatoy, *The New Sweden: A Vindication of Democracy*, London: Thomas Nelson, 1939, ch. 1.

[24] Actually the antidepression policy of 1933 caused some splits in all the major parties; cf. pp. 171 f. infra.

policies. The Liberal party as a whole, however, from this time has definitely been to the "right" of the Agrarians (that is to say, it has shown less inclination to cooperate with the Socialists than have the Agrarians). Meanwhile the economy had begun to recover, and by the end of 1934 both employment and agricultural prices were back to their predepression levels. Economists have debated whether this recovery was due primarily to governmental policies or to other factors,[25] yet the economic laymen, who make up the overwhelming majority of the Swedish as of any other electorate, at the time were very largely inclined to give the government and its supporters full credit. In the local elections of 1934 both Agrarians and Socialists made small but significant gains as compared with the local elections of 1930.

As the riksdag's attention turned away from economic questions the farmer-labor alliance began to show signs of strain. On a number of minor questions the Agrarians joined the opposition; the government, as a result, suffered a series of reversals in connection with proposals for legislative protection from secondary boycotts for so-called "neutral third parties" in labor disputes and in connection with a vote of censure against the Socialist minister of justice.[26] In the summer of 1936 the Hansson cabinet suffered a major defeat on a question of military appropriations. In view of signs of increasing international tension, such as German rearmament and the Sino-Japanese, Ethiopian, and Spanish wars, the government earlier in 1936 had proposed a certain increase in Swedish defense expenditures. The three opposition parties (Conservatives, Liberals, and Agrarians), however, insisted on more substantial increases and gathered a majority for their counterproposal.[27] Hansson declared that the government would be willing to go

[25] See, e.g., Arthur Montgomery, *How Sweden Overcame the Depression 1930–1933*, Stockholm: Bonnier, 1938; *Annals of the American Academy of Political and Social Science*, vol. 197 (May 1938); Clark, *op.cit.*; and Brinley Thomas, *Monetary Policy and Crises: A Study of Swedish Experience*, London: Routledge, 1936.

[26] On secondary boycotts see Westerståhl, *op.cit.*, pp. 383 ff., and Robbins, *op.cit.*, pp. 173 ff. On the censure motion see Nyman, *Svensk parlamentarism, 1932–1936, op.cit.*, pp. 340 ff.

[27] On the defense debate of the nineteen-thirties see Tingsten, *The Debate on the Foreign Policy of Sweden 1918–1939, op.cit.*, pp. 277 ff.

along with a further increase provided the opposition would support an upward revision of government old age and disability pensions that was to come up for legislative action shortly afterward. When the three non-Socialist parties at the end of the 1936 session rejected the government's pension plan he ministry finally resigned.

Since the Agrarians had decisively contributed to Hansson's fall, their leader Pehrsson i Bramstorp was charged with the formation of a new cabinet. The numerical strength of the Agrarians in the riksdag was very small, almost as small as that of the Liberals when Ekman formed his two cabinets in 1926 and 1930. Bramstorp merely went through the motions of trying to bring about a bourgeois coalition and meanwhile went ahead with plans for a purely Agrarian ministry. It was therefore generally assumed that Bramstorp wished to resume Ekman's familiar see-saw tactics. Yet the new Agrarian ministry took office during the parliamentary recess, and before the government had even met the riksdag the lower chamber elections of 1936 frustrated any such plans. The Socialists returned with 112 mandates, while the three bourgeois parties were reduced to a total of 107 mandates. (The Kilbom Socialists and Communists divided the remaining 11 seats.) Even a coalition of all three non-Socialist parties would thus have been insufficient to counterbalance Social Democratic strength. Bramstorp's balancing act had to be called off even before the spectators had taken their seats. His "Vacation Government" resigned in September 1936 after a mere three months in office.

Hansson, who was the obvious choice for the premiership, might well have formed another purely Socialist government. His first cabinet had remained in office longer than any previous parliamentary cabinet and, in spite of some difficulties, had maintained its leadership in parliament during four entire sessions. The position of his party in the lower chamber after the Socialist election victory was greatly strengthened. Only an unlikely alliance of the three bourgeois parties with the two Communist groups could have defeated the Socialists in the lower house. In the senate, on the other hand, the Socialists still faced a bourgeois majority. If the party wished to carry out any long-range legislative program it would have to prevent the Agrarians from aligning with the two parties of the right.

In consultation with the highest party organs, Hansson therefore decided to offer the Agrarians a share in the government. Bramstorp, who favored cooperation with the Socialists, had to overcome considerable opposition within his own party, but in the end a coalition was formed.[28]

During the following years (1937–1939) the Socialist-Agrarian government enacted a broad program of social legislation. An act to improve old age and disability benefits met a long-stand ing Socialist demand, and the Agrarians obtained a broadening of the existing agricultural price support system. The riksdag passed several measures extending the rights of the working class: existing maximum-hour regulations were widened so as to guarantee an eight-hour day to agricultural workers, seamen, and employees in the retail trade; and government employees won the right of collective bargaining. The government removed an old grievance of the labor unions when it proposed the repeal of an act of 1899 which provided penalties not only for coercion but also for attempted coercion of workers by other workers in connection with labor disputes.[29] The riksdag also adopted a series of new laws providing for free maternity care; subsidies to fatherless children, orphans, and children of disabled parents; rent allowances for large families; and dental care for the entire population at nominal charges.[30] By 1939, however, the approaching international crisis began to preoccupy Swedish lawmakers. In the spring the riksdag passed additional military appropriations and price control measures. As the international situation grew tenser the Agrarians began to plead that the government coalition be enlarged so as to include members of the Liberal and Conservative parties. Yet both the Socialists and the two right wing parties were reluctant to take this step; their leaders declared publicly that for the time being they considered existing methods of informal

[28] See *Socialdemokratiska partistyrelsens berättelse för år 1936*, Stockholm: Tiden, 1937, pp. 105 ff.; cf. Nyman, *Svensk parlamentarism, 1932–1936, op.cit.*, pp. 466 ff.

[29] See Westerståhl, *op.cit.*, pp. 214 ff., 415 ff., and Robbins, *op.cit.*, pp. 246 ff.

[30] The present Swedish system of social benefits, developed partly during this period and partly since the Second World War, is described in Karl J. Höjer, *Social Welfare in Sweden*, Stockholm: Swedish Institute, 1949, and [Sweden, Socialstyrelsen,] *Social Sweden*, Stockholm, 1952.

cooperation between government and opposition adequate.[31] Nevertheless, negotiations continued behind the scenes and, following Russia's attack on Finland in December 1939, Premier Hansson finally formed a national coalition cabinet. The new government included the leaders of the four major parties —Prime Minister Hansson of the Socialists; Professor Gösta Bagge, minister of education, of the Conservatives; Gustaf Andersson i Rasjön, minister of communications, of the Liberals; and Axel Pehrsson-Bramstorp,[32] minister of agriculture, of the Agrarians. In addition the ministry included three prominent Socialists and one additional member of each of the other three parties. The important foreign portfolio went to a career diplomat, and two other nonpartisans sat in the cabinet.[33] This ministry, with some changes in personnel, stayed in office until the end of the Second World War.

From the beginning Sweden proclaimed her complete neutrality in the conflict. The German invasion of Poland in September

[31] See Hansson's speech of August 27, 1939, reprinted in Per Albin Hansson, *Svensk hållning och handling*, Stockholm: Tiden, 1945, pp. 14f.; and statements by Bagge (Conservative) and Andersson i Rasjön (Liberal) in the lower chamber on September 12, in *Riksdagens protokoll, Andra kammaren, 1939U*, no. 2, pp. 1, 9. On the latter occasion the Agrarian floor leader, Hjalmar Svensson i Grönvik, replied tersely: "I believe, in contrast to Messrs. Bagge and Andersson i Rasjön, {that the time [for forming a national coalition] has come." *Riksdagens protokoll, Andra kammaren, 1939U, op.cit.*, no. 2, pp. 10f.

[32] A note on certain usages regarding Swedish family names may be in order. Bearers of patronymics such as Pehrsson, Gustafsson, Olsson, and Svensson are commonly distinguished by appending to their last name that of their farm or residence preceded by "i" (meaning "in"). Since these names are extraordinarily common (among the 230 lower chamber members there were, in 1949, 15 Anderssons, 14 Johanssons or Jo[h]nssons, 12 Petter[s]sons or Pe[h]rssons, eight Nil[s]sons, and seven Ericssons or Erikssons) there has been an increasing tendency to exchange them for more distinguishing, as well as distinguished, names. Often the farm name is substituted (thus the Conservative leader Fritiof Domö entered politics as Fritiof Gustafson i Domö); occasionally the two are hyphenated (thus Axel Pehrsson, long known after his farm as Pehrsson i Bramstorp or simply Bramstorp, in 1937 adopted the name Pehrsson-Bramstorp).

[33] There was Conservative criticism because Hansson, with the king's consent, delayed his resignation until the new cabinet was formed (see the remarks by Carl Gustaf Sundberg in *Riksdagens protokoll, Första kammaren, 1940*, no. 3, p. 84). This procedure naturally strengthened the premier's hand in negotiating with the Conservatives and Liberals.

1939 and Russia's attack on Finland in December of that year brought the war into Sweden's immediate vicinity. Shortly after the outbreak of the Finno-Russian War, Sweden, anxious to maintain her neutrality, rejected a request by Britain and France to allow the passage of an expeditionary corps through Swedish territory into Finland. As a result of the German occupation of Denmark and Norway in the spring of 1940, and Germany's attack on Russia in June 1941 (in which Finland joined), Sweden was surrounded on all sides by Axis-held territory until the time of Allied victory in the spring of 1945. The wartime situation not only brought many material deprivations but also made necessary certain limitations on peacetime political procedures. A number of wartime constitutional amendments were passed in 1940 and ratified in 1941. These authorized the government, with the consent of three fourths of the riksdag, to introduce preliminary censorship and to postpone parliamentary elections by one year. Yet this authority was never invoked: except for the confiscation of individual issues of newspapers containing attacks on the belligerents and for the banning from the mails of Communist newspapers, the press remained free; and three general elections—two for the lower chamber and one for the provincial and municipal assemblies—were held on schedule during the war. At the end of the emergency, in 1945, the wartime constitutional amendments were promptly repealed. Although the sympathies of the government and the people were no doubt preponderantly on the Allied side, the government saw itself forced to yield to German demands that troops moving from Norway to Finland be allowed to pass through Swedish territory—a privilege that the government had previously denied to the Western allies. Sweden also allowed German troops on leave to travel on the Swedish railways. On the other hand the Swedish government supported the Norwegian cause by allowing the formation and training of a Norwegian police force on Swedish territory. As Axis military power declined the earlier concessions to the Germans were revoked.

During this trying time of external tension the Swedish people manifested a remarkable spirit of unity. In its first declaration before the riksdag the wartime cabinet announced that "one of the preconditions for the work of the national coalition government is that internal differences of political opinion be set aside."[34] Although the government received periodic declarations of support and solidarity from all major parties, it also faced many individual critics both inside and outside parliament. Most of the criticism was restrained and related to details of policy, yet some members of parliament and some newspapers adopted a more fundamentally critical attitude. Many of the critics complained that the government did not give enough moral and material assistance to Finland at the time of the Russian attack in the winter of 1939–1940, and to Norway after her occupation by the Germans; that it did not communicate fully enough with the riksdag on decisions of foreign policy and generally kept the people inadequately informed; and that it yielded too readily to German pressure in the question of troop transports through Swedish territory. Significantly, the most outspoken criticism along these lines came not from the few extremists of the right and left but from individuals and newspapers affiliated with the government parties, notably the Liberals and Social Democrats.[35] There were other differences of opinion that largely remained unexpressed; for example, between those who continued to believe in Allied victory when Axis power was at its zenith and those who—more or less reluctantly—accepted a Nazi victory as inevitable.[36] For all alike the feeling of being condemned to

[34] *Riksdagens protokoll, Andra kammaren, 1939U*, no. 26, p. 1, and *Första kammaren, 1939U*, no. 26, p. 1.

[35] As early as January 1940 Rickard Sandler, ex-premier and foreign minister in the second Hansson cabinet, declared: "Since all parties are now officially represented in the government there is all the more occasion for individual members of parliament from all parties to express their opinion on national policy...." *ibid., Första kammaren, 1940*, no. 3, pp. 33 f. Among the most vigorous critics were the Socialists Erik Brandt and Ture Nerman (editor of the newspaper *Trots Allt*) and one of the leading Liberal dailies, *Göteborgs Handels- och Sjöfartstidning*, edited by Torgny Segerstedt. The government point of view is represented in two collections of speeches by Premier Hansson, *op.cit.*, and the foreign minister, Christian Günther, *Tal i en tung tid*, Stockholm: Bonnier, 1945; see also the compilation of official communiqués and riksdag debates, *Svensk utrikespolitik under andra världskriget*, ed. Utrikespolitiska institutet, Stockholm: KF, 1946.

[36] See Herbert Tingsten, "Swedish Foreign Policy after the Second World War," *American Scandinavian Review*, 33:308 (1945), and Rowland Kenney, *The Northern Tangle*, London: Dent, 1946, pp. 179 ff.

inaction in one of the greatest struggles in world history was a trying experience the nervous strain of which it is hard for the outsider fully to appreciate.

During the last two years of the war, as the foreign threat diminished, disagreements within the cabinet on questions of internal policy began to come to the fore. All parties used the period of forced leisure during the war for major program revisions. Although a comparison of these programs reveals a large area of interparty agreement, the remaining points of disagreement now appeared in clearer relief. The Communists in the 1944 elections scored a major victory by agitating against the wartime wage ceiling imposed by the government (their vote rose from 3.5 per cent of the electorate in 1940 to 10.3 per cent in 1944), and thereby caused the Socialists to veer sharply to the left. During the early war years prominent members of all major parties had expressed themselves in favor of continuing the national coalition even in peacetime;[37] now the non-Socialists insisted that continued cooperation was impossible unless the Social Democrats ceased their "propaganda socialization." Thus disagreements on internal policy finally led to the dissolution of the national coalition after the end of the emergency. In July 1945 Premier Hansson formed another purely Socialist government—his fourth cabinet.

In a conciliatory policy declaration the new government announced that it would continue the Social Democratic policy of the last thirteen years and indicated that it proposed to adopt the party's Postwar Program of 1944 as its guide; it summarized the principles of that program as "progressive democratization of society, politically, economically, and socially."[38] In accordance with this program the government expanded the structure of social legislation that had been begun before the war. A series of laws provided for "general child allowances" (consisting of subsidies of 260 crowns—about $72—per annum paid to parents for each child under sixteen years of age),[39] ex-

[37] Cf. chapter VIII infra.
[38] Socialdemokratiska partistyrelsen, *Berättelse för år 1945*, Stockholm: Tiden, 1946, p. 45.
[39] The general child allowances replaced the traditional system of income tax exemptions for dependent children, which was held to favor the upper income groups; see Höjer, *op.cit.*, pp. 126f.

tended the vacation rights of workers, and arranged vacations at government expense for housewives. To pay for these and other social benefits the riksdag adopted a revised system of taxation, including withholding taxes on income, more steeply progressive income tax rates, and a new inheritance tax.

During the postwar years the government gradually lifted wartime rationing but maintained government controls over exports and imports. Under the leadership of the Socialist minister of commerce, Gunnar Myrdal, Sweden concluded a six-year trade and credit agreement with the Soviet Union. This last measure, together with the new tax system, provoked the most vigorous criticism from the bourgeois opposition. In 1948 the riksdag adopted a major revision of the criminal code of 1864 and in 1950 passed a school reform bill in an effort to equalize educational opportunities. The Socialist Postwar Program, beyond the improvement of social services and the equalization of income and educational opportunity, demanded "socialization where private enterprise entails abuses or monopolism."[40] The government, however, took no major steps toward realizing this sweeping demand, which has been seriously criticized by the non-Socialist parties. In her external policy Sweden has resolutely kept aloof from alliances. Thus she has fully participated in recent agreements for European economic cooperation but has refused to join the North Atlantic pact. Although vocal minorities have sharply attacked this decision, the leaders of the major parties stand united behind the traditional foreign policy.[41]

A shift of generations in the Socialist leadership resulted in a number of personnel changes in the postwar cabinet. Per Albin Hansson died in Oktober 1946 at the age of sixty. His place as premier and party leader was taken by Tage Erlander, a man in his forties who had only recently taken over the educational

[40] *The Postwar Programme of Swedish Labor*, Stockholm: Landsorganisationen, 1948, p. 28.

[41] On Sweden's recent foreign policy and her impressive defense effort see, e.g., Henning Friis, ed., *Scandinavia between East and West*, Ithaca: Cornell University Press, 1951, pp. 255 ff.; Royal Institute of International Affairs, *The Scandinavian States and Finland*, London, 1951, pp. 267 ff.; Harald Wigforss, "Sweden and the Atlantic Pact," *International Organization*, 3:434–443 (1949); and William L. Shirer, *The Callenge of Scandinavia*, Boston: Little, Brown, 1955, pp. 125–143.

portfolio. In 1949 and 1951 two of Hansson's contemporaries, Ernst Wigforss and Gustav Möller, retired from the cabinet, both in their late sixties. Wigforss, a philologist by training, was one of the most vigorous intellects in the party, headed the finance department in every Socialist cabinet after 1925, and won fame as the originator of Sweden's double budget and as one of the chief authors of the party's Postwar Program of 1944. Möller had been Hansson's close friend and associate since their days in the Socialist youth movement and later became the main architect of Sweden's social welfare program. By 1952 only two members of Hansson's team of 1932 were still in the cabinet. One was Östen Undén, who once, in 1917, had been Sweden's youngest cabinet minister and who in 1945 took over the foreign office. The other was Per Edvin Sköld, successively minister of agriculture, of "economic coordination," and of finance, and in recent years perhaps the strongest political force in the cabinet.

The postwar situation has been characterized by an almost equal balance between Socialists and bourgeois parties in the riksdag. The Socialists had an ample majority in the lower house from 1941 to 1944. When the wartime coalition dissolved they held an even half of the lower chamber seats, and the remarkable Liberal victory of 1948 cost them another three seats. In the senate the Socialists have held a majority since 1941, which diminished only slightly as a result of subsequent local elections (1946, 1950, and 1954). The Erlander cabinet, by virtue of its senate support, was assured of a margin—though a dwindling one—on joint votes. Yet its position was tenuous enough to prompt negotiations for a broader coalition. The Agrarians, after turning down a previous offer in 1948, joined the Erlander cabinet late in 1951. This timely realignment forestalled a change of regime as a result of the bourgeois election victory in 1952. The situation since 1945 has been like that of the nineteen-twenties, except that this time the Socialists rather than the Liberals found themselves in the position of balancer.

CHAPTER IV

THE ELECTORATE

EVEN the casual observer of Swedish politics will be impressed with the stability of the four-party system in recent decades. Since the First World War the Swedish government has been based on the democratic right of every adult citizen to participate in the selection of his rulers. Election administration is efficient and orderly; complaints of fraud or corruption are all but unknown. Candidates are elected by proportional representation rather than plurality vote. As in other European countries, proportionalism in Sweden has encouraged and confirmed the division of the electorate into more than two parties. Yet a number of specific features have mitigated the divisive effects of the system. Proportionality is attained in relatively small districts, so that a party must build up a sizable national following or achieve strong local concentration to compete with its rivals on equal terms. Until recently the device of election cartels put a premium on interparty cooperation, and hence on moderation. Since then the premium has been on size alone. Either way extremist groups, with whom others will not cooperate and who start from small beginnings, have been the losers. Thus the Swedish variant of proportional representation has buttressed the four-party system implicit in the country's social structure. Although the party hierarchies in fact control the nomination of candidates, this control is at the sufferance of the voters. Hence Sweden, unlike some other countries using the list system of elections, has not cut the bond between the voter and his representative. Party alignments in the senate continue to lag behind those in the chamber; yet the strong bicameral contrast that bedevilled Swedish politics in the late nineteenth century is now a thing of the past. The absence of substantial national and religious minorities and of strong regional contrast also has contributed to stability and moderation. Following the settlement of the fundamental constitutional issues of the turn of the century party distinctions have largely coincided with economic and social differences. Conservatives, Agrarians, and Socialists speak for the interests of employers, farmers, and workers respectively. Those middle class elements not readily identified with any of these groups provide the chief support for the Liberal party. Variations in party preference from region to region, between the sexes, and among various age groups have been slight but remarkably persistent.

STABILITY OF PARTY STRENGTH

A comparison of the party vote in the first election based on universal suffrage, in 1921, with that in the lower chamber election of 1952 illustrates the stability of party strength in Sweden (table 1):

TABLE 1

PARTY STRENGTH IN 1921 AND 1952 ELECTIONS

Party	Vote for Party as Per Cent of Total Vote	
	1921	1952
Conservatives	25.8	14.4
Agrarians	11.1	10.7
Liberals	19.1	24.4
Social Democrats	36.2	46.1
Communists (including Left Socialists)	7.8	4.4

The *net* change in party strength over a period of thirty-one years amounted to a little over 15 per cent of the electorate. Disregarding compensating gains and losses in party strength, this means that in 1952 six Swedish voters out of seven voted as their parents did a generation earlier. Naturally, a juxtaposition of election returns three decades apart gives an over-simplified view; the figures nevertheless correctly indicate the trend. The Conservatives have been the main losers in the political arena: in 1921 the second largest party, they had by 1952 dropped to third place and lost nearly half their former strength. The Social Democrats, for over three decades the largest party, have been the principal gainers. A slight net advance was registered by the Liberals and a slight loss by the

Communists, whereas the net long-term change in Agrarian strength has been negligible.

Although the trend has been toward the left, there have been some crosscurrents.[1] The Conservatives registered some slight gains during two separate periods, in the nineteen-twenties and during the later 'thirties; each time, however, they lost more in the following period (the early 'thirties and the 'forties) than they had previously gained. The Liberals, on the other hand, lost continuously during the 'twenties, stabilized their following during the 'thirties, and have made a considerable advance since 1944. The Social Democrats have gained in all the elections, except for minor setbacks in 1926, 1928, and 1952 and three more serious successive defeats in 1942, 1944, and 1946. Of all the parties the Agrarians have had the most stable electoral support; they have never polled more than 14.3 or less than 10.3 per cent of the total vote (1936, 1954). The groups on the extreme left, on the other hand, have had the most fickle popular following; they reached their low (4.0 per cent) in 1930 and their high (11.2 per cent) in 1946. After the last in a series of splits, the reconstituted Communist party since 1929 has closely followed every shift and turn in the Kremlin's tactics. As a result its electoral success has largely been a function of popular reaction to Soviet policies. The Communist vote declined sharply following the Soviet attack on Finland (1939–1940) and the Czechoslovak coup (1948); its all-time high came in the wake of the victory of the USSR and the Western allies over Nazi Germany.

Even more important than individual party strengths have been the shifts in majority-minority alignments. Until 1932 the nonsocialist parties (Conservatives, Agrarians, and the two Liberal groups) polled a clear majority (of 54 to 57 per cent); in 1932 nonsocialists and socialists (the latter including the

---

[1] The above generalizations are based on all election returns for the lower chamber and the senate electoral colleges since 1921, with the sole exception of the local election of 1922. That election was the sixth in seven years, and participation marked a record low for this century. The returns deviated so markedly from the general trend that it can fairly be assumed that the active voters at that time did not constitute a representative sample of the normally active electorate. Cf. J. L. Hartmann, "Första kammarens partipolitiska sammansättning 1922–1945," in *Statsvetenskapliga studier*, Uppsala: Almqvist & Wiksell, 1944, p. 306.

Social Democrats and the Kilbom and Sillén Communists) stood almost evenly divided, with a mere sixty-five-vote margin for the socialists. After a slight setback in 1934, the socialist parties gained a majority in 1936 and have held it ever since. (Their total vote has ranged from 50.4 to 56.9 per cent.)

These figures show that landslides are virtually unknown to Swedish politics. The greatest single changes in electoral strength experienced by any party in recent deades were the Conservative setback in 1917 (from 35.5 per cent in the fall of 1914 to 24.7 per cent) and the Liberal gain in 1948 (from 12.9 per cent in 1944 and 15.6 per cent in 1946 to 22.8 per cent). No party has ever lost or gained more than 14 per cent of the lower chamber seats in a single election: this percentage was recorded when the Liberals lost thirty-one seats as a result of the elections in the spring of 1914 and gained a similar number in 1948 elections. In the upper chamber, shifts in party strength as a result of the staggered elections have been extremely small— the Social Democrats in 1943 set the record when they gained four seats (2.3 per cent of the total) at once.

The absence of landslides in Sweden is due partly to the electoral system and partly to the rigidity of traditional party alignments. In translating votes into parliamentary strength proportional representation, unlike the single-member plurality system, does not magnify slight gains and losses.[2] By creating conditions favorable to the survival of more than two parties, moreover, proportionalism provides a subtler instrument for recording the electorate's preference. The independent (or "marginal") voter, who causes shifts in electoral strength in two-party countries, is likely to find a party of the center more nearly to his liking; this in turn will relieve him of the necessity

[2] This disregards, of course, gains and losses due mostly to extensions of the franchise, such as the senate realignment in 1919. In a two-party country with single-member plurality elections, such as the United States, a far greater proportion of seats changes hands from election to election. The Republicans, for instance, gained 78 seats in the house of representatives in 1924 and lost 97 seats in 1932 (or 18 and 22 per cent of the total house membership). Over four-year periods the shifts have been even greater—the Republican losses between 1929 and 1933 totalled 150 seats (or 34 per cent). See U.S. Department of Commerce, Bureau of the Census, *Historical Statistics of the United States 1789–1945*, Washington: Government Printing Office, 1949, p. 293.

of changing parties frequently. Again, the monarch is not now in the habit of dissolving parliament in order to settle a conflict between two of the three top organs of government (king, cabinet, and parliament). Insofar as dissolutions of this kind tend to precipitate landslides, Sweden is less exposed to them than, say, Britian. The heavy losses of the Liberals in the spring of 1914—one of the closest Swedish approximations to a landslide—were the result of an election that followed immediately upon the second (and last) instance in Swedish history of a dissolution of parliament over a sharp issue.

Small fluctuations in the electoral tide may cause somewhat greater realignments in the lower chamber, but their full force is never felt in the senate. Large or locally concentrated parties are generally "overrepresented" in the lower chamber, so that a small variation in the following of such a party may result in a slightly greater change in its lower house delegation. In the senate such changes are both delayed and reduced. A vast majority of voters, in any case, remain loyal to their party, so that the parties can count on a relatively stable following in election after election.

VOTING

Since the introduction of a fully democratic suffrage in 1921 all adult Swedish citizens, both men and women, have been entitled to vote for the lower chamber and for the senate electoral colleges.[3] The voting age for the chamber was fixed at twenty-three in 1921 and reduced to twenty-one in 1945; that for the senate was set successively at twenty-seven (1921), twenty-three (1937), and twenty-one (1941).[4] Originally a

[3] The relevant statutes are the parliament act of 1866 and the election law of 1909. Both are reprinted, with amendments through 1949, in Robert Malmgren, ed., *Sveriges grundlagar*, 6th edn., Stockholm: Norstedt, 1951. On the amendment of 1951 concerning the distribution of a district's seats among the parties see infra.

[4] The senate electoral colleges consist of twenty-five provincial assemblies and six municipal councils in some of the largest cities. As early as 1921 the voting age in all municipalities was reduced to twenty-three. For the next sixteen years voters over twenty-seven in the six cities participating directly in senate elections had to vote for special senate electors. The statistics show that the younger voters who used their franchise were more inclined than their elders to vote for the Social

number of minor disqualifications limited the franchise for both houses: persons who had not performed their military duty, who were bankrupt, who were permanent public charges, or who were under legal guardianship were denied the right to vote. These restrictions were lifted one by one, with the exception of the last. Today therefore any man or woman who is a Swedish citizen, who at the end of the year preceding the election has reached the age of twenty-one, and who is not under guardianship may vote in any local or national election. As in most other European countries, voters are permanently registered. Public officials periodically prepare lists of all persons of twenty years and over.[5] They then check off the names of all persons not yet of voting age, of foreign citizens, and of persons under legal guardianship. Anyone whose name has been omitted, or who believes that the list contains names that it ought not to, may take his complaint to the responsible officials and, if necessary, to the courts. All those listed on the election register as voters are automatically entitled to vote. Elaborate provisions for absentee voting guarantee that anyone who fulfills the constitutional requirements for voters and cares to cast his ballot can do so. The terms "potential voter" and "registered voter" are synonymous in Sweden.

Elections must be held on a Sunday, and polling places usually are open from eight to ten hours on election day. Elections to the lower chamber are held on the third Sunday in September in every leap year (unless a dissolution intervenes); all local elections (for provincial, municipal, and township assemblies) take place in September of the intervening even years. The lower chamber includes 230 members elected for four-year terms. The twenty-eight constituencies, as a rule, coincide with the provinces; the two largest cities (Stockholm and Göteborg) form separate constituencies, and the third largest city, Malmö, is combined with three other cities in Malmöhus Province to form a single district. This four-city

Democrats, Communists, or National Socialists. The total number of voters between twenty-three and twenty-seven was so small, however, that their exclusion did not appreciably affect the composition of the senate.

[5] Census officials keep a continuous check of population changes due to births, deaths, and changes of residence. This facilitates both voter registration and the periodic reapportionment of riksdag seats.

district is the only constituency whose parts are not contiguous. Lower chamber seats are apportioned every four years among the constituencies according to their population.[6] In 1952 the number of representatives per district varied from three to twenty-four.

The 150 senators are elected for eight-year periods by the members of provincial assemblies and of certain municipal councils. There are nineteen senatorial constituencies (each of them including one or two provinces and in 1950 electing five to fourteen senators). Senate seats were apportioned in 1921 and are reapportioned every ten years. Unlike the lower chamber members, the senators are not all elected at the same time.[7] The nineteen constituencies are divided into eight groups, which take turns in electing about one eighth of the senate every year. Senators are thus replaced continuously. Since a complete renewal of the senate takes eight years and since the local assemblies serve for four years, only one half of the local assemblies chosen in any one local election have an opportunity to elect senators for their districts. The results of a local election do not affect the senate immediately, but they continue to be felt over a twelve-year period. The local assemblies elected in September 1938, for instance, served from January 1939 to January 1943. In September 1939 the first group of these assemblies elected senators who served from January 1940 to January 1948. In the fall of 1940, 1941, and 1942, additional senators were elected by three other groups of the local assemblies of 1938; the last of them served from

[6] The apportionment is not strictly proportional to the *voting* population. (1) Every district must receive at least three seats. (2) Seats are apportioned according to resident population (including both foreigners and those below voting age). (3) Those seats which remain undistributed after every district has received one seat for every two-hundred-and-thirtieth of the country's population it contains (or at least three seats) are assigned according to a formula that slightly favors the smaller districts. Under the first rule the island of Gotland has regularly received one more seat than it would otherwise have. The other two rules favor the predominantly rural districts. These include a larger proportion of children (which more than compensates for the greater concentration of foreigners in the large cities) and turn out a lighter vote; they also happen to be the smaller districts. Among the four major parties, the apportionment thus slightly favors the Agrarians—the only purely rural party.

[7] Except in the case of dissolution, on which cf. chapter VII infra.

January 1943 to January 1951. Thus the first senators who owed their seats to the 1938 assemblies did not enter the upper house until sixteen months after that local election, and the last senators chosen by the assemblies of 1938 did not leave the upper house until twelve years and four months after the popular election to which they indirectly owed their seats.

Not every voter may run for parliament. Candidates for the lower chamber must be at least twenty-three years of age and must reside in the constituency for which they run, while any voter over thirty-five years of age may run for the senate in any constituency, regardless of residence. In the last thirty years, however, an increasing proportion of senators have been residents of their constituencies.[8] Until 1949 lower chamber members had to be at least twenty-five years old, and until 1933 candidates for the senate had to have an annual taxable income of at least 3,000 crowns or own taxable property assessed at a minimum of 50,000 crowns. While these economic qualifications have been abolished, other restrictions on eligibility for both houses remain: no one against whom bankruptcy proceedings are pending and no one who has ever been convicted of election fraud may run for office.

PROPORTIONAL REPRESENTATION

The election procedure under any system of proportional representation differs considerably from the procedure under the Anglo-American single-member plurality system. Proportionality can be attained only in multiple-member constituencies. There are two main variants of proportionalism. Some American cities have adopted the so-called Hare (or single-transferable-vote) system, while Sweden and several other European countries use the list system. In Sweden every voter in a lower chamber or local election and every assemblyman in a senate election must indicate, first, his party preference and, second, a list of candidates in the order in which he wishes

[8] The proportion of senators residing outside their districts fell from 31 per cent in 1920 to 22 in 1930 and 17 in 1945. These figures are based on a study by Arne Björnberg, "Riksdagsproblem," *Tiden*, 37:452 (1945). Björnberg shows that the figures given in the official election statistics are not always reliable.

to see them elected. There are no official ballots listing all the possible choices of parties and candidates; any piece of white paper may be used.[9] Nor are there any legal provisions regulating the nomination of candidates. The law permits any party to register its official name in advance and to list its official candidates, so that other parties will be prevented from taking over its name and recruiting the involuntary support of its followers. The voter, nevertheless, remains free to vote for a party that has not been registered in this manner, or to vote for a registered party name while disregarding that party's official list. In the latter case the ballot is invalid unless the first name on it is that of a candidate approved by the party. In practice the parties hand out printed ballots to their followers, and most voters simply cast one of these; yet the voters' freedom to draw up their own list of candidates, though exercised within narrow limits, provides a valuable check on the parties' nomination precedure.[10]

[9] To preserve the secrecy of the vote, the law requires that ballots not contain any individual identifying marks. In the polling place every voter obtains an envelope from the election official, retires into a booth where he encloses the ballot in the envelope, and hands the envelope back to the official. The latter makes sure it is sealed, checks off the voter's name on the register, and drops the envelope into the ballotbox.

[10] Before 1952 the bourgeois parties frequently put up several alternative lists for the same party. One list, for instance, might be labelled "Conservative—Townsfolk," another "Conservative—Farmers." The first few names on all these lists usually were the same, but further down each list contained names that were designed to appeal to local or professional interests. The voters were given an illusion of choice among candidates for the same party—an illusion because only the top names had any chance of being elected. See Elis Håstad, *Det moderna partiväsendets organisation*, 2d edn., Stockholm: Bonnier, 1949, pp. 72 ff. Professor Friedrich asserts that in Sweden "the social-democratic electorate (labor) is very loyal," whereas "the conservative and liberal groups are more ready to bolt." Carl J. Friedrich, *Constitutional Government and Democracy*, rev. edn., Boston: Ginn, 1950, pp. 287 f. He may have been misled by the election statisticians who faithfully record the votes cast for such alternative lists of one party and, with a straight face, proceed to calculate indices of "party cohesion" on that basis. See, e.g., *Sveriges officiella statistik, Allmänna val, Riksdagsmannaval åren 1945–1948*, Stockholm, 1949, p. 43* [sic]. Genuine bolting is a rare phenomenon among bourgeois and Socialist voters alike. There have been a few isolated instances—e.g. in lower chamber elections among the Stockholm Löfgrenites in 1928 (see page 98 supra) and among the Norrköping Liberals in 1920, and in senate elections among the Örebro Socialists in 1934 and the Uppsala Agrarians in 1938 (see pages 150 n., 171 infra).

Once all the ballots have been cast they are totalled within each constituency. Since the number of seats for each constituency is given by nation-wide apportionment, their distribution among the various parties must now be determined. Until 1952 this was achieved by a mathematical formula known as the d'Hondt rule, which insures that the ratio of votes per seat will be as nearly equal as possible for all parties competing in a given district: the number of votes cast for each party is divided successively by the series of cardinal numbers (1, 2, etc.); among the quotients thus obtained, as many are selected as there are seats, beginning with the largest quotient; and each party receives one seat for every quotient that contains its vote as numerator.[11] Once the seats have been distributed among the parties it remains to assign them to individual candidates. If all ballots cast for a party contain the same names in the same sequence, this operation is simple: the names of the elected candidates are taken from the top of the list. If, on the other hand, the ballots contain different names or the same names in different sequence, the order of precedence among the various candidates is determined by a series of complex operations designed to reflect the voters' preferences as accurately as possible.

The major purpose of any system of proportionalism is to insure that all parties will be represented in the legislature in fairly exact proportion to their popular following. In a large electorate choosing a small number of representatives, the chances that perfect proportionality can be ensured are infinitesimal.[12] In practice, then, even the most elaborate system of proportional representation will fall short of its ideal—at least (to use Karl Braunias' phrase) as long as "representatives cannot be divided into fractions."[13] The Swedish system was

[11] For a more complete account of the details of the procedure see Robert Malmgren, *Sveriges författning*, vol. 1, 2d edn., Malmö, 1948, pp. 241–259.

[12] This would require that the total number of seats equalled a quotient obtained by dividing the total vote by the highest integral factor contained in each of the party votes. In most cases there would have to be as many seats as there are voters. Every voter would have to represent himself, and representation would be reduced *ad absurdum*.

[13] Or, one might add, as long as parliamentary representation is not superseded by an elaborate system of procuration such as is used at stock-

never designed to approach nation-wide proportionality, and it has thereby avoided what are often considered the major shortcomings of proportionalism.

The d'Hondt rule, as just mentioned, distributes seats as proportionately as possible among the parties *within a given district*. The laws of some countries, e.g. the Netherlands, treat the entire country as a single constituency, thus coming as close to proportionality as is humanly possible. Swedish legislators have hesitated to take this step, fearing that the task of voting for some 200 candidates would baffle the voter, that party hierarchies would gain exclusive control over nominations, and that any personal ties between voter and representative would be cut off. District-wide proportionality, however, will not en- sure nation-wide proportionality. Two observations are perti- nent in this connection. First, the ratio of votes per seat will in practice vary among the parties in a single constituency; as a result they will be left, in each district, with unused "surpluses" of different sizes—i.e. with votes that they might have foregone while retaining the same number of seats. Small parties are especially likely to accumulate sizable surpluses throughout the country; and since the total number of seats in Sweden is con- stant, the larger parties gain whatever the smaller ones lose. Second, the loss to the smaller and the gain to the larger parties will vary directly with the number of constituencies and in- versely with the number of seats per district. For instance, Sweden from 1911 to 1921 had 56 lower chamber districts electing from 3 to 8 members apiece; a majority of the chamber represented 3- and 4-member districts. In 1921 the number of constituencies was reduced by half, and since then a majority of the lower chamber has been chosen in districts with 9 seats or more. The older constituency division inhibited the growth of splinter parties far more effectively: before 1921, parties re- ceiving less than 30 per cent of the national vote were generally "underrepresented," and parties obtaining a larger vote "over- represented"; since then the threshold has been around 12 per cent of the national vote. It is no coincidence, therefore, that the three-party system, which survived in recognizable if

holders' meetings. The quote is from Karl Braunias, *Das parlamentarische Wahlrecht*, Berlin: De Gruyter, 1932, I, 219.

diluted form until 1921, since that time has been replaced by a four- to five-party system.[14]

From 1921 to 1951 the electoral law provided a partial remedy for the loss of "surpluses" by allowing them to be pooled. Unlike the system of the Weimar Republic, which enabled each party to use its own "surpluses" from the constituencies in order to elect additional candidates from a national list, the Swedish system permitted several parties within the same constituency to pool their remainders by forming a so-called cartel. Whenever several parties entered a cartel agreement the d'Hondt rule was first applied to all the cartels and any independent parties competing in a district, whereupon the seats of each cartel were distributed among the participant groups.[15] While the Weimar system led to a far-reaching splintering of parties, the Swedish cartel system encouraged a measure of cooperation among parties of similar complexion. From 1911 to 1924 the Liberals and Socialists frequently cooperated in elections (first by submitting their lists under the same party name, later by concluding cartels), whereas a "bourgeois" cartel of Conservatives, Agrarians, and Liberals became a standard feature after 1928.[16] The bourgeois cartel constituted a recurrent source of

[14] The effect of the enlargement of the districts is apparent in the following pairs of figures, the first in each pair representing the number of seats actually won in the 1921 elections and the second the number each party would have won under the old plan; Conservatives — 62, 59; Agrarians — 21, 16; Liberals — 41, 40; Socialists — 93, 105; Left Socialists — 6, 6; Communists — 7, 4. See Ernst von Heidenstam, "Andra kammaren och valkretsindelningen," *Statsvetenskaplig tidskrift*, 26:237f. (1923).

[15] Two numerical examples may illustrate the gain that smaller parties were able to derive from cartels. Suppose 2 parties in a 10-member district polled 6 and 5 per cent respectively. Running independently they would both go empty-handed. As partners in a cartel they would receive 1 seat, which eventually would go to the larger of the 2. Or suppose there are 4 parties, A, B, C, and D, competing for 5 seats and polling respectively 66, 13, 11, and 10 per cent. If all ran independently A would occupy all 5 seats. If B and C cooperated, B would gain 1 seat from A. If the 3 smaller parties formed a cartel, B and C would obtain 1 seat each, leaving A with only 3.

[16] The party composition of the senate electoral colleges is known in advance. Since the effect of all possible cartels can thus be calculated exactly, the parties have often resorted to fairly intricate patterns of cooperation. A party with a few "surplus" votes in one district may "loan" these to

irritation between Socialists and Agrarians. In the early 'thirties the Agrarians were in the anomalous position of cooperating with the Socialists in the riksdag and with the Liberals and Conservatives at election time. A Socialist-Agrarian cartel would have been of no use to the Agrarians, since the system operated in such a way as to make cooperation most advantageous to parties of roughly equal size. When the Socialists in 1936 offered to the Agrarians a role in the government the former stated as a "self-evident" condition that neither party was to form any cartels with outside groups.[17] In the 1938 local election the Agrarians suffered a slight setback, aggravated by their abstention from the bourgeois cartel, and this was one of the considerations that prompted their insistence on a national coalition in 1939. In 1948 the cartel question once again was one of the main obstacles to the conclusion of a new Socialist-Agrarian government coalition. When the coalition at length was formed, the two parties carried out a substantial modification of the relevant provisions of the electoral law. The amendment, first applied in the 1952 elections, prohibited the formation of cartels and replaced the d'Hondt rule by a new formula that tended to compensate the Agrarians for the losses they would otherwise have incurred.[18]

another party—that is to say, instruct a few of its members to vote for the other party's list; the other party will return the favor elsewhere. Or two parties may agree to "split" a mandate in such a fashion that the candidate of the first resigns his seat after four years in favor of a member of the second who has been elected as his alternate. Such loan and split-mandate arrangements have by no means been limited to closely related parties. In 1942, for example, the Conservatives in Göteborg formed a cartel to help the Socialists win a seat from the Communists; on another occasion the same two parties split a mandate which they gained at Liberal expense (Värmland, 1949).

[17] *Socialdemokratiska partistyrelsens berättelse för år 1936*, Stockholm; Tiden, 1937, p. 106.

[18] Under the new rule the votes obtained by each party in a district are divided not by the cardinal numbers but by 1.4, 3, 5, and successive odd numbers. The resulting distribution of seats favors the larger parties to about the same extent as the d'Hondt-cartel system but bears no direct relationship to either district-wide or nation-wide proportionality. Conservative critics were quick to calculate that the new system, if applied to elections from 1932 to 1948, would have given an average of seven extra seats to the Socialists and Agrarians and of two seats to the Liberals — all this at Conservative expense. See "Rädd regering," *Svensk tidskrift,*

IMPLICATIONS OF THE ELECTORAL SYSTEM

The division of the country into constituencies and the provisions for party cartels have tended to discourage the growth of small extremist parties—a tendency reinforced, if anything, by the recent election law amendment. The election statistics indicate that, from 1921 to 1948, parties polling less than 11 per cent of the national vote have consistently been "underrepresented" in the lower chamber, while parties polling more than 13 per cent have been "overrepresented."[19] The losses inflicted by the electoral system on small parties have been somewhat greater for parties evenly distributed throughout the country than for parties with strong regional concentration. This circumstance has regularly benefited the Agrarians, who are the most unevenly distributed of the major parties.[20]

Every seat gained by a cartel constitutes a loss to one of the parties outside the cartel. Usually a cartel will gain additional seats at the expense of a large party which runs independently. However, a small extremist party which has been unable to arrange a cartel agreement with another party may be at a double disadvantage, both because of its size and because of losses to the cartel. The total effect of the electoral system on small extremist parties can be measured by comparing the

39:311-313 (1952). As early as 1948 one of the chief Socialist strategists, Finance Minister Sköld, had proposed a change in the election system that would have "brought about greater political independence of the parties toward one another" by making cartels superfluous while maintaining previous standards of proportionality. See Per Edvin Sköld and Lars Sköld, "Valkarteller och valmetoder," *Tiden*, 40:520-530 (1948).

[19] A party receiving a larger share of parliamentary seats than of the national vote is said to be "overrepresented," one receiving a smaller share "underrepresented." In using these terms the writer does not mean to imply that a party *ought* to receive a number of seats exactly proportional to its vote. He believes, on the contrary, that many who defend proportionalism as the "fairest" system of representation would have to withdraw that claim once they spelled out what they mean by "fairness." Cf. Dankwart A. Rustow, "Some Observations on Proportional Representation," *Journal of Politics*, 12:109 ff. (1950).

[20] In 1948 the Agrarians and the Conservatives polled almost exactly the same proportion of the national vote—12.4 and 12.3 per cent respectively. The Agrarians received only a handful of votes in the three purely urban districts, while the Conservative vote was more evenly distributed. The Conservatives, as a result, received only 10.0 per cent of the seats as against the Agrarians' 13.0 per cent.

number of lower chamber seats that they would have received in proportion to their national vote with the number of seats they actually did receive (table 2). Such a comparison clearly indicates that the Swedish electoral system has effectively discouraged the growth of small extremist parties, or rather (since all extremist parties started out as small parties) of extremist parties in general.

TABLE 2

UNDERREPRESENTATION OF EXTREMIST PARTIES IN THE LOWER CHAMBER, 1921–1952

Election	Number of Seats Proportinal to Vote						Number of Seats Actually Received						Underrepresentation					
	National Socialists	Nationalists	Left Socialists	Kilbom Socialists	Communists	All Extremists	National Socialists	Nationalists	Left Socialists	Kilbom Socialists	Communists	All Extremists	National Socialists	Nationalists	Left Socialists	Kilbom Socialists	Communists	All Extremists
1921	.	.	7	.	11	18	.	.	6	.	7	13	.	.	1	.	4	5
1924	.	.	.	11a	.	11	.	.	.	5a	.	5	.	.	.	.	6a	6
1928	.	.	.	.	14	14	.	.	.	.	8	8	.	.	.	.	6	6
1932	1	.	.	12	6	19	0	.	.	6	2	8	1	.	.	6	4	11
1936	1	2	.	10	7	20	0	0	.	6	5	11	1	2	.	4	2	9
1940	.	.	.	1	8	9	.	.	.	0	3	3	.	.	.	1	5	6
1944	.	.	.	.	24	24	.	.	.	.	15	15	.	.	.	.	9	9
1948	.	.	.	.	14	14	.	.	.	.	8	8	.	.	.	.	6	6
1952	.	.	.	.	10	10	.	.	.	.	5	5	.	.	.	.	5	5

a Höglund and Kilbom factions.
Source: My calculations from the official election statistics.

Since the early nineteen-twenties the upper and lower chambers have very nearly represented the same electorate. As a result the strong political contrast between the two houses—a major source of conflict in Swedish politics from 1867 to 1918—has almost disappeared. A party or combination of parties with an *ample* majority in one house is now almost certain to have a majority in the other house too. On the other hand, significant differences between the two houses remain, and a party or a coalition which has a *narrow* margin over its opponents in one house may well find itself in a minority in the other. The differences in party alignments between the two houses have been due to two factors: (1) Longer terms for the members of the upper house in combination with the system of periodic partial renewal have caused senate alignments to lag an average of about four years behind alignments in the lower chamber. As a result contracting parties have maintained their old strength in the senate for several years, while expanding parties have been stronger in the lower chamber. (2) The indirect election of senators has reinforced the tendency toward "overrepresentation" of large parties and "underrepresentation" of small parties that can be observed in the lower chamber. As mentioned above, the division of the country into constituencies tends to result in the accumulation of a surplus vote by the smaller parties. A small party that attempts to make its way into the senate will accumulate such surpluses on two occasions, first in the election of the local assemblymen and second in the election of the senators themselves. A small party that fails to secure any cartel agreements with other parties will incur especially heavy losses both times.[21]

Indirect election of senators has reduced the representation of extremists in the senate even below the level they have attained in the lower house. In 1946, for instance, the Communists polled a record vote of 11.2 per cent; in 1951, however, when all the senators owing their election to the 1946 assemblies had taken their seats, they held merely 2.7 per cent of the senate seats. The two results of the senate electoral system outlined above may in some instances cancel out and in others reinforce each other. The Socialists in the late nineteen-thirties were a large, expanding party. The overrepresentation of large parties and the underrepresentation of expanding parties balanced each other almost completely in their case, and the Socialists received a majority of senate seats in 1942, only a year after they had attained a majority position in the lower house.[22] The Liberals in the 'twenties were a large party which lost ground in every election. As a result they were doubly overrepresented.

[21] Other factors may influence senate representation. A low voter turnout in a local election may decimate the delegation of a working class party for over a decade—something the Socialists experienced after 1922.

[22] Cf. J. L. Hartmann in *Statsvetenskapliga studier, op.cit.*, pp. 297-323.

In the late 'forties they were a small but rapidly expanding party; again the two effects cumulated, this time making for heavy Liberal underrepresentation in the senate.[23] The significance of such discrepancies in the party composition of the two houses was touched upon briefly in the preceding chapter, where it was pointed out that the recent postwar Socialist cabinet owed its strong position in the legislature largely to such a discrepancy.

ETHNIC AND RELIGIOUS HOMOGENEITY

In many countries parties are largely based on differences of language and religion. In some cases, e.g. Belgium, Czechoslovakia, and Finland, differences of language have been the more prominent factor; in others, e.g. the Netherlands, Yugoslavia, and Germany, religious distinctions have constituted the more serious cleavage. Even in countries where parties have not as a rule been founded on an ethnic or denominational basis, such as Switzerland, Great Britain, Canada, and the United States, the voter's native language, national origin, and religious affiliation are known to have a marked effect on his party preference.[24]

In a second group of countries, including among others the Catholic countries of southern and western Europe and the Lutheran countries of Scandinavia, national and religious minorities are almost entirely absent; hence wherever parties exist in these countries they must appeal to other distinctions among the voters—social, economic, or ideological.

Perhaps, then, the first fact about Sweden that most strikes the student of party formation is the country's linguistic and religious homogeneity. About 95 Swedes out of 100 are Luther-

[23] The following figures indicate the percentage of seats held by the Liberals in the lower and upper chambers during these periods: 1922 — 17.8, 25.3; 1925 (Ekman and Löfgren groups) — 14.3, 23.3; 1949 — 24.8, 12.0.

[24] See, e.g., the article "Parties, Political," in *Encyclopaedia of the Social Sciences*, New York: Macmillan, XI, 590–632 (1937), esp. pp. 593 and 600 (United States), 602f. (Great Britain), 605 (Canada), 608 ff. (South Africa), 613 ff. (Belgium), 615f. (Germany), 620 (Switzerland), 624 (Finland), 626f. (Czechoslovakia, Yugoslavia); cf. Rudolf Heberle, *Social Movements*, New York: Appleton-Century, 1951, pp. 143 ff.

ans and members of the state church, and as many as 99 out of
100 speak Swedish as their native language. With one exception
the ethnic and denominational differences appear to have no
influence on party formation. There are two small ethnic
minority groups in Sweden—some 30,000 Finns and some
10,000 Lapps. Both groups live in the extreme north of the
country. Most of the Finnish population is concentrated in the
Torne Valley on the Swedish-Finnish border, whereas the
Lapps are scattered over the three northern provinces of Norrbotten, Västerbotten, and Jämtland. Nearly one third of the
Lapps are nomads; those who are sedentary derive their
livelihood from agriculture, forestry, and fishing. Not all of the
Lapp population is a linguistic minority: in 1945 only about
4,000 of them spoke Lappish in their homes. Even if the Swe-
dish-speaking Lapps are added to the ethnic minorities, the
total minority population still amounts to less than 1 per cent
of Sweden's population. The Finnish group in the province of
Norrbotten is just large enough so that it would permit the
Finns, by pooling their votes, to elect one of their number to
the lower chamber. But there has never been a "Finnish Nationalist party" in Sweden, and apparently no candidate of Finnish
origin has ever been elected to parliament. In recent elections, voting behavior in the districts with a Finnish majority
did not differ appreciably from that in the neighboring districts.[25]

Approximately 3 Swedes in 1,000 are outside the state
church.[26] There is, however, a somewhat larger group of Protestant dissenters, or non-conformists, who are organized in
separate sects but mostly have not severed their connection
with the state church. These sectarian groups within the state
church amount to nearly 4 per cent of the population; the
largest among these sects is the Swedish Missionary Union

[25] The latest census of ethnic minorities was taken in 1930, when the
Finnish- and Lappish-speaking groups amounted to .7 per cent of the
population. By 1945 the Lappish-speaking population had declined by
about one third. For the Finnish vote in 1948 see the returns for Torneå,
Pajala, and Korpilombolo in *Sveriges officiella statistik, Allmänna val,
Riksdagsmannavalen åren 1945–1948, op.cit.*, pp. 128f. Sweden's only
bilingual newspaper, *Haparandabladet*, serves this Finnish border region;
see Ingvar Andersson et al., *Introduction to Sweden*, 2d edn., Stockholm:
Swedish Institute, 1951, p. 181.

[26] The latest census of religious groups also was taken in 1930.

(1.6 per cent), followed by the Baptists (.9 per cent), Pentecost Revivalists (.5 per cent), Methodists (.2 per cent), and followers of the Salvation Army (.2 per cent). Unlike the ethnic minorities or the Jewish and Catholic groups, the Protestant sects have had a profound effect on Swedish political life. The Free Church movement, like the temperance and suffrage movements, became a major social force toward the end of the last century, and there has been ever since a close connection between the Free Church and temperance movements on the one hand and Swedish liberalism on the other. The early annals of the Liberal party are full of the internal struggle between the sectarian and temperance groups and the secularist intellectuals in the party. The split of 1923 showed that the sectarian-prohibitionist wing of the party had by far the more numerous following, especially in rural areas.

REGIONAL DISTRIBUTION OF PARTY STRENGTH

Regional differences in voting behavior are hardly more pronounced than those based on ethnic and religious factors. In most countries political sectionalism can be attributed to one or more of several causes: (a) the concentration of certain religious or national minorities in one particular region, (b) differences in the historical traditions of various areas, (c) marked differences in the economic pursuits and interests of the inhabitants of various sections; and the foregoing may be reinforced be (d) a regional distribution of power within the country's government. If this list be exhaustive, there is little reason to expect any strong regionalism in Swedish politics. In the first place, ethnic and denominational minorities in Sweden, with one exception, are too small to affect party development; the Free Church groups, the only exception to this rule, are scattered all over the country and hence do not provide any basis for regional politics. Second, Sweden has a longer continuous history of territorial unity than any other European country except Norway, Iceland, and Portugal.[27] Third, although Swe-

[27] All of present-day Sweden has been part of the same realm for 300 years or more. The last permanent additions were the northern mountain regions of Härjedalen and Jämtland and the island of Gotland (1645) and the southern coastal regions of Bohuslän, Halland, Blekinge, and Skåne

den includes some predominantly agricultural and some predominantly industrial regions, the contrast between these is not nearly as sharp as in many other countries. (Economic differences nevertheless largely account for such rudimentary political regionalism as one finds in Sweden.) Last, Swedish government for centuries has been of the unitary rather than the federal type.

Norrland is the only possible exception to this rule of territorial homogeneity. It is the most sparsely populated section of the country, with 1.9 inhabitants per square mile as against Götaland's 14.8 and Svealand's 11.6. In many parts communications are poor, especially when lakes and rivers melt in the summer. Although Norrland's population has increased, and its economy has expanded, more rapidly than those of the other sections, it is still often considered an "underdeveloped area." Parliament periodically takes time to discuss the pressing problems of the section, and occasionally it has been suggested that Norrland should always have a representative in the cabinet.[28] Yet all parties alike are aware of the special problems of this section and generally agree to treat them as nonpartisan questions; nor has any one party a monopoly over the Norrlanders' loyalty. Hence one can hardly speak of a Norrland "sectionalism" in Swedish politics.

Sectional or regional parties are entirely unknown in Sweden. Squire and yeoman, rustic and townsman, employer and employee, high churchman and sectarian, dry and wet have met in the political arena, have founded parties or sought to influence the policies of existing parties. But there has never been a party of the North or the South, the mountain or the plain, and parties originating in one particular region have always spread within a few years to the rest. As a result no Swedish region has ever been as firmly committed to any one

(1658)—all of them acquired from Denmark-Norway. Today's Great Britain is entirely made up of territory that has had a common ruler for three and a half centuries; yet England and Scotland were separate political entities until 1603 (formally until 1701), while Swedish unity was achieved many centuries earlier.

[28] Upon leaving the cabinet in 1939, Rickard Sandler, himself a Norrlander, commented with some bitterness on the fact that the new national coalition included no representative of his region; see *Riksdagens protokoll, Första kammaren, 1940,* no. 3, p. 34 (January 17, 1940).

party as, say, the South of the United States to the Democratic party, the province of Quebec to the Canadian Liberals, or the Rhineland to the German Center party. The strength of the four major parties is fairly evenly spread over the country. Regional variations are least among the Social Democrats. The Agrarians tend to be somewhat more concentrated in a few regions; yet only the regional distribution of the Communists is markedly uneven.

Such slight differences in the political complexion of the sections and regions as exist, however, have proved remarkably persistent. For over half a century the Göta Canal from the Baltic to Lake Väner, and the Göta River thence to the North Sea, have formed what has been called a political "watershed."[29] South of this line, in agricultural Götaland, the Conservatives, Agrarians, and various parties of the extreme right have been stronger, while the Liberals, Social Democrats, and Communists have had their strongholds in the central and northern sections. Thus the old division of parties into right and left, which in this particular form has been obsolete for nearly thirty years, persists in the regional party alignments.

Even within each of the sections, geographical distribution of party strength has been quite stable. Thus the Conservatives have their traditional strongholds in Västergötland, Stockholm, and Malmö, the Liberals theirs in Bohuslän and Västerbotten, the Communists in Norrbotten, Gävleborg, Göteborg, and Stockholm. The strength of the Agrarian party is as a rule closely correlated with the size of the farming population, whereas the strength of the Social Democrats varies (though somewhat less closely) with the size of the industrial population. The strength of these two parties is a function of both region and occupation. In nearly all of Götaland the Agrarians have attracted considerably more than the average share of the farming population, while throughout Norrland the party's strength lags considerably behind. Conversely, the Social Democratic vote in relation to the industrial population is larger in Norrland than in the nation as a whole, and considerably smaller in western Götaland (Göteborg-Bohuslän, Älvsborg, Jönköping).

[29] Cf. Arne Wåhlstrand, "Andra kammaren under tiden omkring sekelskiftet," in *Studier över den svenska riksdagens sociala sammansättning*, Uppsala: Almqvist & Wiksell, 1936, pp. 178 ff.

Of the five present-day parties the Communists have the most irregular geographical distribution, and earlier extremist parties—such as the Nationalists, National Socialists, and Kilbom Socialists—followed a similar pattern of dispersion. The extremist parties, too, illustrate the general rule that in Sweden parties of the left are stronger in the North and parties of the right stronger in the South, except that the province of Norrbotten and the cities of Göteborg and Stockholm are traditionally strongholds of extremist parties of both right and left.[30]

ECONOMIC AND SOCIAL FACTORS
AFFECTING VOTING BEHAVIOR

There are two sources of data on the influence of occupation, income, sex, age, and marital status on the behavior of Swedish voters. (1) For many years the Swedish Central Statistical Bureau has published, as part of its quadrennial summary of lower chamber election returns, tables showing the voting participation of the two sexes and of the various age and occupational groups, along with a breakdown of the party vote according to different types of communities, urban and rural, agricultural and industrial. (2) More recently the Swedish Gallup Institute has undertaken a series of polls in which it has tried to ascertain the correlation within a small sample of the electorate between party preference and each of the following: income, age, sex, and marital status.[31]

Voting participation in Sweden has increased considerably since the beginning of the bicameral period. In 1872 less than one fifth of all eligible voters participated in the lower chamber elections; not until 1905 did the participation figure pass the

[30] A constituency-by-constituency comparison of the vote on either extreme of the spectrum in 1936 shows a clear if none too strong positive correlation. The phenomenon is analogous to the bipolarization of parties (i.e. the simultaneous growth of the two extremes) which Germany experienced before 1933 and France after 1945. For a detailed ecology of Swedish Communism see Sven Rydenfelt, *Kommunismen i Sverige*, Lund: Gleerup, 1954.

[31] The major results of the polls are analyzed, and a large number of them summarized, in Elis Håstad et al., *"Gallup" och den svenska väljarkåren*, Stockholm: Geber, 1950.

50 per cent mark. The election of 1908 (largely a plebiscite on the pending constitutional amendments providing for manhood suffrage and proportional representation) and the dissolution election of 1914 brought two new highs of 61.3 and 69.9 per cent respectively. The First World War and the introduction of woman suffrage in 1921 brought a slight decline in voter interest. From 1924 (when participation was as low as 53.0 per cent) to the present there has been a steady rise which was interrupted only by the Second World War. The first postwar lower chamber elections, in 1948, set an all-time high of 82.7 per cent.

In Sweden, as in the United States, there is a temporary decline of voter interest in "off-year" elections. The turnout at the polls in the lower chamber elections (which since 1924 have come every leap year) has generally been from 5 to 10 percentage points higher than that in the preceding local elections at midterm.

As in many other countries, voting participation in Sweden has been greater among men than among women, greater in the cities than in rural areas; middle-aged voters (between thirty-five and fifty-five) have shown greater interest than either the young or the aged; married persons have voted more regularly than either unmarried, widowed, or divorced persons; and persons of higher social status have participated more eagerly than members of the working class. Nevertheless, many of these differentials, especially the ones between the sexes and between the various social classes, have tended to diminish as time has gone on.[32]

Since election officials must respect the secrecy of the ballot, they cannot obtain any data relating party preference to sex, age, marital status, or occupation. But the election statistics regularly include information concerning the party vote in

[32] The following percentages of various social groups went to the polls in 1948: men — 84.9, women — 80.7, urban residents — 84.1, rural residents — 81.6, upper class — 92.8, middle class — 85.7, working class — 80.0 The three classes in the official statistics are distinguished primarily by training and occupation rather than income. The following occupational groups had the highest rates of participation (in approximately this order): landowners, industrialists, civil servants and white collar workers in higher positions, schoolteachers, and foremen. For comparative data on other countries see Herbert Tingsten, *Political Behavior*, London: P. S. King, 1937.

cities and rural districts and in communities with varying proportions of working class residents and residents engaged in agriculture.[33] It appears, in the first place, that both the Conservatives and the Social Democrats have a stronger appeal in the cities than in the rural districts, although Conservative losses in the cities and Socialist advances in rural areas recently have narrowed both these gaps. Second, two other parties, the Liberals and Communists, have undergone a process of gradual urbanization. The Liberals up to the nineteen-twenties were a predominantly rural party; from 1936 to 1944 they polled, roughly, an equal proportion of urban and rural votes, but in 1948 they received 27.0 per cent of the city vote as against 18.6 of the rural vote. Similarly, the Communists, whose supporters until 1940 were distributed evenly, have since then made greater gains among the townsfolk. Third, the Agrarians have drawn their supporters almost exclusively from rural areas. Their city support never exceeded 1.2 per cent of the total urban vote, and for many years the party did not even trouble to run candidates in two of the three purely urban constituencies (Stockholm and Göteborg).

All parties except the Agrarians have in recent elections polled a greater proportion of the urban than of the rural vote; yet since the rural residents constitute about 55 per cent of the total population this does not imply that in all four parties the urban supporters outnumber those in the country. On the contrary, both Liberals and Socialists had a majority of rural followers until 1944, and as late as 1948 the urban Social Democrats constituted only 48.6 per cent of their party's total support.

The election returns for various types of agricultural and industrial communities over a period of more than twenty years show that the vote of the socialist parties (that of the Social Democrats always, that of the Communists and Kilbom

[33] The term "urban" vote as used in the official statistics refers to the cumulative vote in all "cities" (*städer*). A city in turn is an administrative rather than a statistical concept. The dividing line between cities on the one hand and towns (*köpingar* and *municipalsamhällen*) on the other is around 5,000 inhabitants; yet there were, in 1949, 20 cities (out of a total of 130) with a smaller and 18 towns with a larger population than 5,000. Cf. *Statistik årsbok för Sverige 1949*, Stockholm, 1949, pp. 326 ff. All towns and other places not incorporated into cities are considered rural.

Socialists nearly always) has stood in direct relation to the working class population, whereas the strength of the three "bourgeois" parties (that of the Conservatives and Agrarians always, that of the Liberals with one or two exceptions) has varied inversely with that of the workers. Throughout the years the Agrarians have been strongest in the purely agricultural districts, and their strength has declined steeply in mixed agricultural-industrial and nonagricultural communities. The Prohibitionist Liberals, up to the Liberal merger in 1934, were also stronger in the more purely agricultural districts; yet the Löfgren Liberals in 1932 were, and the reunited Liberals since 1936 have generally been, weaker in the pure farming districts than in the mixed districts. This development parallels the gradual urbanization of the party which has been noted above. The strength of the Conservatives, Social Democrats, and Communists has usually been inversely related to the size of the farming population.

The election returns provide mere clues for a study of the influence of income and occupation on party preference. The figures of the Swedish Gallup Institute, on the other hand, give specific information on this point, as well as on the relation between party preference and age, sex, and marital status; yet it must be remembered that the Gallup figures refer only to a small group of persons, namely those members of the sample willing to answer the relevant questions.[34]

The Gallup figures for 1944, 1946, and 1948 show that the Conservatives are predominantly an upper and middle class party, that about four fifths of the Agrarians belong to the middle class, and that about three fourths of all Social Democrats and around four fifths of all Communists are working class people. The Liberal party, especially in the 1948 elections,

---

[34] See Håstad et al., *op.cit.*, pp. 123–181. The samples included about 3,000 persons each, of whom three fourths responded. The responsive part of the sample seems to have represented the two center parties accurately (within about 1 percentage point), but underrepresented the extremes (Communists and Conservatives) by about 3 to 4 percentage points each and overrepresented the Socialists (by 4 to 9 percentage points). In 1944 the Gallup Institute nonetheless published a remarkably accurate forecast coming within 4/10 of 1 percentage point of each party's vote. In 1948 it overcorrected the known biases of the sample and hence predicted a bourgeois majority. Cf. *ibid.*, pp. 124 ff.

has had a rather strong working class following (28 per cent of the party in 1944 and 1946, and 34 per cent in 1948) in addition to its solid middle class core (62 per cent in 1944 and 1946, and 58 per cent in 1948). Nearly one half of the upper class voted Conservative in 1946, whereas in 1948 the Liberals ran a close second in the competition for the upper class vote (each party attracting about two fifths of it).[35] In 1946 the Social Democrats attracted about one third of the middle class vote, while the Liberals counted less than one fourth of that class among their supporters; in 1948, however, the roles were reversed. The Conservatives and Agrarians in both elections obtained the same share of the middle class vote (about one sixth for the former and one fourth for the latter). About seven tenths of the working class voted for the Social Democrats in both elections; yet the figures indicate that the Socialists in 1948 lost a substantial part (about one tenth) of their working class supporters to the Liberals but received an equal reinforcement from former Communist voters.[36]

While the Gallup figures on the relation between class status and party affiliation largely confirm what is generally known about Swedish parties from other sources (such as the official statistics and their programs), the figures on party preference in various income groups reveal one unexpected deviation from the general pattern in that the Conservatives and Liberals attract a larger share of the voters in the lowest income group (under 2,000 crowns per year)[37] than of those in the next two higher groups (2,000 to 6,000 crowns). A breakdown of the sample according to both income and class status shows further that this group of Liberals and Conservatives within the lowest income bracket consists largely of workers rather than of members of the middle and upper class. Conversely, the Social Democrats are strongest not in the lowest but in the 2,000-to-6,000 group. Preference for the Agrarian party is greatest in

[35] The middle and lower class following of the Liberals increased even more sharply so that the proportion of upper class voters within the party declined slightly.

[36] *ibid.*, pp. 126, 169.

[37] The official exchange rate of the Swedish crown was about $.28 in U.S. currency until September 1949; since then it has been about $.19. Internal purchasing power, however, is greater than either of these figures would indicate.

the lowest income group and decreases slightly but steadily with increasing income. The Communists, finally, seem to be spread very evenly throughout the income pyramid.[38] The median income for supporters of the various parties appears to have been within the following ranges in 1946: Conservatives, 6,000–8,000 crowns per year; Liberals and Communists, 4,000–6,000 crowns; Socialists and Agrarians, 2,000–4,000 crowns.[39]

The average age of followers of the various parties in 1948 was highest for the Conservatives (46.6 years), next for the Agrarians, Liberals, and Social Democrats (in that order), and lowest for the Communists (about 40 years).[40] Women are more likely to vote for one of the "bourgeois" parties than men, and married people more likely to be Social Democrats than unmarried ones. One of the most surprising findings of the polls is that a greater proportion of married women than of either unmarried (single, divorced, widowed) women or married men vote for the Social Democratic party.[41] Several explanations seem possible: (1) women who before marriage either voted for a non-Socialist party, or did not vote at all, after marriage vote Socialist under the influence of their husbands; (2) married women, independently of their husbands' party preference, turn to Socialism; (3) women who support the Social Democratic party get married more readily than female supporters of other parties.[42]

When the various data on the correlations between party preference and geographical, social, and economic conditions

[38] ibid., pp. 162–164, 174–176; the data are based on a series of surveys conducted in 1946.

[39] My computation from ibid., p. 174.

[40] ibid., pp. 138, 140f., 166f. These data bear out the results of an earlier investigation based on the returns for elections for municipal councillors and senate electors in six large cities from 1921 to 1936; see Tingsten, Political Behavior, op.cit., pp. 111f.

[41] Håstad et al., op.cit., pp. 143ff., 171, 173. In 1946 the following percentages of groups included in the sample expressed a preference for the Socialists: unmarried women—41.3, unmarried men—48.5, married women—58.1, married men—53.4.

[42] Håstad et al. (ibid., p. 166) consider only the first hypothesis. In view of the figures cited in the preceding note the second seems likelier: it does not seem implausible that free vacations, child allowances, and similar benefits should have earned the Socialists the special gratitude of wives and mothers.

are drawn together, the following picture emerges: All of the five present-day Swedish parties have a relatively stable and well-defined social base. The Conservatives are a party of the upper and upper middle classes, appeal strongly to the higher age and income groups, and have their main strongholds in the south of the country and in the large cities; however, they receive some support from the poorest workers. The Liberal party, although built around a strong middle class core, is the only major party to receive substantial support from all three social classes.[43] It appeals to both urban agnostics and rural nonconformists, and to farmers as well as to small merchants; its strongholds are in the North and in the cities. The Agrarian party is almost exclusively a countryside party of small farmers; it is strongest in the southern rather than northern agricultural districts. The Social Democrats are predominantly a working class party with support from both industrial and agricultural workers; they appeal more successfully to young people than to old, and to married couples (especially to the wives) than to single persons. The Communists derive their main support from workers of all income groups; they are strongest in the extreme North and in the two largest cities (Stockholm and Göteborg).

[43] Liberals are fond of adducing this as evidence that they have a better claim to the name *Folkpartiet* (People's party) than any of their rivals.

CHAPTER V

PARTY ORGANIZATION

EARLIER chapters of this study have traced the historical origin of the present Swedish parties in the parliamentary feuds of the eighteen-sixties and 'seventies and in the popular mass movements of the eighteen-eighties and 'nineties; observed their subsequent entrenchment as a result of universal suffrage, proportional representation, and parliamentary cabinet government; described their interaction in recent Swedish politics; and analyzed the social composition of their present following. Parties in Sweden elect candidates, devise legislative programs, and form cabinets; yet in turning to a survey of the structure of party organization it is important to remember that this list of purely political activities does not exhaust their functions.

A party in Sweden as elsewhere in Europe is not only a political apparatus; it is also a civic club, a pressure group, and an organization for the pursuit of various leisure-time interests. The parties have separate women's and youth organizations; they sponsor boy scout groups, summer camps, civic training centers for party workers and others interested in public affairs, and adult education classes in subjects as nonpolitical mathematics and foreign languages. Nearly all the daily newspapers are closely identified with one or another of the parties, and a large array of political and literary magazines are published by them or give them consistent editorial support. The parties, finally, have established intimate ties with economic and other interest groups. It goes without saying that a Swedish party consists not merely of professional politicians. A large proportion of all adult citizens hold party membership cards and pay their annual dues. Every party, moreover, has developed a distinct philosophy or *Weltanschauung*—or if it has not done so it will tend to be apologetic about this deficiency. A politically conscious citizen therefore does not just "vote for" or "register in" a party at stated intervals: he *is* a Socialist or Agrarian, a Liberal or Conservative. In the national party organizations the welter of proliferating activities finds a center of coordination, and through their leaders and parliamentary groups the organizations become articulate in national politics.

NATIONAL ORGANIZATIONS

National party hierarchies are built on three levels: local organizations, district organizations, and a central organization.[1] In rural areas a party local may include one or two parishes; the larger towns, on the other hand, are subdivided into a great number of local branches. Each of the four large parties has from 1,000 to 3,000 local organizations spread throughout the country. Party bylaws usually specify a minimum of ten members for each new local organization. Most locals hold at least one meeting a year; their main functions are to recruit new members, to organize political discussion groups, to collect dues and other contributions, and to assist in campaign work. Party dues range from 1 to 3 crowns (about $.20 to $.60) per member per year, but some parties provide a sliding scale according to the member's income. The locals remit all dues to the districts, which retain a certain amount to defray their own expenses and forward the balance to national headquarters. None of the parties can cover their expenses from dues alone, and all of them have to rely on contributions from wealthy supporters and friendly organizations, such as business or labor groups.[2]

[1] Edvard Thermænius's *Sveriges politiska partier*, Stockholm: Geber, 1933, though outdated, remains a useful reference work. For a more up-to-date survey see Gunnar Heckscher and Verner Helte, *De politiska åskådningar och partierna*, Stockholm: Studieförbundet Medborgarskolan, 1950. Elis Håstad offers a concise analysis of party structure and activity inside and outside parliament in two small works: *Partierna i regering och riksdag*, 2d edn., Stockholm: Bonnier, 1949, and *Det moderna partiväsendets organisation*, 2d edn., Stockholm: Bonnier, 1949. For a study of Social Democratic organization see Raymond Fusilier, *Le Parti Socialiste Suédois*, Paris: Les Editions Ouvrières, 1954.

[2] The Social Democratic party is the only one which regularly publishes a summary of its accounts. In 1948, for instance, it collected a total of 775,000 kronor in dues, or an average of 1.20 kronor per member, of which 684,000 went to central headquarters. See Socialdemokratiska partistyrelsen, *Berättelse för år 1948*, Stockholm: Tiden, 1949, pp. 92 ff. Håstad estimates that in 1948 the total campaign expenditures of all parties and subsidiary organizations amounted to 15 or 16 million kronor, or

Each local organization appoints a committee which calls meetings and coordinates the activities of members during election campaigns. Representatives elected by the locals meet for an annual district convention. The districts usually coincide with the provinces or lower chamber constituencies, so that each party has twenty-five to twenty-eight district organizations. At the district convention, questions of party policy in the province are discussed; a district committee, elected by the annual convention, handles routine business during the year. All districts have a permanent staff, which usually includes a full-time secretary. In some provinces the parties have set up intermediate organizations between the districts and the locals, covering the area of a provincial assembly constituency; these organizations, however, function only during the campaign periods preceding provincial elections.

Each party has a women's organization and a youth organization operating side by side with the network of district and local organizations. These groups generally have a smaller membership than the main party organization but are set up on similar lines of local and district hierarchy. The youth organizations recruit members who have not yet reached voting age, the minimum age for membership being fifteen to sixteen. Upon reaching voting age members are expected to join the local party organization, but many stay within the youth organization until their thirty-fifth or fortieth year. The youth organizations also serve as training grounds for future leaders. Both Per Albin Hansson and Bertil Ohlin won their spurs as chairmen of their party's youth organization; so did Gustav Möller, Rickard Lindström (former Social Democratic party secretary), Torsten Nilsson (party secretary and postwar Socialist minister of communications and defense), Folke Kyling (second vice-chairman of the Conservative party in 1950), and Waldemar Svensson (Liberal party vice-chairman).[3] In past decades serious tensions have at times developed between a youth organization

about 4 kronor per vote. Håstad, *Det moderna partiväsendets organisation*, *op.cit.*, p. 67; for a similar estimate for 1932 see Thermænius, *op.cit.*, pp. 129f.

[3] Heckscher and Helte, *op.cit.*, passim, and Olle Nyman, *Parlamentarism i Sverige*, Stockholm: Ehlins, 1950, pp. 126 ff., have convenient tables showing the party leadership personnel in recent decades.

and its parent party, and in the case of the Socialists in 1908 and 1917 and the Conservatives in 1934 these led to an eventual secession. Each time, however, a new youth organization was built up, and today the ties between the parties and their affiliates seem close enough to prevent similar defections.

The highest authority in every party is its national convention, whose members are elected by the district organizations.[4] The Liberals and Agrarians meet every year, the Conservatives every two years (several months before a local or lower chamber election),[5] the Socialists every four years (in the spring before a lower chamber election). The conventions usually consist of 100 to 400 delegates; the districts are represented according to a system of basic quotas to which bonuses for districts with a large party membership or a large party vote are added. The convention also includes representatives from the women's and youth divisions and the party's parliamentary group. Usually other local and national party officials (or, as in the case of the Agrarians, any party member) may participate without a vote. When the convention is not in session, party activity is directed by a national committee which consists of from twenty-five to sixty members. The Socialist and Conservative national committee are elected by the convention, the Agrarian committee by the districts, and the Liberal committee partly by the convention and partly by the districts. The convention has jurisdiction over the formulation of the party's program, campaign platforms, and the bylaws concerning party organization; it also may lay down major policy directives.

In practice, however, major lines of policy can hardly be determined by an assembly of several hundred persons that meets for only a few days at intervals of one to four years. The business of the convention is therefore prepared in detail by the national committee, and policy decisions are likely to be made by an even smaller circle of leaders in parliament. In the Social Democratic party, resolutions originating in the

[4] The Socialists elect their convention delegates by district-wide mail ballot among the party members. The other parties allow the district committees, or a combination of district and local committees, to perform the selection.

[5] During the intervening years the Conservatives hold a kind of rump convention, including one representative from each district.

districts or locals are generally submitted in advance to the national committee, which presents these resolutions to the convention together with its own comments and recommendations. National conventions, nevertheless, are more than mere ratifying bodies for prearranged decisions. They constitute a valuable link between the central leadership on the one hand and the party membership in the districts and locals on the other. At the convention the delegates inform the leaders of the feelings and views prevalent among the party following throughout the country; they thus enable the leaders to formulate an over-all policy which will have the backing of a majority of the rank and file. Back home the delegates interpret the leadership's policy to the membership at large. The convention also gives dissatisfied party members a chance to air their dissident views. If there is any serious split within the party leadership itself, the issue may be decided at a national convention.

The national committee is the highest party organ in the interval between conventions. Even the committee, however, is too unwieldy a body for day-to-day political decisions, especially since its members reside in various parts of the country. All parties, therefore, have a smaller executive committee of seven to twenty members. Members are elected either by the convention itself or by the national committee; they sit on the national committee ex officio. The Socialist party provides specifically that the executive committee may include only residents of Stockholm and its suburbs, so that meetings can be called at short notice.

The organizational pattern so far described applies, with minor variations, to the four major parties, Social Democrats, Liberals, Conservatives, and Agrarians. The organization of the Communist party also follows this pattern. Like the other parties, the Communists have a hierarchy which includes, at the top, a national executive committee and a national committee and, at the lower levels, a network of district and local organizations. Within each local organization the party members form so-called cells whose task it is to infiltrate labor unions, civic clubs, neighborhood groups, and so on. The Communists have a youth organization, but there is no separate Communist women's movement. There is reason to believe that the Communist party in Sweden, as in other countries, has a secret organization operating side by side with the legal party structure.[6]

NOMINATIONS

One of the most important functions of the party organizations is to nominate candidates for parliament and for the provincial and local assemblies. The decision on nominations is always in the hands of the organization corresponding to the area for which the candidates are to run: candidates for the lower chamber are nominated in the district organizations, candidates for the provincial and city councils in the local organizations corresponding to the assembly constituencies. The national organizations have no official control over these nominations, although they may, and frequently do, make suggestions. All national organizations lay down certain standard procedures but leave the districts and locals to work out the details of the nomination process. As a result the actual procedure varies greatly from party to party and from district to district. For lower chamber nominations the district committees usually receive preliminary suggestions from individual party members and local organizations; a final list is drawn up either by the committee itself or by a special district convention composed of representatives from the local organizations. The district committees of the nonsocialist parties usually consult the entire party membership in the district by mail ballot but reserve the final decision. Until 1940 the Socialist districts were required to call a convention to make up a preliminary slate; this slate was then submitted to the party members at a district-wide primary in which they could either endorse the convention slate, or rearrange the order of candidates, or write in candidates of their own choice. A majority vote in the primary always determined the final composition of the list. Since 1940 the preliminary slate adopted at the convention has been submitted to a

---

[6] See Leif Kihlberg, *Den ryska agenturen i Sverige*, Stockholm: Norstedt, 1950—a critical exposé—and Björn Hallström, *I Believed in Moscow*, London: Lutterworth Press, 1953—the memoirs of a disenchanted former Communist youth leader in northern Sweden. The secret operations of the party were in part exposed in a series of espionage trials in 1952.

primary only if at least one fourth of the convention delegates request it; otherwise the preliminary list becomes final.[7] Similar procedures apply to the nomination of candidates for the provincial and municipal assemblies. The nomination of senatorial candidates is usually left to the senatorial electors. Yet party groups in the senate electoral colleges will as a rule consult with the district committee of their area and frequently will receive suggestions from national party headquarters, which are rarely disregarded.

EXTENT OF PARTY MEMBERSHIP

The national party organizations and their direct affiliates include within their ranks a considerable proportion of Swedish citizens. The "membership ratio"[8]—that is to say, the proportion of active voters enrolled as card-holding members in the various parties—indeed provides an excellent measure of the degree of control which parties exercise over a country's political life. The cumulative membership claimed by the five national party organizations and their women's and youth auxiliaries in 1948 was close to 1.4 million. Since in the lower chamber elections that year 3.9 million voters went to the polls, this would mean that about 35 per cent of the active Swedish voters are affiliated with parties. Similar figures for 1932 give a membership ratio of 28 per cent for all parties (disregarding National Socialists and splinters). The figures almost certainly are somewhat too high, since the membership of national parties in part overlaps with that of the women's and youth groups, and since many youth members are below voting age. Clearly, however, the party organizations in the last two decades have not merely kept pace with rising voting participation but succeeded in recruiting an increasing proportion of active supporters. The membership ratio has consistently been lowest among the Liberals; yet "certain Free Church and temperance

[7] Occasionally, disgruntled party members whose wishes have been disregarded in making up the official party list vote for candidates of a rival party. Thus in 1938 one Agrarian senate elector in Uppsala deserted his party to vote with the Liberals; cf. also the 1934 Örebro election discussed on page 171.

[8] The term is used by Maurice Duverger, *Political Parties*, tr. B. and R. North, London: Methuen, 1954, pp. 94 ff.

organizations probably include substantial portions of the party's unorganized voters."[9] The ratio for Conservatives and Communists has been close to the average. The Social Democrats in 1932 had the highest ratio and since then have shown a considerable increase. The Agrarians, finally, who began with one of the lowest ratios, registered a spectacular increase. Although almost half the total Agrarian membership was in the youth organization, it seems likely that the party today has the highest proportion of affiliated voters.

TABLE 3

MEMBERSHIP CLAIMED BY PARTIES, 1932 AND 1948

Party	Membership 1932 in Thousands				Membership in % of Vote, 1932	Membership 1948 in Thousands				Membership in % of Vote, 1948
	National	Women	Youth	Total		National	Women	Youth	Total	
Conservatives	106	20	36	162	28	74	42	23	139	28
Agrarians	33	.	28	61	17	116	38	115	269	56
Liberals	.	.	.	.	.	75	11	13	99	11
Prohibitionists	18	3	3.	24	10	.	.	.	.	.
Löfgrenites	7	.	.	7	14	.	.	.	.	.
Socialists	297	8	64	369	35	636	50	101	787	44
Communists	.	.	.	.	.	52	.	20	72	29
Sillén group	15	.	8	23	17	.	.	.	.	.
Kilbom group	16	.	7	23	31	.	.	.	.	.
All parties	492	31	146	669	28	953	141	272	1366	35

Source: Figures for 1932 according to Edvard Thermænius, *Sveriges politiska partier*, Stockholm: Geber, 1933. Figures for 1948 for Socialists according to party reports; for Communists and Liberal women according to Elis Håstad, *Det moderna partiväsendets organisation*, 2d edn., Stockholm: Bonnier, 1949; and for all others according to Gunnar Heckscher and Verner Helte, *De politiska åskådningar och partierna*, Stockholm: Studieförbundet Megborgarskolan 1950.

The true significance of these figures can be appreciated only in comparing the Swedish situation with that in other European countries. Unfortunately, detailed data seem to be available only for the labor parties; yet these in most countries

[9] Håstad, *Det moderna partiväsendets organisation*, *op.cit.*, p. 39.

appear to have the most extensive organization. Figures compiled by Maurice Duverger[10] show that among the European Social Democratic parties the Swedes since the First World War have had one of the highest membership ratios, exceeded only by the Austrians and in 1949 the British. After the Second World War these three, together with the Danes, showed by far the highest figures, followed at some distance by the Norwegians and the Swiss (25.7 and 22.0 per cent). The French Socialists (SFIO) rarely managed to enroll as many as one tenth, the Germans as many as one eighth, of the voters for their parties; in both cases theirs was the highest ratio for any party.[11] Other German parties, including the National Socialists in 1932 and the contemporary Christian Democrats and Free Democrats, counted twenty or more voters for every card-holding member. For the British Conservatives in 1950 and 1951 the ratio of voters to members was about five to one.[12]

These data, sketchy as they are, support the conclusion that in few if any other democratic countries is party organization as inclusive as in Sweden.[13] It is difficult to follow Professor

[10] Duverger, *op.cit.*, pp. 93, 95. On Britain cf. Allen M. Potter, "British Party Organization 1950," *Political Science Quarterly*, 66:74 (1951), and D. E. Butler, *The British General Election of 1951*, London: Macmillan, 1952.

[11] For France see Duverger, *op.cit.*, pp. 93 ff.; for Germany, Sigmund Neumann, *Die deutschen Parteien*, Berlin: Junker und Dünnhaupt, 1932, p. 123. Today the (paid-up) membership of the German Social Democrats amounts to 10.4 per cent of their electorate; see Rudolf Wildenmann, *Partei und Fraktion*, Meisenheim am Glan: Anton Hein, 1954, p. 37.

[12] The ratios were 5.8 per cent for the National Socialists, 4.8 per cent for the Christian Democrats, and 2.9 per cent for the Free Democrats; my calculations from Neumann, *op.cit.*, p. 134, and Wildenmann, *op.cit.*, pp. 68, 81. For the British Conservatives see Butler, *op.cit.*, pp. 22 f., 251.

[13] Denmark probably exceeds Sweden, with Britain and Norway running closely behind. Figures for four of the six Danish parties indicate that in 1948–1949 about 38 per cent of the active (or about 30 per cent of the potential) voters were enrolled; see [Denmark, Statsministeriet,] *Den Danske Rigsdag 1848–1948*, vol. 3, Köbenhavn: J. H. Schultz, 1950, pp. 191 ff. Membership in the two major British parties in 1950–1951 amounted to about one third of their vote; see Butler, *op.cit.*, pp. 22 f., 251. For Norway cf. Berndt A. Nissen, *Politikk for Alle*, Oslo, 1949. The slightly lower estimates for the three Scandinavian countries given in my contribution to Sigmund Neumann, ed., *Modern Political Parties*, Chicago: University of Chicago Press, 1956, refer to the ratio of party members to *potential* rather than active voters.

Håstad's reasoning that the Swedish proportion of party-affiliated voters "is not particularly high," so that "there is still much virgin soil to be brought under the parties' plow."[14] In proportion as the parties achieve complete tillage, the political community is transformed into what German political scientists call a *parteienstaat*. "In the *parteienstaat*," Karl Braunias warns eloquently, "the constructive principles of representation and integration vanish; for the aim is no longer a community of the people or a unification of wills.... When the ideal of a *parteienstaat* has been accomplished and all voters are politically organized, elections might well be dispensed with altogether. The idea of representation, taken over from monarchy or democracy, has been hollowed out at the core and only a series of fictions can keep it intact. The independent representatives of the nation have made room for party agents subject to recall without notice. The electoral system no longer serves the purpose of recruiting leaders. For the party leadership renews itself by cooptation, and within the party the electoral principle retains a merely decorative significance."[15]

THE PARTIES AND ORGANIZED INTERESTS

The national parties are only one among many types of associations which have proliferated in Sweden. By establishing close ties with many of the nonpolitical organizations the parties have further tightened their grip on the country's public life. As noted in an earlier chapter, progressive industrialization and urbanization in the late nineteenth century transformed the old estate commonwealth into the "Sweden of the organizations." The nonconformist sects were among the earliest popular movements, but others soon followed. Most spectacular has been the growth of economic association. The first labor unions entered the scene in the eighteen-eighties, and in 1898 a majority of these formed the Swedish Federation of Labor.[16] A

14 Håstad, *Det moderna partiväsendets organisation, op.cit.*, p. 41.

15 Karl Braunias, *Das parlamentarische Wahlrecht*, Berlin: De Gruyter, 1932, II, 22f.

16 See Jörgen Westerståhl, *Svensk fackföreningsrörelse*, Stockholm: Tiden, 1945, pp. 58ff., and James J. Robbins, *The Government of Labor Relations in Sweden*, Chapel Hill: University of North Carolina Press, 1942, pp. 42ff.

Cooperative Wholesale Society was formed in 1899,[17] a Swedish Employers' Association in 1902, a Swedish Farmers' Association in 1905. The white collar workers were last to be organized. In 1944 two separate organizations of government and private employees that had been formed in the nineteen-thirties consolidated in the Central Organization of Salaried Employees. The membership in these various organizations rose sharply during the period between the two World Wars; today each one of them represents a vast network of affiliated organizations and local associations, and their total membership comprises an overwhelming majority of the entire working population. "Strictly speaking, the labor market in·industry and commerce no longer includes any one unorganized sector. In large parts of agriculture, economic associations are in charge of distribution almost in its entirety. The activity of the consumers' cooperative societies extends to all parts of the retail trade. Those portions of private trade that fall outside the sphere of influence of the cooperatives are almost entirely regulated by various merchant associations... Comparing the situation in Sweden with that in other countries, it can be stated that the Swedish organizational structure is unique...in its inclusiveness."[18]

Side by side with these economic organizations, which have revolutionized the entire structure of the Swedish economy, cultural and religious organizations have attracted a membership running into the tens and hundreds of thousands.[19] The

[17] For a popular account of the growth and activity of the consumers' cooperatives see, e.g., Marquis W. Childs, *Sweden: The Middle Way*, New Haven: Yale University Press, 1937; rev. edn., 1947; Penguin edn., 1948.

[18] Gunnar Heckscher, *Staten och organisationerna*, 2d edn., Stockholm: KF, 1951, pp. 77f. The following are recent membership figures for the largest employees' and farmers' organizations (1949–1950): Swedish Federation of Labor — 1,278,000; Central Organization of Salaried Employees — 271,000; Swedish Farming Association — 1,063,000. *ibid.*, pp. 50, 55, 70. These three alone included over three fourths of the gainfully employed population.

[19] Membership in the major temperance societies totalled nearly 300,000 in 1935; see Mauritz Enander, "Nykterhetsrörelsen," in *Svenska folkrörelser*, Stockholm, 1936–1937, I, 16. According to the 1930 census the various sectarian groups had a total of about 225,000 members; the present figure is nearly double that.

emergence of all these religious, economic, and other organizations during the last decades of the nineteenth century coincided, as we have seen, with the early growth of organized parties within the constituencies, and from the beginning there has been a close relationship between political and nonpolitical organizations. This relationship has been most intimate in the case of the Socialist party and the labor unions. In 1898 the founding congress of the Swedish Federation of Labor adopted a resolution which required all member unions to affiliate *en bloc* with the Social Democratic party within three years of their admission to the Federation. Although this sweeping rule was repealed two years later, individual unions within the Federation have at various times decided to join the Social Democratic party as a body; on the other hand, union members who disapproved of such a decision have always been granted the right to refuse party membership while remaining in the union. In 1939 about 300,000 union members were "collectively affiliated" with the Socialist party in this manner, a figure corresponding to about two thirds of the party's membership and one third of the membership of all unions in the confederation. Some 13,000 members of these affiliated unions had chosen to remain outside the party.[20]

The connection between the Liberal party and the sectarian organizations has never been institutionalized through formal affiliation. It can safely be assumed, however, that a large proportion of those Liberal voters who do not pay dues belong to one of the nonconformist or temperance societies.[21] In 1936 the Liberal party instructed its campaign workers to approach all persons on membership lists of "sectarian and temperance societies and other groups that are close to us."[22] The organ of the largest nonconformist group, *Svenska Morgonbladet*, is one of the most widely read Liberal dailies, and for a long time was considered the official mouthpiece of the Prohibitionist party's leadership. At the same time the Liberal movement has always included a substantial group of intellectuals who have been quite aloof from the nonconformist and temperance movements,

[20] Westerståhl, *op.cit.*, p. 222.
[21] Håstad, *Det moderna partiväsendets organisation, op. cit.*, p. 39, and Heckscher and Helte, *op.cit.*, p. 39.
[22] *Folkpartiets valhandbok 1936*, Stockholm, 1936, p. 42.

and it appears that since the reunification of the party in 1934 the two groups have been cooperating fairly harmoniously. While the Liberals are the most vocal spokesmen of nonconformist and temperance interests, many sectarians and prohibitionists have supported the Socialist and Agrarian parties.

The organizations that regulate the economic activities of farmers naturally have many interests in common with the Agrarian party. Nevertheless, the Swedish Farmers' Association, with which most of these organizations are affiliated, has always stressed its nonpartisan character and has attempted to function as a pressure group within each of the four major parties. Since all of these compete actively for the rural vote, this strategy has met with considerable success. The Consumers' Cooperatives and the employers' associations have remained aloof from partisan politics, although a majority of the members of the former support the Socialists, and a majority of the latter the Conservatives.

Cooperation between the parties and the various economic and cultural organizations finds expression in frequent combination of leadership posts. The second Socialist cabinet (1921-1923) included Herman Lindqvist, longtime chairman fo the Swedish Federation of Labor, as minister of social affairs and Anders Örne, secretary general of the Cooperative Society, as minister of communications. The chairman of the Metal Workers' Union, Fritjof Ekman, and the secretary of the Union of Railroad Engineers, Henning Leo, were members of a Socialist cabinet in 1932-1936. In the fall of 1936, union leaders within the Social Democratic national committee formally demanded the inclusion of a union man in the cabinet, and in deference to their wishes the chairman of the Swedish Federation of Labor, Albert Forslund, was made minister of communications.[23] Axel Gjöres, Socialist minister of civilian supply from 1941 to 1947, was secretary general of the Cooperative Society, and his successor Gunnar Sträng chairman of the Farm Workers' Union. The Liberal parliamentary delegation has included at different times the chairman of the Association of Swedish Dairies and the chairman of the largest nonconformist association (the Swedish Missionary Union). Three successive

[23] Olle Nyman, *Svensk parlamentarism, 1932-1936*, Uppsala: Almqvist & Wiksell, 1947, p. 472.

leaders of the Prohibitionist-Liberal party, Carl Ekman,
Felix Hamrin, and Gustaf Andersson i Rasjön, were active in
the temperance movement. The board of directors of the
Swedish Farmers' Association has usually included up to a
dozen riksdag members—some belonging to the Agrarian,
some to the Liberal, and some to the Socialist party;[24] the
Agrarian leader Axel Pehrsson-Bramstorp was elected chairman of its board in 1946. Hjalmar von Sydow, for many decades chairman of the Swedish Employers' Association, was a
prominent Conservative parliamentarian.

Many observers have been tempted to interpret the close
personal and organizational ties between the major economic
interest groups on the one hand and the political parties on the
other as a revival of the corporate or estate principle.[25] According
to this view, Swedish development during the last 100 years
has come full circle. After a long struggle the estates were
finally abolished in the eighteen-sixties to make room for a
representative system conforming to more individualistic
notions. After some fifty years, however, they had crept back
into Swedish politics, having changed their names, to be sure,
from Nobles, Clergymen, Burghers, and Peasants, to Conservatives, Liberals, Agrarians, and Socialists. Many of the
facts reviewed in the last two chapters lend support to this
thesis—whatever may be said about the obvious differences
between the estates of a semifeudal era and modern democratic
mass parties.[26] Only the recent rapid growth of the Liberal

[24] See the yearbook *Svenska landsbygdens kalender.*

[25] Heckscher, *Staten och organisationerna, op.cit.*, pp. 187f. For similar
views see Håstad, *Partierna i regering och riksdag, op.cit.* pp. 50f., and
Nils Herlitz, *Svenskt författningsliv,* Stockholm: Norstedt, 1947, pp. 20f.
Cf. the following articles by Gunnar Heckscher: "Pluralist Democracy,
The Swedish Experience," *Social Research,* 15:417-461 (1948), and
"Organisationsväsendet i svensk folkstyrelse," in Hal Koch and Alf Ross,
eds., *Nordisk demokrati,* Oslo, Stockholm, and Köbenhavn, 1949, pp. 134-
153.

[26] See Robbins, *op.cit.*, pp. 338f. In recent years the leaders of economic
interest groups have found it increasingly difficult to combine their duties
with active participation in party politics. A leading union spokesman
recently complained that "the special interests of the employers [*sic*] in
legislation" were no longer adequately represented in the riksdag (cited
by Heckscher, *Staten och organisationerna, op.cit.*, p. 185). A full evaluation
of the estate thesis would require a detailed examination of economic data
beyond the scope of the present study.

party into a movement supported by segments of all major social gruops would seem to contradict the estate thesis.

PARLIAMENTARY PARTIES

The party groups in parliament form distinct and highly influential units within the wider structure. Until the beginning of this century parliamentary parties were restricted to either the lower chamber or the senate, and the groups in both houses had little connection with the nascent national organizations. Since then a gradual integration has taken place, both between groups in the two houses and between the parliamentary and national party branches. When the Socialists and Liberals after 1909 elected their first senators these joined in a single party group with their colleagues in the chamber. This precedent was followed later by the Agrarians, Left Socialists, and Communists. Only among the Conservatives was full integration delayed until as late as 1935.

Today the full caucus, composed of all party members in both chambers, is the highest authority in the parliamentary party. Each major party has its parliamentary executive committee. Its membership, about a dozen, is apportioned between the chambers according to the party's strength in each. The executive committee formulates parliamentary strategy and prepares slates for committee assignments. All major decisions, however, including the final nomination of candidates for the parliamentary standing committees, are subject to ratification by the caucus. In addition to the executive committee, each parliamentary group appoints a number of specialized committees to discuss specific legislative questions, to prepare party motions and interpellations, and to consult with the party's members on the standing committees. In 1942, for example, the Conservatives chose seven specialized committees. Each of these included from fifteen to twenty members, so that most served on more than one committee. The assignments included defense and foreign policy, economic legislation and taxes, agriculture, and so forth. Any Conservative parliamentarian, whether or not he was a committee member, was free to participate in the proceedings. At regular intervals the committees reported to the caucus at one of its weekly meetings. A so-called "autumn committee" met during the parliamentary recess to prepare party resolutions for the following session.[27]

LEADERSHIP

The activities of the national party organization and its parliamentary representatives are integrated primarily in the persons of the party leader and his chief lieutenants. This unified leadership, which differentiates Swedish parties from those in Denmark and Norway,[28] is a relatively recent phenomenon. The oldest party in the bicameral riksdag, the Ruralists, refused to appoint a single chairman and instead elected a Council of Seven (later of Nine) to call caucus meetings and to draw up lists for committee nominations. The Social Democrats, the first national party, at their opening convention rejected a proposal to create an executive committee with wide powers over policy and discipline; the only body appointed was a continuation committee to serve in the interim between conventions. Other parties displayed a similar diffidence. The senate Conservatives in 1912 experimented with a leading triumvirate before picking a single chairman the following year;[29] the officers of the Agrarian party well into the nineteen-twenties exercised a purely nominal leadership; the Left Socialists started out with two coequal chairmen and, to the very end, rotated their chairmanship in parliament from year to year. The reconciliation of divergent views and rival personalities in a nascent party (it would seem) requires considerable effort; a further effort is needed to persuade the newly consolidated body to accept unified direction. Since in a new

[27] Elis Håstad, for many years the secretary and later a member of the Conservative parliamentary party, has described its internal structure in "Hur ett riksdagsparti arbetar internt," *Medborgaren*, 1942, no. 4½ [*sic*], pp. 25–28.

[28] See my article in Neumann, *Modern Political Parties, op.cit.*

[29] On the Ruralists see Edvard Thermænius, *Lantmannapartiet*, Uppsala: Almqvist & Wiksell, 1928, pp. 343 ff.; on the Socialists, John Lindgren, *Det socialdemokratiska arbetarpartiets uppkomst i Sverige*, Stockholm: Tiden, 1927, pp. 279 ff., and G. Hilding Nordström, *Sveriges socialdemokratiska arbetareparti under genombrottsåren*, Stockholm: KF, 1938, pp. 185 ff.; on the Conservatives, [Sweden, Riksdagen,] *Sveriges riksdag*, Stockholm: Victor Petterson, 1931–1938, XVII, 208.

organization no one has as yet demonstrated his leadership capacities this interim allows for a "natural selection" among the aspirants. Even mature parties have put their chairmanship in commission when the death or unexpected resignation of a leader has left a sudden vacuum. Thus the Liberals upon Staaff's death appointed a committee of five; and the Socialists after Branting's death and the Liberals after the Ekman debacle for a time had separate parliamentary and national chairmen.

In the end the principle of unified leadership has always won out. Although the Ruralists, down to their split in 1888, never appointed a permanent chairman, Carl Ifvarsson and to a lesser extent Arvid Posse and Emil Key emerged as the real chiefs. (By 1883 Ifvarsson and Key were the only original members still on the Committee of Nine.)[30] And when the Socialist congress of 1907 elected Hjalmar Branting to the new post of party chairman it merely confirmed what for nearly two decades had been a fact.

Once installed in office a leader is almost invariably reelected as long as he desires. Lindman and Trygger, Branting and Hansson led their parties for two or three decades, and Tage Erlander today is only the third leader in sixty-odd years of Social Democratic history. Although the seemingly voluntary resignation of a leader may at times have been due to subtle pressure from the members,[31] the dethronement of Olsson i Kullenbergstorp seems to have been the only instance of open revolt against a leader in recent decades. The vested interest which party chairmen acquire in their positions regularly has presented a major obstacle to party mergers. Such was the story of the Ruralists' reunification (1895), engineered by Olof Jonsson at a time when illness kept his rival Anders Peter Danielson away from Stockholm; of the Agrarian fusion in 1921;[32] and of the Liberal and Conservative mergers in 1934–1935, which were delayed for many years until one or both of the original leaders had retired.

[30] On the changing personnel of that body see Thermænius, *Lantmann-apartiet, op.cit.*, pp. 211, 219, 233, 242, and Emil Key, *Minnen*, Stockholm: Bonnier, 1915–1917, II, 244.

[31] As in the case of the seventy-six-year-old Ernst Trygger. See Nyman, *Svensk parlamentarism, 1932–1936, op.cit.*, p. 165. For an earlier instance of open rift between leader and followers see page 63 supra.

[32] See *Sveriges riksdag, op.cit.*, XVII, 133 ff., 275.

Parties, as we have seen, arose independently in the lower chamber, the senate, and the constituencies. The election of the first Liberal and Socialist senators inaugurated an era of bicameral parties (although the Conservatives did not follow suit until 1935), and today the chairman of the parliamentary group is also the national chairman. The latter principle was adopted by the Socialists in 1907, the Conservatives in 1913, and the Liberals and Agrarians in 1924. The selection of a new leader therefore requires a concurrent vote of the parliamentary caucus and the national committee, and it is not always easy to determine which of these carries the greater weight. Lindman, Bagge, Ekman, Ohlin, and Hansson were first elected by their national organizations and later endorsed by the riksdag group; in the case of the Agrarian leaders Kälkebo, Kullenbergstorp, and Bramstorp the order was reversed.[33] Further integration between the two main branches of the party is commonly achieved through overlapping personnel at the level immediately below the leader. In 1932, for instance, half the members of the executive committee of the Social Democratic caucus also sat on the national committee; in 1948 the proportion was nine out of seventeen.

The social origin of party leaders has not always reflected the composition of the membership. The attack on the narrow oligarchic system of the late nineteenth century came in two major waves, the first from the Ruralist farmers, the second from the Liberal lower middle class and the Socialist workers. In both instances a surprisingly large number of the leaders were recruited from the upper middle class or the ruling class itself. Arvid Posse was a scion of the oldest nobility and one of the country's largest landowners, and Emil Key a landed squire and litterateur who refused to "fraternize" with his party colleagues because he found their rustic habits of drinking

[33] After Hansson's death in 1946, the Socialist national committee took a preliminary vote but delayed final action until the riksdag group had met. As it happened both groups concurred in selecting Erlander. The executive committee of the riksdag group had favored Gustav Möller but was overruled by the full caucus. See Lars Sköld, "Förfaringssättet vid svenska statsministervakanser efter parlamentarismens genombrott," *Statsvetenskaplig tidskrift*, 51:62 ff. (1948); Ernst Wigforss, *Minnen*, 3 vols., Stockholm: Tiden, 1951–1954, III, 326 ff.; and Fusilier, *op.cit.*, pp. 189 ff.

and checker playing thoroughly distasteful. The early Liberal leaders almost without exception were members of the professions—teachers (von Friesen, Fridtjuv Berg) journalists, (Bergström, Mauritz Hellberg), and lawyers (Staaff). The Socialist press might boast that the party congress of 1889 consisted almost entirely of workers and artisans; yet of the two delegates of middle class origin one was Fredrik Sterky, later the first chairman of the Swedish Federation of Labor, and the other was Hjalmar Branting.[34]

Differences in social standing such as these have at times sharpened the latent rebelliousness of a party's rank and file against its own leaders. Emil Key complained bitterly of the farmers' "peevish sense of independence" and explained that every time they had supported him on a major question they would be sure to oppose him on a minor one to show that they were not "dancing after the gentlemen's tune."[35] It was in part the same jealousy that turned the Ruralist representatives against the aristocratic Posse government. More recently the Liberal split of 1923 was in part a rebellion of the lower middle class membership against the upper middle class intellectuals who held many of the leading positions within the party organization. No similar conflicts are recorded in Social Democratic annals—a circumstance which caused Erik Hedén (himself a middle class intellectual prominent in the Left Socialist movement) to remark wistfully that the Ruralist farmers "were decidedly less inclined to obey upper class leaders" than the Socialist workers.[36] Be that as it may, there is little doubt that Branting's unparalleled prestige within the party was due as much to his conciliatory manner and his personal modesty[37] as

---

[34] The press comments are quoted in Lindgren, *op.cit.*, p. 277. For the role that leaders of middle or upper class origin have played in the international socialist movement see Robert Michels, *Political Parties*, Glencoe, Ill.: Free Press, 1949, pp. 248 ff.

[35] Emil Key, *Minnen*, Stockholm: Bonnier: 1915–1917, II, 239.

[36] Erik Hedén, *Politiska essayer*, Stockholm: Tiden, 1927, p. 130. For a similar remark see E. H. Thörnberg, *Samhällsklasser och politiska partier i Sverige*, Stockholm: Bonnier, 1917, p. 34.

[37] Axel Danielsson, his most serious rival for the leadership of the early Socialist party, attested that Branting was the kind of person "who never makes personal enemies." Quoted by Zeth Höglund, *Hjalmar Branting och hans livsgärning*, 3d edn., Stockholm: Tiden, 1939, p. 91.

to any supposedly inveterate subservience among the Swedish working class.

The inclination of lower class political movements to select their leaders from among the higher social strata probably played its part in making the momentous transition from oligarchy to democracy toward the turn of the century relatively harmonious. It thus helped preserve many of the older political customs, especially within the riksdag and its committees. The historian of the Ruralist party notes that the farmers in the riksdag, "as a result among other things of their long sojourns in the capital, began to approximate both the living habits and the ways of thinking of the townsfolk and the gentlemen."[38] Conservative aristocrats might well have been terrified at the thought of seeing the representatives of a professedly revolutionary labor movement intrude into the parliamentary inner sanctum. Yet their terror must have given way to agreeable surprise when the first intruder turned out to be a highly educated, well-mannered gentleman who had gone to school together with the crown prince. Bishop Billing later was to remark that if Sweden had to have a Socialist movement it was fortunate that its leader should have been Hjalmar Branting.[39]

The democratization of the franchise and the progressive narrowing of class differences in Swedish society naturally have left their mark. The transition within the Conservative leadership from large landowners to industrial managers has been noted in an earlier context. Of the groups active in nineteenth century Swedish politics only the civil servants, including university professors, have retained their old influence, and several among the latter (Trygger, Edén, Bagge, Ohlin) have attained top positions within their parties.[40] In marked

[38] *Sveriges riksdag, op.cit.*, XVII, 106f. Sten Carlsson notes a similar tendency among the peasant representatives in the estate parliament; see his book *Svensk ståndscirkulation, 1680–1950*, Uppsala: J. A. Lindblad, 1950, pp. 106 ff.

[39] On Branting's schooling see Höglund, *op.cit.*, pp. 42f.; Billing's remark is quoted *ibid.*, p. 528.

[40] Claes Lindskog, professor of classics at Lund and a Conservative member of the riksdag, has recorded some interesting reflections on the question "Do professors make good politicians?" See his *Bokslut: Hågkomster och människor*, Stockholm: Bonnier, 1949, pp. 11 ff.

contrast to the situation in France and the United States, lawyers have played almost no part in Swedish politics— Staaff and Löfgren being among the rare exceptions. Since Key's and Posse's days the political leaders of the rural population have nearly all been farmers. Although the Agrarian riksdag delegation has included a number of influential urban middle class members (such as the famous trio of professors in the interwar period, Carl-Axel Reuterskiöld, Nils Wohlin, and Karl Gustaf Westman), the party has long been reluctant to confer any offices on its "gentlemen peasants."[41] To this day persons who derive their livelihood from politics are in a minority in public life; it remains to be seen whether such recent innovations as all-year riksdag sessions and retirement pay for members of long service will produce a change in this regard. The Social Democrats are the only major party in which professional politicians—journalists, party secretaries, and union officials—have played a dominant role. Manual workers, unlike farmers, businessmen, or civil servants, cannot retain their jobs during prolonged absences;[42] and as the oldest and largest of the present-day parties the Social Democrats have developed a more elaborate hierarchy than any of their rivals.[43] Many of their leaders have been editors of party newspapers— and some in this group have been sons of middle class parents (Branting, Höglund), others of workers (Hansson, Möller) and farmers (Engberg, Sköld).[44] Teachers also have been prominent within the party (Sandler, Wigforss, Erlander), whereas university professors (Undén, Myrdal) and career civil servants

[41] On Wohlin see note 56 infra. Bramstorp's successor as party leader since 1949, Dr. Gunnar Hedlund, was the first exception to the rule.

[42] Cf. Thörnberg, op.cit., pp. 34 ff.

[43] For similar tendencies in Socialist parties elsewhere on the Continent see Michels, op.cit. As a result of their progressive bureaucratization the Social Democrats today have the oldest riksdag delegation of any party. Since their constituents are on the average younger than the followers of the other major parties there has been some grumbling among the younger generation. See Arne Björnberg, "Generationsväxlingen i politiken," Tiden, 37:321–328 (1945).

[44] Elfred Kunn, "Vem var Per Albins farfars far?" Tiden, 37:490–493 (1945), gives some interesting data on the occupations of Socialist members of parliament as well as of their lineal ancestors. On the occupational background of the present Socialist executive commitee see Fusilier, op. cit., table facing p. 168.

(Schlyter, Nothin) have served in Socialist cabinets without penetrating into the party's inner circle.

PARTY DISCIPLINE

The expansion of party organization since the mid-nineteenth century has gone hand in hand with a steady tightening of party discipline in parliament. The parties of the early bicameral period tended to be regarded as at best a necessary evil; their membership fluctuated rapidly and the leaders had no effective means of securing unity even on major questions. It was not unusual for members of the riksdag to shop around among several parties until they found one to their liking. One northern farmer, Per Olof Hörnfelt, joined a different party at each of the first three sessions of the lower chamber (Ministerials, New Liberals, Ruralists). That endearing busybody Per Nilsson i Espö was "sufficiently enterprising and open-minded to participate in the founding of two opposing parties [Ministerials and Ruralists], in each case as a member of the innermost circle." As soon as the New Liberal party formed he was frequenting its meetings as well—all the time rendering an inestimable service to future historiographers by keeping a faithful diary.[45] For many decades the appearance of a new political issue, such as tariff protection or suffrage reform, would set off a chain reaction of splits and mergers, individual reaffiliations and formation of new groups. The confusion and instability of the political situation toward the turn of the century is illustrated by the career of August Henricson i Karlslund: having entered the lower chamber as a Ruralist free-trader in 1887, he stayed with the Old Ruralists (1888), joined the reunited Ruralist party (1895), later was a member of a loosely organized group of Agrarian independents, and in 1900 became a cofounder of the Liberal Union party. Few have matched this record of four parties in five years, yet a good many underwent a similar metamorphosis over a longer period.[46] Many representatives,

[45] On Hörnfelt and Espö see *Sveriges riksdag, op.cit.*, XVII, 48, 50 (the quote is from *ibid.*, p. 35); see also Thermænius, *Lantmannapartiet, op.cit.*, pp. 26, 215.

[46] Because of the split, remerger, and final disintegration of the Ruralist party its followers contributed more than their share to the floating party membership. Petersson i Påboda was a Ruralist (1897), National Progres-

moreover, remained aloof from all parties. The number of independents in the 1897 lower chamber has been estimated at about seventy—almost a third of the total. During the next decade this number varied between twelve and thirty.[47] Since the introduction of PR, on the other hand, the independents have almost disappeared, and transitions from one party to another have become far less frequent.

Some of the leading statesmen of the late nineteenth and early twentieth centuries considered the need to join a party an intolerable restriction which they did their best to avoid. Louis De Geer (the Elder) expressed an "insuperable aversion to all partisanship."[48] Repeatedly he passed up the opportunity of becoming a party leader, and once when asked to preside over a caucus of senators who favored a compromise on defense and land tax he accepted only on condition that the opposition be invited to attend. Two decades later Bishop Billing found it "very distasteful to participate in party meetings," since he cherished his "complete independence and freedom of action."[49] And Hugo Hamilton, who in 1901 bolted the newly formed Liberal party, considered himself fortunate to escape any party ties in his later career as cabinet minister (1907–1911) and senate speaker (1916–1928).[50] It is no coincidence, however, that this testimony comes from members of the traditional upper class, which well into the twentieth century exercised an influence in politics out of all proportion to its numbers. Although not always averse to change, this group had ample reason to be content with the existing order; nor did it harbor fundamental differences of opinion or interest in its own midst. The lower

sive (1906), and Liberal (1910); Andersson i Nöbbelöf a Ruralist (1882 and again in 1895), Old Ruralist (1888–1895), National Progressive (1906), and Conservative (1912). A late and extreme example is that of Gösta Tamm, minister of agriculture in Staaff's first cabinet: Liberal (1903), Liberal Defense Supporter (1914), Independent (1915), Agrarian (1917).

[47] For later developments cf. page 86, note 73.

[48] Louis De Geer, *Minnen*, Stockholm: Norstedt, 1892, II, 48; cf. I, 156; II, 158.

[49] Gottfrid Billing, *Anteckningar från riksdagar och kyrkomöten, 1893–1906*, Stockholm: Norstedt, 1928, p. 38.

[50] Hugo Hamilton, *Hågkomster*, Stockholm: Bonnier, 1928, pp. 253 ff. On the early depreciation of partisanship in general, both in Sweden and elsewhere, see Carl Gösta Widell, *Staten och partiväsendet*, Lund: Sundqvist & Edmond, 1939, pp. 109 ff.

classes—farmers, sharecroppers, and industrial workers—knew from personal experience from childhood on that only disciplined organization could force a hearing for their most urgent demands. They could hence ill afford the luxury of condemning partisanship in principle, and it is not surprising that successive impulses to party formation came largely from these same groups as represented by the Ruralists, the suffrage societies, and the Social Democrats.

Even where the need for party solidarity was acknowledged it was no mean task to maintain it in practice. Carl Ifvarsson used to carry handkerchiefs of different colors to signal to his followers whether they were to vote "aye" or "nay" in a division;[51] yet the recalcitrant Ruralist in his days risked nothing but his committee assignment. Even when the parties began to organize the constituencies a representative could calmly defy the leaders as long as he was assured of his electors' loyalty back home. The senate Protectionist leader Patrik Reuterswärd, on a visit to the rural residences of some of his party friends, let out a deep sigh and told his chief lieutenant: "Now you see—here they all live in their estates and mansions like so many princes; it's no use trying to keep discipline in a party such as this."[52] In these days of proportionalism, on the other hand, he who breaks with his party generally faces political retirement unless he finds shelter with another group. Time was when a member of parliament could select his party; now it is the parties that select those who will become members of parliament. There is no legal obligation for a candidate to join the party group on whose ticket he has been elected or to resign his seat when he severs his party ties. Nonetheless it takes a serious disagreement over a deeply felt issue to precipitate an open break, such as the controversies among the Liberals over the defense question in 1914 and over temperance in 1923. (The secession of the Left Socialists in 1917 and the Nationalists in 1934, both of which had the backing of an existing organization, belong in a somewhat different category.) That there have been no similar splits since the early 'thirties probably is due both to increased party cohesion and to the absence of new divisive issues.

[51] Håstad, *Partierna i regering och riksdag, op.cit.*, pp. 56f.
[52] Quoted in Billing, *op.cit.*, p. 36, editor's note.

A party occasionally may use a reputation for poor discipline to good advantage. Conservative critics thus suspected Pehrsson-Bramstorp of staging periodic "rebellions" among his Agrarian followers as a means of exacting concessions from his Socialist allies.[53] But this was an unusual situation where a large—and well-disciplined—party depended on a much smaller group for the few extra votes that it fell short of a majority. And in any case such tactical "rebellions," to serve their end, require close teamwork. Generally a parliamentary group that is divided on a major issue is likely to undermine its bargaining position in negotiation with other parties, both in the committee room and in decisive informal conferences in the lobby. A party that fails to maintain intimate contact with its cadres in the constituency, or with the organized interests it represents, courts defeat at the polls.

Swedish parliamentary parties have no formal rules that would compel members to support the party in a debate or on a vote. The equivalent of the whips in the riksdag are known as "pair secretaries"; their job is to alert members for important votes and to arrange pairs for those who cannot be on hand. The Social Democrats in 1915, when faced with the systematic opposition of a radical minority, adopted a rule under which the caucus majority could endorse a policy and require all members, under penalty of exclusion, to refrain from speaking or voting against that policy. This "gag rule,"[54] however, was never invoked and was promptly repealed after the rebels had left the party. No such rule has ever been adopted by another party. The labelling of the riksdag as "His Majesty's Transport Company," popular with right wing cartoonists in recent years, is not descriptive of the real situation. The leaders may decide to commit the party to a strong unified stand, but the decision will be preceded by consultation and discussion within the party.

Just how a party will react when its unity is challenged depends both on the seriousness and the magnitude of the opposition. Well-known personalities with independent views have

[53] See the editorial "Mysteriespelet om Bramstorp," *Svensk tidskrift*, 28:73–75 (1941).

[54] Reprinted in Ragnar Edenman, *Socialdemokratiska riksdagsgruppen 1903–1920*, Uppsala: Almqvist & Wiksell, 1946, pp. 287f.

at times been allowed to remain outside the parliamentary party without penalty. Thus Kerstin Hesselgren, first woman senator, and ex-Premier Hammarskjöld served for several terms in the senate as, respectively, Independent Liberal and Independent Conservative. Similarly, a speaker who chooses to leave his party group has always been renominated for his seat in the riksdag as a matter of course, even though to a dwindling party, such as the senate Conservatives since the nineteen-thirties, this represents a considerable sacrifice. The Socialists have welcomed many prominent dissenters back into their ranks and conferred important offices upon them. Thus Assar Åkerman, who had served as an Independent in 1909–1914, was renominated by them in 1919 and later became Branting's minister of justice. Of the former Left Socialists Zeth Höglund became a member of the Social Democratic executive committee (1928–1944) and Ivar Vennerström minister of defense in Hansson's first cabinet. At a time when the party was embarked upon a course of moderate reform, patience with left wing critics within its ranks may have served both to ransom its own Socialist conscience and to attract votes from the Communists.

Organized opposition within the party is of course far more serious than individual deviation. Nevertheless, while the leadership may move swiftly against a small group of rebels, it may show great leniency when the party is about evenly divided. If a majority of the rank and file refuse to heed the official signals, a change in leadership may be indicated. During the First World War the Social Democrats expelled three of their riksdag members who had failed to purge themselves of charges of pro-German propagandizing; but the leadership moved with extreme caution against the left wing, which, backed by the youth movement and several major party newspapers, had systematically set out to capture the top leadership. The tariff vote of 1930 (when a substantial number of Conservatives joined with the opposition in defeating the Lindman cabinet) and that on salary increases for the clergy in 1950 (when the Erlander government carried the day with bourgeois support against almost solid opposition from its own party) show that even wholesale defection need not entail any grave consequences.

Recent Swedish history, as Professor Håstad has pointed out,[55] records fewer instances of transition from one party to another than that of a two-party country like Britain, where a constant reshuffling of top leadership personnel is taking place. Even so, converts are not infrequent and have generally been received with even more alacrity than repentant rebels—despite the mutterings of many an organization regular who has failed to see what good such "turncoats" could do for a party.[56] Carl Lindhagen and Baron Erik Palmstierna joined the leading circle of the Social Democratic party almost immediately after abandoning the Liberal cause (1910–1911), and the Liberals in turn elected Petersson i Påboda to their national executive committee (1910) the year after he had resigned from Lindman's government. Of the three Social Democrats expelled in 1915, one (Yngve Larsson) for many years was the Liberal leader in the Stockholm city council; another (Otto Järte) in 1932 became political editor of the Conservative *Svenska Dagbladet*.[57] Järte's example finds a recent parallel in Professor Herbert Tingsten, who left the Social Democratic party to become editor in chief of the largest Swedish daily, the Liberal *Dagens Nyheter* (1945–1946). It is not surprising that the youngest of the major parties more than any other has recruited its leaders among converts from other camps: the four men who led the Agrarian party from its unification in 1921 until 1948 all had served their apprenticeship as Liberals or Conservatives; Axel Pehrsson i Bramstorp, who took over in 1934, had sat as a Liberal member of the lower house as late as 1918–1921.[58]

[55] Håstad, *Partierna i regering och riksdag, op.cit.*, p. 55.

[56] See Karl Magnusson's acid comment (*Vid spade och riksdagspulpet*, Malmö: Gleerup, 1950, p. 202) about Professor Nils Wohlin. Wohlin in twenty-three years in the riksdag built up a unique record of vacillation: Agrarian senator (1919–1927) and floor leader (1922–1923); "nonpartisan" member of one and Conservative member of a second Conservative cabinet (1923–1924, 1928–1929); independent senator (1928); Conservative member of the lower chamber (1929–1931) and senate (1932–1933); again an independent (1934) and once more an Agrarian (1935–1942) in the senate. Wohlin resigned his senate seat after each conversion (1928, 1934) to seek reelection under his new label.

[57] See *Vem är det*, Stockholm: Norstedt, every other year 1912–1920 and since 1923.

[58] Among his predecessors, Johan Andersson i Raklösen (1921–1924) and Johan Johansson i Kälkebo (1924–1928) had been Liberal members

Party cohesion is put to its severest test at times when major political realignments are taking place. The political aftermath of the "Swedish New Deal" thus provides some further illustrations of the devices by which parties insure both internal discipline and responsible leadership. The Socialist Hansson government had secured passage for its program thanks to a palace revolt in the Agrarian party and a serious split among the Liberals. Actually the events of 1933 caused some tensions within each of the four major parties and these in turn precipitated the following reactions: (1) Early in 1934 the Agrarian riksdag group refused to reelect its aging leader, Olsson i Kullenbergstorp, who had denounced the Socialist-Agrarian agreement as a "horse-trading deal," and instead by acclamation selected Axel Pehrsson, who had negotiated this very deal behind his back.[59] (2) In the fall of 1934 a senate election in the district of Örebro provided a minor test of strength between the supporters and opponents of the government's crisis policy. The candidates included Anders Örne, one of the leaders of the cooperative movement and a long-time Social Democrat, and Professor Nils Wohlin. Wohlin had been the only Conservative to vote for the New Deal measures, had been denied his traditional committee seat by the Conservative caucus, had thereupon resigned his mandate, and now was seeking reelection as an Agrarian. Örne, on the other hand, was one of the few Socialist opponents of the government's crisis policy but had been renominated by his party. Faced with this choice, four Socialist electors joined with four Agrarians in electing the ex-Conservative Wohlin, thereby defeating their own party's candidate.[60] (3) Two left wing Social Democrats who also had opposed the "New Deal" policies joined the Communist Kilbom faction. One of them was formally expelled from the party by the national committee for "systematically disloyal conduct" —an action which the next national convention confirmed.[61]

of the riksdag (1912–1914 and 1907–1908 respectively), whereas Olof Olsson i Kullenbergstorp (1928–1934) had been an independent Conservative (1909–1911).

[59] Nyman, *Svensk parlamentarism, 1932–1936, op.cit.*, pp. 167f.

[60] Cf. *Sveriges officiella statistik, Allmänna val, Riksdagsmannavalen åren 1933–1936*, Stockholm, 1937.

[61] *Protokoll från Sveriges socialdemokratiska arbetarepartis 15:e kongress*, Stockholm: Tiden, 1937, pp. 333f.

(4) The Liberals, anxious to preserve outward unity, distributed their top offices both in parliament and within the national organization among the two rival factions. At the party's national convention of 1934 the right wing leader Felix Hamrin and the left winger Ola Jeppsson were elected chairmen, respectively, of the national and the executive committee with equal powers in party affairs. The election of Andersson i Rasjön as party leader in 1935 finally healed the rift.[62]

The relationship between leaders and followers within the major Swedish parties is not one of command and unquestioned obedience, but one of cooperation and constructive interplay within a hierarchical structure. Party discipline is maintained not so much by drastic sanction as by long-formed habit stemming from a recognition of its value for every member. Most Swedish politicians would concur in Branting's dictum: "The party does not wish to do violence to anyone's conscience, but a party that wants to go ahead and reach its goals must demand respect for its decisions."[63] Just as the major parties attempt to reconcile the imperatives of unity within the organization and of individual conscience, so they preserve a respect for the opinions of other parties while engaged in the intense power competition that permeates the legislative process.

[62] Nyman, *Svensk parlamentarism, 1932–1936, op.cit.*, pp. 168 ff., 222 f.
[63] Remark at the 1917 party congress, at which the Left Socialists seceded, quoted by Edenman, *op.cit.*, p. 133.

CHAPTER VI

THE LEGISLATIVE PROCESS

THE legislative process is one of the most distinctive features of the Swedish governmental system. American observers particularly will be impressed with the purposefulness of procedure, the careful attention customarily given to relevant facts and to a great variety of interested opinion, and the complete absence of the cruder forms of obstruction. The cabinet, the parliamentary committees, and the two chambers are the main partners in this process. There is an inverse relation between the compactness of each of these groups and the length and complexity of the task it is expected to perform. The preparatory investigations, which may extend over many weeks and months (in some cases years) are conducted by the cabinet, usually under the immediate direction of a single minister. Being a small and homogeneous body the cabinet is well equipped to integrate the divergent views presented by the administration and by private interest groups, and to resist and channel the many conflicting pressures that arise. The committees are not much larger than the cabinet but are far less homogeneous, since they reflect all the major political tendencies present in the legislature. In a period of several days or a few weeks they attempt to clarify and, as far as possible, reconcile partisan views on the bill as it has emerged from the cabinet. Although committees may conduct their own investigations, they deliberate in a secluded atmosphere and generally are content to supplement the material gathered by the cabinet at a few crucial points. The two houses, finally, debate the committee report for a few hours or at most two or three days. The debate merely sums up arguments that have been expressed earlier in the cabinet, in committee, and in the press. There is little time now for major changes in the text of the bill, and on the final vote the chambers usually have a choice only of adopting or rejecting the bill, or approving it with any amendments suggested in the committee report.

EVOLUTION OF LEGISLATIVE POWER

The cabinet's central role in the preparation of legislation has been the result of a slow evolutionary process extending over the last 150 years. The constitutional fathers of 1809, in their efforts to establish a system of checks and balances, had assigned some legislative functions to the king, others to parliament, and still others to both jointly. All laws affecting the rights and duties of subjects toward each other—that is to say, all criminal and civil legislation—required concurrent action by king and parliament; the initiative for bills of this kind might come from either side. Within a vaguely defined sphere of public economy the king could legislate by decree. The crown also could rely on certain fixed incomes from the royal domains and from excises, stamp duties, and other traditional levies not subject to parliamentary control. The riksdag, on the other hand, had exclusive power to levy taxes over and above such "ordinary income." The cabinet, within this constitutional scheme, was to be merely a body of royal advisers whose advice the king, in exercising his legislative and executive functions, must ask but need not follow.

Successive constitutional amendments and the slow accretion of custom have changed many of these provisions and in some respects simplified the original scheme. First, the king's executive and legislative power has, in fact though not in law, devolved upon the cabinet. Second, two secular trends—a steady expansion of government activity and a continuous fall in the value of the monetary unit—have brought all but a small fraction of state revenues within the purview of the riksdag. Third, some categories of law have been transferred by constitutional amendment from royal to joint legislation, and since the late nineteenth century the cabinet has generally obtained the riksdag's consent even for such economic legislation as remains the king's exclusive province. Fourth, the riksdag has given up the practice of writing new legislation; since about 1920 it has restricted itself to requesting the government to prepare bills on matters which in the riksdag's judgment require action and to approving, amending, and rejecting government bills. Finally, the royal veto, always applied sparingly, has not been used since 1913. In short, the cabinet has replaced the king; the distinction between joint legislation and other legislation has virtually disappeared; and the original division of *powers* between the government and parliament has given way to a division of *labor*.

THE CABINET AND ADMINISTRATION

The cabinet today consists of a prime minister, eleven department heads, and from two to five ministers without portfolio. The competence of the eleven departments largely follows the pattern familiar in other countries. There are ministers of foreign affairs, finance, justice, defense, the interior, agriculture, and commerce. Other department titles reflect particular concerns of Swedish government: A minister of social welfare is in charge of the elaborate scheme of benefits evolved during the last few decades. His colleague in the communications department handles matters connected with the state-owned railroad, telephone, telegraph, and broadcasting systems. The department of education also is concerned with the State Church and is officially styled the "ecclesiastic department." Finally, a wage department, added in 1950, represents the government in collective bargaining negotiations. At least two of the ministers without portfolio must have had some administrative or judicial experience at the time of their appointment;[1] they are expected to assist their colleagues with the technical aspects of drafting bills. Other ministers without portfolio may act as assistants to overburdened department chiefs. During the recent world war some of them took on special emergency functions, such as allocation of scarce fuel, and more recently Dag Hammarskjöld served as deputy foreign minister until his appointment as United Nations secretary general (1953). Occasionally the premier himself may head one of the departments, in which case the cabinet will include one additional minister without portfolio. Such an arrangement enables the premier to take direct charge of a subject that he considers to be of acute political importance—e.g. the defense portfolio in 1914, the foreign office during the Åland conflict (1921–1923), or the agriculture department in the Agrarian cabinet of 1936.

[1] *RF,* §6. For the abbreviations used in notes to this chapter cf. page 13, note 3, supra.

Unlike the cabinet departments of other countries, the Swedish ministries act almost exclusively as policy-planning staffs. Some fifty administrative agencies—including, for instance, the treasury, the customs office, the social welfare administration, the public health service, and the state railways—carry out the actual administration. The cabinet formulates the general instructions that govern the activity of these agencies, makes the higher-level appointments, and passes on budget requests before they are incorporated in the appropriation bill that goes to the riksdag. But within such wide limits the agency heads (whether an individual director or a commission) are generally free to interpret the statutes and decrees for whose application they are responsible. The foreign service, which is directly subordinated to the minister of foreign affairs, provides the chief exception to the general rule of administrative independence;[2] and the king, advised by the defense minister, is of course the commander in chief of the armed forces. Two agencies—the bank of Sweden and the national debt office—are governed by boards appointed by the riksdag.[3]

The cabinet has very little patronage to dispense. Subordinate officials in the administration are selected by open competition and normally acquire tenure. The highest officials—heads of administrative agencies, provincial governors, undersecretaries in the cabinet departments, and all diplomats—may be freely removed by the king upon the cabinet's advice.[4] In practice, however, most of these, too, come from the ranks of the professional service and serve during good behavior.

Two examples—that of the undersecretaries and that of the provincial governors—may illustrate the strong tradition of nonpolitical appointment and the limitations of patronage. The undersecretaries are the highest officials in each department immediately under the minister, and the law itself defines their function as "political."[5] An overwhelming majority, nevertheless, have in fact been recruited from the civil service

[2] For other exceptions see Herbert Tingsten, *Studier rörande ministerstyrelse*, Uddevalla, 1928.

[3] See [Sweden, Riksdagen,] *Sveriges riksdag*, Stockholm: Victor Petterson, 1931–1938, vol. XIII.

[4] *RF*, § 35; cf. Robert Malmgren, *Sveriges författning*, vol, II, Malmö, 1941, pp. 183 ff.

[5] Malmgren, *Sveriges författning, op.cit.*, II, 187.

and judicial careers. Of the fifty-odd undersecretaries who served in the various departments from 1917 (when the posts were created) until 1936, only four or five had any apparent party connections. Since 1936 the number of political under-secretaries has somewhat increased, yet they have always been a minority.[6] As a result most undersecretaries retain their posts regardless of changes in the political complexion of the cabinet.

The governors of Stockholm and the twenty-five provinces, by contrast, perform chiefly routine administrative and cere-monial functions. Yet it is among these rather than within the government chancellery that political appointments have been prevalent. Traditionally these posts have been considered suit-able sinecures for retired cabinet ministers, and more recently other veteran politicians have been similarly rewarded. The general trend toward a slight increase in the proportion of "political" governors may be gathered from table 4. It should be noted, however, that ex-ministers have been appointed to

TABLE 4

POLITICAL APPOINTMENTS TO GOVERNORSHIPS, 1900–1952

	1900-1916	1917-1931	1932-1952	1900-1952
1. Number of governors appointed[a]	31	28	43	102
Thereof:				
2. Ex-ministers with riksdag service	12.9%	10.7%	27.9%	18.6%
3. Others with riksdag service	24.8	21.4	16.3	20.6
4. Total politicians	37.7	32.1	44.2	39.2
5. Other ex-ministers	12.9	14.3	7.0	10.8
6. Total (lines 2, 3, and 5)	50.6	46.4	51.2	50.0

[a]Disregarding temporary appointments, reappointments, and trans-fers.

Source: As in note 6, below.

[6] My calculations from the government manual (*Sveriges Statskalen-der*, annually), the Swedish who's who (*Vem är det?* Stockholm: Nor-stedt, biennially), and *Vem var det?* (Stockholm: Norstedt, 1944).

governorships regardless of party; among the governors appointed by Socialist or Socialist-Agrarian cabinets since 1932 have been the Liberal leaders Hamrin and Jeppsson and the Conservatives Fritiof Domö and Georg Andrén. Even here, then, the cabinet's patronage power has not been used to promote the exclusive interests of the government party.

Unity within the administration is achieved not by detailed direction from the cabinet, but rather by a quasi-judicial procedure that can here be outlined but briefly. All administrative agencies must keep their records open for public inspection; exceptions to this rule, again notably regarding foreign office and military documents, are defined by law.[7] Any person whose interests are directly affected by an administrative decision may appeal to the agency head and, after that, either to a supreme administrative tribunal or to the cabinet. Broadly speaking, the tribunal reviews mandatory, the cabinet discretionary, decisions.[8] But parliament too has an important share in the indirect supervision of the administration. Every four years the riksdag appoints two supervisory officials, one for the judiciary and civil service, one for the armed forces, who are charged with the legal prosecution of officials guilty of misconduct; and a parliamentary board of auditors checks the expenditures of public agencies.[9]

To the foreign observer the Swedish system of administrative independence with its corollaries of publicity of administration and administrative appeals may seem circuitous and wasteful. But the separation of administration and policy making is deeply rooted in Swedish history; and most Swedes consider the right "to go to the king" with their complaints an essential guarantee of individual freedom, just as Americans tend to see their liberty closely linked to the bill of rights and an independent judiciary. The political significance of the system may be illustrated by a concrete example. In 1926 a number of unemployed refused to take work in a struck mine to which the unemployment commission had assigned them. When the com-

[7] See *Lag om inskränkningar i rätten att utbekomma allmänna handlingar*, reprinted in Robert Malmgren, ed., *Sveriges grundlagar*, 6th edn., Stockholm: Norstedt, 1951.

[8] Cf. Gunnar Heckscher, *Svensk statsförvaltning i arbete*, Stockholm: Näringsliv och samhälle, 1952, pp. 172 ff.

[9] *Sveriges riksdag, op.cit.*, vol. XVI.

mission cancelled their unemployment benefits they complained, and the Sandler government overruled the decision. Yet the bourgeois riksdag majority reinterpreted the relevant statute in accordance with the original ruling, thereby causing the government's resignation.

THE CABINET AND LEGISLATION

Another necessary bridge across the gap between ministry and administration is the constitutional requirement that the minister in charge of preparing a bill or decree must "obtain all necessary information from interested administrative agencies."[10] Although the constitution does not specify what information is "necessary" or which agencies are "interested," ministers, eager to forestall parliamentary and public criticism, have interpreted these terms broadly. Two main procedures have evolved in the course of more than a century: (1) After a cabinet department has drafted a bill or decree the minister may ask one or several administrative agencies to comment; more recently draft bills have circulated in the same manner among private organizations—labor unions, employers' and farm producers' associations, and consumers' cooperatives. The reports received may range from simple endorsements to detailed critiques or counterproposals. (2) The minister or the entire cabinet may appoint some private individual or a commission to prepare a report on some legislative or administrative question, or to draft a measure in keeping with certain general directives.[11] These "royal commissions" may include administrators, scholars and other private experts, representatives of the public, and members of parliament; today more than 100 such commissions may be active at any given time. Whichever procedure is followed, the cabinet usually sends all reports to the riksdag along with the text of the bill and the cabinet's own exposition of its rationale. Although some governments have used royal commissions as a favorite device for procrastinating, or otherwise sidetracking demands for reform, their chief pur-

[10] RF, § 10.
[11] For the earlier history of the commissions see Gunnar Hesslén, *Det svenska kommittéväsendet intill år 1905*, Uppsala: Almqvist & Wiksell, 1927; for recent developments, Heckscher, *op.cit.*, pp. 206 ff.

pose has been to gather factual information for the guidance of the cabinet and the legislators, to predict the probable effects of a proposed measure, and to test public reaction. The most important commission reports are printed at public expense, and these constitute a voluminous library of basic information on public affairs.

In addition to the administration, private organizations, and royal commissions, one other body often examines a legislative measure before it reaches the riksdag. This is the law council, consisting of three judges of the supreme court and one from the administrative tribunal. Judicial preview—as we may call this process of preliminary scrutiny of legislation by the judges—is required for all civil and criminal legislation and is optional at the king's (i.e. the cabinet's) discretion for all other matters. The judges are free to comment on any aspect of the bill but in practice have limited themselves to opinions concerning the consistency of the bill with statutes already on the book and concerning the adequacy of the wording from a technical viewpoint. As a result the judges' opinions, though merely advisory, have carried great weight with both the cabinet and the riksdag.

THE COMMITTEE SYSTEM

Of all modern parliaments the riksdag has perhaps one of the oldest and most elaborate committee systems, and to this day Swedish parliamentarians perform much of their most important work in the committee room. The fact that the constitution itself regulates the composition, jurisdiction, and much of the procedure of the committees attests to—and enhances—their importance. Within the legislative process their main function has traditionally been to serve as mediators—first among the four estates, later between two antithetic chambers, and more recently among the four major parties in the riksdag. During periods of minority government the power of the committees in the riksdag has often exceeded that of the cabinet itself.[12]

[12] Cf. Neil C. M. Elder, "The Parliamentary Role of Joint Standing Committees in Sweden," *American Political Science Review*, 45:464–473 (1951), and Herbert Tingsten, "Utskottsväsendet," in *Sveriges riksdag*, *op.cit.*, vol. XI.

Foremost among the committees are the nine joint standing committees—on foreign relations, appropriations, ways and means, banking, and agriculture; a constitutional committee; and three law committees. The constitutional committee handles proposed constitutional amendments and other bills relating to governmental machinery (elections, parliamentary procedure, administrative and local government organization). Until the final settlement of the great constitutional questions after the First World War it was considered the most important committee, and many of the ablest riksdag members vied for a place on it; since then it has sunk to comparative insignificance, and its former prestige has largely devolved upon the appropriations committee. The three law committees consider all bills relating to civil, criminal, and social welfare legislation. The agriculture committee was created in 1900, that on foreign relations in 1937, and the second and third law committees in 1909 and 1949 respectively. The other five were already enumerated in the original version of the 1809 constitution—though the committee system itself goes back at least to the eighteenth century.

Although the lines of jurisdiction among the standing committees rest upon a complete enumeration of all types of bills, the constitution also admits of more flexible arrangements. Two standing committees may designate a composite committee to consider a bill that concerns them both. Or the two chambers, by concurrent resolution, may appoint a select committee and refer to it any bills that normally fall in the province of one or several standing committees. This device gives the parties a chance to pool their best talent; and select committees have therefore often handled highly controversial legislation, such as the electoral reform of 1918 or the antidepression program of 1933. Finally, there are two general-purpose committees which consider private members' requests for government legislation.

All standing, composite, and select committees include an equal number of members from the senate and the lower house. Most standing committees today have sixteen members; the constitutional and ways and means committees have twenty each, and the appropriations committee as many as thirty. These larger committees assign much of their work to subcommittees.

Until 1909 each chamber elected its committee members by majority—a method that promoted party discipline but often eliminated the representatives of minority groups at the center who might have effectively mediated between the chamber majorities. Since then committee elections have been proportional. Because the party composition of each committee is thus predetermined, the parties occasionally since 1918 and consistently since the late nineteen-twenties have agreed on "common lists" which have been approved by the chambers without opposition.[13] In addition to these regular members each chamber may appoint an indefinite number of alternates. In practice these sit in on committee sessions without a vote. When a full member is absent, an alternate from the same party leaves his seat near the wall to take his place at the table with full voting rights. All standing committees, as a rule, meet on the same days and hours. Since any absence from committee work must be specifically excused, the members of the foreign relations committee (which meets infrequently) and alternates are the only ones who combine several standing committee assignments.

The limited size of the joint committees has tended to exclude representatives of extremist parties. A party today has to muster at least one fifteenth of a chamber's vote to obtain a seat even on the largest committee, and the Communists and other minor parties so far have fallen short of that ratio. Occasionally a large party may cede a few of its committee seats to one of the minor factions. Thus Branting and some of his Socialist colleagues obtained their first committee assignments with Liberal support, and in the nineteen-twenties the Social Democrats and bourgeois parties elected a few Left Socialists and Löfgrenites respectively. The Communists, Kilbomites, and Nationalists, on the other hand, have never been the object of such generosity, and their absence has no doubt helped to preserve harmony within the committee room.

Before 1909 any change in parliamentary majorities was likely to produce a wholesale turnover of committee member-

[13] See the summaries of committee elections in the yearbook *Lagtima riksdagen*. For nonpartisan elections in the eighteen-seventies see page 37 supra. An amendment to *RO*, § 75, adopted in 1949, for the first time sanctions acclamation as a method of committee election.

ship. With proportional committee-elections, however, membership has been very stable. Although assignments run for only one year, a committee member can expect to be renominated as long as his party keeps its claim to the same number of committee seats. Alternates are generally first in line for vacancies within their party delegations. Four to six years go by before a majority of full members on a permanent committee is replaced. The average full committee member in 1949 was 59 years old, had served in parliament for 21 years (as against 54 and 9 for the average riksdag member), and had held his committee post for almost a decade. A majority of the foreign relations committee, which includes the party floor leaders and their immediate assistants, had served in the riksdag for a quarter century or more.[14]

THE COMMITTEES AND LEGISLATION

Since statute and custom closely regulate committee procedure, the posts of chairman and vice-chairman confer little autonomous power. (If the committee is evenly divided on a vote, the lot decides.) The chambers, nevertheless, have allocated these posts to the parties in rough proportion to numerical strength. By custom the chairman and vice-chairman of a committee belong to different parties and different chambers. Although seniority is an important factor, it is not followed slavishly. Thus in 1949 five of the (then) eight standing committees were headed by men over sixty-five, and five chairmen had attended thirty or more riksdag sessions; yet one was a comparative youngster of forty-eight with only four years of parliamentary experience.

Both statute and custom strengthen the committees' influence. The houses may not adopt any bill or resolution, whether sponsored by a minister or a private member, without a committee report. Although a house may reject a private member's

[14] Elder, *op.cit.*, p. 465, gives a table of average committee tenures. The other figures are my computations from *Lagtima riksdagen*, vol. 44 (1949), for committee members, and from the official election statistics for parliamentarians generally. For a profile of the appropriations committee of 1938–1941 see Georg Andrén, "Några anteckningar angående statsutskottet och dess arbetsformer," in *Festskrift till professor skytteanus Axel Brusewitz*, Uppsala: Almqvist & Wiksell, 1941, pp. 193–211.

resolution that does not fall in the province of a standing committee, even resolutions that have no chance of passing are in practice referred to committee. Only in the cases of the budget and of an occasional controversial bill[15] do the chambers avail themselves of the right to debate a bill before sending it to committee. Since the budget debates in fact tend to deal with everything but the details of the budget, the committees' hands are in no way tied. The final debate on the floor is based on the committee report. If the committee, that is to say, rejects or amends a bill, the original version does not even come up for a vote unless someone specifically moves its adoption from the floor. Three of the committees (constitution, appropriations, and ways and means), moreover, may initiate legislation on certain matters. The committees have regular staffs and frequently employ administrative officials or private experts on a temporary basis. They may obtain information, oral and written, from any cabinet department or agency; yet cabinet members are barred from attending the meetings of any committee except that on foreign affairs.[16] The committees, furthermore, participate directly in the supervision of the administration. The constitutional committee examines the official cabinet minutes; the ways and means committee, in cooperation with the parliamentary auditors, examines the accounts of the executive branch; and the foreign relations committee receives periodic reports on the conduct of foreign policy.[17] There is,

[15] Such as the Socialist defense bill of 1936, whose eventual rejection caused Hansson's fall.

[16] The same rule applies to judges of the highest courts. The constitution carries this antiquated bit of "separation of powers" to the extreme of excluding ministers and high judges who may have seats in parliament from participating in the selection of committee personnel (*RO*, § 36:3). A strict application of this rule in the recent postwar period would have enabled the bourgeois parties in the lower chamber, though in a minority, to elect a majority of committee members. By voluntary agreement, however, the principle that the committees ought to reflect the alignments in the chamber was made to prevail.

[17] A foreign relations commission, set up in 1921, antedated the committee, established in 1937; their personnel is identical (*RF*, § 54). The functions of both are discussed in two works by Axel Brusewitz: "Riksdagen och utrikespolitiken," *Sveriges riksdag, op.cit.*, vol. xv, and *Studier över riksdagen och utrikespolitiken*, Uppsala: Almqvist & Wiksell, 1933–1941.

however, none of the French tradition of petty and sustained
rivalry between individual committees and cabinet departments—partly, no doubt, because the patterns of committee
and cabinet organization do not coincide, partly because the
ministries do not administer.

The traditional atmosphere of the committees is conducive
to mutual understanding, and they have not arrogated to themselves the corrupting power of obstruction. All committee
meetings are closed. There are no formal hearings; no verba-
tim minutes are kept; and no account of the committee's
deliberations is allowed to appear in the press before the
official report to the chambers is published. Deliberations, as
a result, are at once informal and restrained. There is little point
in trying to excite with flamboyant oratory a select and intimate
group made up mostly of elderly and highly seasoned politicians. Objectivity (or rather *saklighet*—a term untranslatable
with its full connotations) is the prime virtue that will earn a
committee freshman the respect of his seniors. In intensive
discussion of a wide variety of subjects, week after week and
year after year, members of different political persuasions
have an opportunity to become thoroughly familiar with their
opponents' viewpoint and to appreciate its sincerity. In his
committee work "Many a newly elected Socialist deputy has
found..., upon closer contact with his bourgeois colleagues,
that these are not quite as impossible as he had imagined; and
many bourgeois members have been surprised...when they
got to know Social Democrats who turned out to be decent as
well as reasonable people."[18] Many personal friendships across
party lines have had their origin in the committee room.

Strict regulation of the riksdag's calendar facilitates the
committees' work. The government normally is required to
submit all tax and appropriations bills within seventy, and all
other bills within ninety, days of the opening of the session
unless there are urgent reasons for delay;[19] the moral pressure
on the government to stay within these limits is strong. Private
members must introduce their bills or resolutions within
fifteen days after the introduction of the budget bill; they have

[18] Louis De Geer, *Politiska hågkomster från åren 1901–1921*, Stockholm:
Norstedt, 1926, pp. 13f.
[19] *RO*, § 54.

from ten to twenty days to submit amendments to government bills.[20] According to the constitution, committees must report on all matters referred to them "as quickly as possible."[21] If the committee unanimously opposes a measure it may report laconically that "Resolution no. 26 should not cause any action by the riksdag." But it may not kill a bill or resolution by withholding it from floor consideration; and conversely the chambers have no way of bringing a bill to the floor before the committee is ready to report. The committee report often contains a majority opinion and one or more concurring or dissenting opinions. It is always submitted to both chambers simultaneously.

In its committee system the Swedish riksdag possesses both a preventive and a remedy for bicameral disagreements. Where the chambers differ on some minor points, the committee report may offer a synthesis of both views; where there is a wide discrepancy, the committee discussion will bring the essential differences into sharper focus. At any rate joint consideration of all bills removes many petty frictions which intercameral rivalry and ambition might magnify into full-fledged disputes. The committees also have the explicit function of mediating when conflicts between the chambers do arise. If one chamber amends a bill that the other has adopted unchanged, or if each adopts a different amendment, the matter automatically goes back to committee. In a new report the committee will attempt to compromise any points of difference. It may, of course, report that the differences are irreconcilable—in which case the measure falls. During the eighteenth and nineteenth centuries the committees developed a set of standard techniques for performing this task of mediation. These were known as "invitation" (recommendation of a *quid pro quo* by which each chamber would agree to any additional provisions approved by the other[s]), "amputation" (exclusion of conflicting passages), "compromise" (usually in the form of splitting the difference in financial matters, or substituting a new proposal equally far removed from all original positions), and "composite reconciliation" (any combination of the other three).[22]

[20] *ibid.*, § 55.   [21] *ibid.*, § 45.
[22] See Einar J:son Thulin, "Sammanjämkning och gemensam votering," in *Sveriges riksdag, op.cit.*, x, 239–543.

A special procedure known as joint voting is used to resolve disagreements on financial matters, such as appropriations, tax bills, or ordinances concerning the administration of the national debt or the Bank of Sweden. Under this procedure the chambers, in a simultaneous vote taken at separate sittings, choose between the two versions they have previously adopted; a majority of the total ayes and noes decides. Although the constitution presupposes that the committees will attempt reconciliation first and use the joint vote as a last resort, they usually recommend a joint vote at once. Joint voting on financial bills flouts the explicit constitutional provision that "The chambers have equal competence and authority on all questions."[23] For, because of the larger size of the lower chamber, five sixths of its members can outvote a unanimous senate plus one sixth of their own colleagues.[24] In its treatment of financial matters the riksdag is thus in effect a unicameral body deliberating in two sections. Since the equalization of the suffrage for the two chambers, however, disagreements have been rare, and the provisions for their reconciliation have lost much of their practical importance.

THE HOUSES AND THEIR SPEAKERS

The proceedings on the floor, like the work of the committees, are governed by rules and conventions designed to expedite majority decisions while guaranteeing a full hearing for the minority. There is unlimited freedom of debate; yet the position of the speakers, voting procedures, and even seating arrangements all tend to discourage obstruction and to temper partisanship.

The speakership in each house conveys only such powers as are essential to the conduct of business, and Swedish speakers have maintained a high reputation for impartiality. The speaker must preside over the chamber's proceedings whenever he is

[23] *RF*, § 49.
[24] The actual result depends, of course, on party alignments. Since the senate throughout the oligarchic period was far more homogeneous it has done better than might be expected. Although it contains only 39 per cent of the joint membership it carried 43 per cent of all joint votes from 1867 to 1933; see *Sveriges riksdag, op.cit.*, x, 304f.

present; he thus may never participate in a debate or vote. (As in the committees, the lot decides in case of a tie.) When the speaker is detained elsewhere, a deputy speaker takes his place. From 1867 to 1921 the king, upon the recommendation of the cabinet, annually appointed a speaker and a deputy speaker for each chamber. Since 1921 the chambers have elected their own presiding officers, and there now are two deputy speakers for each chamber. Most of the royally appointed speakers were prominent representatives of one of the larger groups in the chamber; yet the posts were never considered a prize for the followers of the cabinet in power. On the contrary, when the leader of the urban free-traders, Carl Herslow, succeeded to the speakership in 1891, the gossipers suspected an "exceptionally astute scheme" of Premier Boström's designed "to fetter his most talented opponent in the speaker's chair."[25] The elected speakers have been men of long parliamentary experience and faithful service to their party who have ascended close to the summit of the organizational hierarchy without having taken a major part in controversy.[26] By informal agreement the six presiding posts are apportioned among the major parties. Although the constitution provides for majority election of the speakers, there have in fact never been any rival candidacies.[27] Incumbent speakers are reelected as a matter of course; when one of them resigns, dies, or declines reelection, the vacany is in effect filled by vote of his party caucus. The speakers customarily resign their party offices and committee assignments; some of them even have severed their formal party affiliation. The deputies (who participate in debates and votes unless they happen to be presiding) retain their party and committee positions. In 1952 three of the deputies were floor leaders of their parties; one was also a committee chairman.

The strict schedule of the riksdag has already been alluded
A chamber may act upon a bill or resolution as soon as it is

[25] Hugo Hamilton, *Hågkomster*, Stockholm: Bonnier, 1928, p. 225.

[26] The situation resembles that in England where, according to Jennings, the speaker "is, usually, a very ordinary member elected to the Chair because he has taken no part in controversy." W. Ivor Jennings, *Parliament*, Cambridge: University Press, 1948, p, 15.

[27] *RO*, § 33. In 1921 each of the three largest parties was given two of the six speakerships and deputy speakerships, one in each house. In 1929 one Liberal deputy speaker was succeeded by an Agrarian.

received but usually allows it to be tabled until the next sitting. On the second day the bill must be referred to committee. Similarly, committee reports must be taken up for final debate and disposition no later than the third business day after they first appear on the agenda.[28] By long-standing custom the chambers sit four times a week during the parliamentary session. The Tuesday and Friday meetings are held so that ministers and private members may introduce bills and resolutions; since there are no quorum requirements committees can deliberate while these "tabling sittings" are in progress. Debates are held on Wednesdays and Saturdays—or more often if the calendar toward the end of the session gets crowded. The parties, by common agreement, hold their weekly caucuses on Thursday afternoons. A "speakers' conference," consisting of the six presiding officers and your additional members (in practice party floor leaders or their assistants), determines the riksdag's agenda from week to week and sees to it that, as the constitution prescribes, all committee reports are "so far as possible taken up simultaneously in both chambers."[29]

In each chamber the members' desks are arranged in rows which, seen from the speaker's chair, form a series of inverted V's; the seating order is by constituencies rather than by parties,[30] so that Socialists will alternate with Conservatives, and Agrarians with Communists or Liberals. To the right of the speaker two rows are reserved for cabinet ministers. Members may speak from their places or from the rostrum. In the early bicameral days Louis De Geer found that members of the riksdag could "at one moment engage in the most heated political disputes and the next moment appear to be the best of friends in their social contacts."[31] This friendly social intercourse was only to be expected among the senators of the eighteen-seventies, who represented a minute and homogeneous aristocratic class closely related by common pursuits and

[28] *ibid.*, §§ 58f.
[29] *ibid.*, § 59.
[30] *Ordningsstadga för riksdagens första (andra) kammare*, reprinted in Malmgren, ed., *Sveriges grundlagar, op.cit.*, appendix. On each provincial bench, senators take their seats according to the number of votes with which they were elected, lower chamber members according to parliamentary seniority and age.
[31] Louis De Geer, *Minnen*, Stockholm: Norstedt, 1892, II, 150.

family ties. But this tradition has survived the bitter conflicts of the turn of the century and seems to continue unimpaired in both houses—for Gottfrid Billing in 1894 and Claes Lindskog in our own day described the personal relations among riksdag members in language almost identical with De Geer's.[32] Like the British house of commons the riksdag thus has "in process of time [become] a club as well as a parliament."[33] It would seem that the nonpartisan seating arrangement has contributed its share to this development.[34]

Debates in the riksdag are orderly and restrained. The constitution specifically guarantees every member the right to speak as often and as long as he wishes. There are no rules whatsoever for closure, guillotine, kangaroo, or moving the previous question. The speaker will see to it that members talk to the subject; he may deny the floor for the remainder of the day to anyone who, after a first warning, persists in using "personally offensive language or otherwise violating good order."[35] But there is little occasion for such drastic discipline. During most debates the speaker will keep the gavel in his desk drawer, and a discreet rattling of it there will often be enough to calm excited tempers. A Conservative member, after thirty-five years of service under Liberal and Socialist speakers (1915–1950), attested to the chair's impartiality and recalled only a single instance where the speaker had to interrupt proceedings to restore order.[36] Since those who wish to speak must enter their names on a roster near the speaker's desk, the problem of

[32] Gottfrid Billing, *Anteckningar från riksdagar och kyrkomöten, 1893–1906*, Stockholm: Norstedt, 1928, pp. 80, 109, and Claes Lindskog, *Bokslut: Hågkomster och människor*, Stockholm: Bonnier, 1949, p. 106 (cf. p. 32).

[33] Ernest Barker, *Principles of Social and Political Theory*, Oxford: Clarendon Press, 1951, p. 51.

[34] Karl Magnusson, *Vid spade och riksdagspulpet*, Malmö: Gleerup, 1950, p. 98.

[35] *RO*, § 52.

[36] Magnusson, *op.cit.*, pp. 148, 245. Axel Brusewitz, *Kungamakt, herremakt, folkmakt*, Stockholm: Tiden, 1951, pp. 153 ff., gives some interesting data on the number of times since 1867 that lower chamber speakers have used their gavel to call members to order. Until 1913, it seems, there were about a dozen such incidents, and since 1933 there have been only five or six. The greatest frequency was attained during the First World War— seventeen in four years.

catching the speaker's eye does not arise The roster is followed strictly except that ministers may take the floor at any time, that anyone may rise to declare his agreement with the preceding speaker, and that anyone who has already spoken in the same debate may take the floor for a three-minute rebuttal.[37] Although there is complete freedom of debate, filibustering is unknown; nor is there any room for other delaying maneuvers. Since no quorum is required, no time is lost on quorum calls; since votes are recorded by electrical apparatus, none is wasted on calling the roll.[38] Once the passions of the constitutional conflict of the early part of this century had ebbed down, the proceedings became utterly undramatic. Since the time before the First World War, ex-Speaker Sävström recalled, "the work of the riksdag has undergone profound changes in important respects... the struggles which formerly were bitter—far too bitter—have given way to a willingness to cooperate. Everything now goes more smoothly than it used to...."[39]

VOTING PROCEDURE AND ITS IMPLICATIONS

The riksdag employs a procedure in debating and voting on floor amendments which differs widely from that of other countries. Since it has some influence on the parliamentary deportment of the parties the system may here be outlined briefly.[40] Perhaps its essential feature can best be explained by saying that the rules do not allow for any amendments from the floor, as the term amendment is understood elsewhere. A motion to amend is a proposal to add new provisions to a measure or to change or delete parts of it. Such a proposal may never be entertained in the riksdag. A member, to be sure, may move that the measure under consideration be adopted in the version proposed by the committee minority; or that a

---

[37] *RO*, § 52, and *Ordningsstadga*, § 12:1.

[38] *Reglementariska föreskrifter för riksdagen*, § 11.

[39] August Sävström, *En talmans levnadsminnen*, Stockholm: Lindfors, 1949, pp. 228 f.

[40] The relevant legal provisions are *RF*, § 60, and *Reglementariska föreskrifter för riksdagen*, § 11. Cf. *Sveriges riksdag, op.cit.*, x, 201 ff.; Robert Malmgren, *Sveriges författning*, vol. 1, 2d edn., Malmö, 1948, pp. 402 ff.; and Ferdinand Vegelow, *Den svenska talmansinstitutionen*, Lund, 1921, pp. 232 ff.

government bill amended in committee be restored to its original wording; or that the bill be adopted in a form resulting from the deletion of such phrases and the substitution of such others; or, for that matter, that the bill be rejected in its entirety. Each motion (*yrkande*), that is to say, refers to the disposition of the bill as a whole rather than only to the parts that are to be changed. Hence there is no occasion for interrupting the main debate in order to discuss and vote on proposed amendments—let alone for opening brackets within a parenthesis to dispose of a motion to amend the amendment. The subject of the debate is the entire bill or resolution,[41] and all motions that have been introduced from the floor with reference to it are voted upon together at the end. When no more members wish to speak, the presiding officer lists all the motions before the house. If adoption of the bill as reported is the only question, a single vote will decide it.[42] If two or more motions have been entered, the speaker asks for a series of votes that amount to a successive elimination contest under the following rules: (1) On each vote the chamber chooses between two alternatives—called "proposition" and "counterproposition." (2) The winning alternative in any one vote appears as the "counterproposition"—that is to say, is paired off against a new motion—on the following vote. Every motion thus enters the contest only once and stays in it until rejected in favor of another. (3) All motions are taken up in reverse order of their support as ascertained by the speaker in a preliminary series of voice votes.

The political significance of the "counterproposition" system of voting is twofold. In the first place, it attenuates the danger to the parliamentary process from a common pattern of obstruction. Many multiparty countries face the constant threat of a "negative majority"—one composed of two minorities who oppose a measure for contrary reasons and hence

---

[41] The chamber may debate the various sections of a committee report separately. In that case the same rules apply to each section.

[42] Here and throughout any vote may have to be taken three times: first, viva voce; next, if the speaker is in doubt as to the outcome or if someone challenges his ruling, a standing vote; finally, upon renewed challenge, a recorded vote by electrical apparatus. Roll calls are taken only when the electrical equipment happens to be out of order.

are unable to agree on any counterproposal.[43] Thus Communists have often voted together with National Socialists in Weimar Germany or with De Gaullists in the French Fourth Republic; but even less extreme cases, which come within the range of Swedish possibilities, have not been uncommon—e.g. German Nationalists and other right wingers joining with Social Democrats in defeating a government of the center on a question of confidence or other crucial measure.[44] While no device of legislative procedure can eliminate the possibility of such a "meeting of extremes,"[45] the Swedish system discourages it to some extent. As soon as two or more alternative proposals for action have been moved, the "counterproposition" method establishes a strong presumption in favor of action of some kind or other. Adoption of the committee report is always one of the questions before the house, even if it has not specifically been moved from the floor; rejection, on the other hand, may not come up for a vote at all unless it has been so moved. If one extreme wants the bill rejected it must enter a motion to that effect; if the other extreme wants to join in this move it has to go on record as supporting its archenemies. The consequences may be unpleasant for both, for Swedish voters—and rival parties in competing for their favor—set a high value upon cooperativeness and react sharply against anything that resembles deliberate obstruction.[46] Support of the opposite extreme may be much harder to explain to the voters than mere opposition to the center.

In the second place, cooperation between the extremes, although unlikely on any final vote, frequently does occur during the earlier stages of the elimination contest. Suppose the choice before the house is between three minority proposals—a Socialist motion for a large public works appropriation, a

[43] Cf. Dankwart A. Rustow, "Some Observations on Proportional Representation," *Journal of Politics*, 12:114 (1950).

[44] For the situation in Weimar Germany see, e.g., Friedrich Glum, *Das parlamentarische Regierungssystem in Deutschland, Grossbritannien und Frankreich*, München: C. H. Beck, 1950, pp. 215 ff.

[45] This is the name under which Maurice Duverger analyses the phenomenon. *Political Parties*, tr. B. and R. North, London: Methuen, 1954, p. 415.

[46] Ernst Wigforss, *Från klasskamp till samverkan*, Stockholm: Tiden, 1941, pp. 262 ff.

Liberal motion for a moderate amount, and a Conservative motion for rejection; and suppose the speaker, on the preliminary round of voice votes, has heard the most ayes on the Socialist motion. The large appropriation will thus appear as the "main proposition" in the final vote. Before that vote is taken, however, the chamber must eliminate one of the other two proposals (smaller appropriation or rejection). If everyone were to state his true preference in the matter, the Liberal compromise proposal would win, first with Socialist support over the Conservative motion and next with Conservative support over the Socialist one. The question to be decided by the first vote, nevertheless, is not "Which of these two motions do you prefer?" but, in effect, "Which of these would you like to see paired off against the 'main proposition' on the final vote?" Now, if the Socialists suspect that the Liberal party will prefer a larger sum to no appropriation at all, they will further their own cause by supporting the Conservatives in the preliminary contest. As a result the motion to reject will win the first round, only to lose out in the next round to the Socialist motion, which will now also receive Liberal support. This type of voting maneuver is older than the bicameral riksdag and has long since become standard practice.[47] To some extent it vitiates the advantage inherent in the Swedish procedure; for it tends to sharpen political contrasts and leave the outcome to caprice. It also confers considerable power on the speaker, since it is he who selects the "main proposition"—i.e. the only motion that cannot be eliminated by any sort of maneuver.[48] The speakers' traditional impartiality and their practice in cases of doubt to make the committee report the "main proposition" make it unlikely that the power will be abused. The center forces, more-

[47] Louis De Geer (*Minnen, op.cit.*, II, 31 f.) recalls an example from the 1865 session of the estates. Although he found such tactics "difficult to reconcile with my conscience," he acknowledged that they had already then become customary. For other examples see Vegelow, *op.cit.*, pp. 212, 214. Kenneth Arrow (in his *Social Choice and Individual Values*, New York: Wiley, 1951, pp. 80f., note) demonstrates the likelihood of such maneuvers under the circumstances. Since neither Arrow nor the author against whom he polemicizes (Duncan Black, "The Decisions of a Committee Using a Special Majority," *Econometrica*, 16:245–261 [1948]) refers to Swedish experience, this would seem to be a neat example of an abstract deduction borne out by empirical evidence.

[48] Vegelow, *op.cit.*, p. 212.

over, can protect themselves against the maneuver by playing their cards close to their chests. This, indeed, is the natural strategy for those at the parliamentary fulcrum, who must appear leftist to the right and rightist to the left so as to draw both of them toward the center. So much so that the chief tactical tenet of the Ekman Liberals in the late 'twenties and early 'thirties was that "it is not really Liberal to commit oneself in advance."[49]

ABSENCE OF OBSTRUCTION

Why has Sweden so largely escaped the bitterness, the wrangling, and the constant attempts at obstruction so characteristic of legislatures both in the United States and on the European continent? The answer of course lies mainly in the broad agreement on fundamentals among the parties, which itself is anchored in the country's social and economic structure. This consensus, however, is of recent origin, and has in part been promoted by traditions of urbanity in politics that evolved during the oligarchic period and have survived both the strain of the constitutional conflict and the successive enlargements of the political arena. As the example of negative majorities shows, procedural devices have been effective where they have operated in conjunction with existing political attitudes. Thus the counterproposition system reinforces the "obstruction taboo"[50] on which its own effectiveness as a safeguard against a negative majority rests.

One further aspect of legislative procedure should be emphasized. The constitutional balance laid down in 1809 operated with only two weights, king and riksdag. Once the separation of powers between these had been overcome, few formal checks remained. The two chambers today are nearly identical in composition; the senate responds to the same electoral impulses as

[49] This charmingly candid remark was made by a member of the Liberal national committee during a post-mortem of the Liberal defeat at the hands of the Hansson-Bramstorp coalition in the riksdag on November 6, 1933, and is reprinted in Olle Nyman, *Svensk parlamentarism, 1932–1936*, Uppsala: Almqvist & Wiksell, 1947, p. 539. Cf. also Carl Ekman's own comments *ibid.*, pp. 538f.

[50] If I may be permitted to coin this term. Ernst Wigforss, *op.cit.*, pp. 261 ff. period, 268f., 272, gives repeated examples of this phenomenon.

the house, with a delay of about four years; they consider legislation simultaneously, and in matters of revenue and expenditure they act as a single body. There is little occasion, therefore, for that "mature afterthought" so dear to the hearts of advocates of bicameralism. The riksdag is the cornerstone of the governmental system. No popularly elected executive competes with it, and the cabinet is wholly dependent on its confidence or toleration. No regional distribution of powers limits the riksdag's ultimate authority and no direct popular legislation encroaches on its law making power. The judiciary, though independent in its own sphere, cannot invalidate statutes as contrary to the constitution. Since the constitution itself may be amended by two successive votes of the chambers separated by a lower chamber election, judicial review (if it were practiced) could not, at any rate, be used to hamper the legislative will. The fusion of political powers in Sweden is not quite as complete as in Britain; yet the majority of the voters, acting through their elected representatives, constant in their determination over a four-year period, and with the king's customary sanction, are fully sovereign. The only effective limitations on their power are found in their own internal divisions and in their own conception of the public good. Formal checks and balances invariably open many avenues for obstruction. While concentration of power does not of itself ensure a sense of responsibility, division of power is apt to thwart it.

CHAPTER VII

CABINET GOVERNMENT

SWEDISH cabinet government combines a number of characteristics of the British prototype with others typical of the countries of continental Europe. As in Britain, the present cabinet system is the product not of legislative fiat but of a slow and continuous process of evolution; to this day some of its principal rules have not been incorporated in the written constitution. Together with her two Scandinavian neighbors, Britain, and the Low Countries, Sweden is the only European nation where hereditary monarchy has weathered the storms of the first half of this century. Like Britain, finally, Sweden has never had to contend with sizable antiparliamentary or antidemocratic parties. On the other hand the Swedish cabinet system conforms to the Continental pattern in that it rests on a multiparty rather than a two party basis.

Among the unique features of Swedish parliamentarism is the almost total absence of procedures by which one of the partners of the team—parliament or cabinet—would impose its will upon the other. Although a fair degree of harmony has obtained, the requirement of cabinet responsibility and parliamentary confidence has been interpreted far less strictly than in other countries. It will be seen that this comparatively loose relationship has constituted at once one of the main strengths and one of the main weaknesses of Swedish government in recent decades.

EVOLUTION OF THE CABINET SYSTEM

The Swedish constitution defines at some length the cabinet's responsibility to the riksdag; yet it is not on these provisions but on a number of largely uncodified practices that the present cabinet system rests. In their attempt to balance legislative against executive power the constitutional fathers of 1809 authorized the riksdag's constitutional committee to make a periodic check of the official cabinet minutes. If this examination revealed any illegal or unconstitutional acts, the committee could bring impeachment proceedings against the erring minister. Even where there was no case for impeachment the riksdag could ask the king to dismiss any cabinet member who in its opinion had "disregarded the true interests of the realm."[1] But the leaders of the "liberal" opposition which formed in the estates during the early nineteenth century soon discovered the futility of these clauses. The ministers were, in law as well as in fact, merely advisers to a king who himself was immune from parliamentary control. Several loopholes, some in the constitution and some in the ministers' responsibility act of 1810,[2] opened avenues of escape, and the biased composition of a royally appointed impeachment court made conviction unlikely in even the most flagrant cases. Under the circumstances a simple request for dismissal, without further sanctions, was even more ludicrously inadequate.[3]

Although the impeachment and dismissal clauses, by about 1870, had fallen into desuetude,[4] several developments during the nineteenth century paved the way for parliamentary cabinet government. The cabinet, in the first place, acquired a corporate personality and increasingly asserted its independence of the king. The first two monarchs under the 1809 constitution both contributed to this gradual change which, a century later and much against their intentions, led to the virtual surrender of royal powers to the cabinet. The senile Karl XIII (1809–1818) displayed "a remarkable tendency to fall asleep during any deliberation."[5] His adopted son, the French marshal Jean

[1] The cabinet's responsibility is defined in *RF*, §§ 106f.; the quote is from § 107. Cf. Axel Brusewitz, "Statsrådets ansvarighet," in [Sweden, Riksdagen,] *Sveriges riksdag*, Stockholm: Victor Petterson, 1931–1938, xv, 245–533.

[2] Reprinted in Robert Malmgren, ed., *Sveriges grundlagar*, 6th edn., Stockholm: Norstedt, 1951, appendix.

[3] *Sveriges riksdag*, op.cit., xv, 459 ff. Cf. Axel Brusewitz, ed., *Studier över den svenska riksdagens kontrollmakt*, Malmö, 1930; Gunnar Heckscher, *Konung och statsråd i 1809 års författning*, Uppsala: Almqvist & Wiksell, 1933; and Ivar Andersson, *Oppositionen och ministeransvarigheten*, Uppsala, 1917.

[4] Robert Malmgren, *Sveriges författning*, vol. II, Malmö, 1941, p. 396, points out that they cannot be considered dead letters—although they will hardly be applied except after an abortive coup.

[5] Gunnar Heckscher, "Konselj och stasrådsberedning," *Statsvetenskaplig tidskrift*, 51:306 (1948).

Baptiste Bernadotte, ruled in Sweden for thirty-four years, first as regent (1810–1818) and later as king (under the name Karl XIV Johan, 1818–1844), but never mastered the language. He therefore encouraged the ministers to meet in his absence so that they could prepare in Swedish all business that was to be submitted to His Majesty in French.[6] The riksdag, secondly, used its control of finance to secure a greater share in the direction of the administration. While earlier estate sessions had appropriated funds under "general headings" only and had allowed the king to transfer funds from one heading to another, the parliaments of the eighteen-thirties and 'forties began to itemize appropriations in detail and to insist on compliance with budgetary ceilings. In 1840 the riksdag, by threatening to withhold all appropriations, obtained the first wholesale resignation of a cabinet. The introduction of annual sessions a quarter century later further served to tighten parliament's budgetary control. Third, Louis De Geer, during his long tenure as minister of state for justice (1858–1870), transformed that office, in effect, into a premiership—an innovation that was confirmed later (1876) by constitutional amendment. A strong premier, by judicious use of the threat of resignation, could force the king to accept both his policies and his nominees for other cabinet posts. In the end the king's independent power was restricted to the dismissal of a premier and the selection of a new one—and even here his discretion was hemmed in by the scarcity of willing candidates. Finally, the introduction of bicameralism and the subsequent growth of parliamentary parties enabled the riksdag to give more consistent direction to national policy. Skill in carrying legislation in the riksdag thus came to be an indispensable qualification for candidates for the ministry.[7]

---

[6] Bernadotte's contribution to the rise of cabinet government offers a striking parallel to that of George I in Great Britain. Cf. Edward Raymond Turner, *The Cabinet Council of England in the Seventeenth and Eighteenth Centuries*, Baltimore: Johns Hopkins University Press, 1930–1932, II, 94 ff.

[7] Gunnar Hesslén has edited a collection of documents illustrating the rise of cabinet government. *Den svenska parlamentarismens uppkomst*, Stockholm: Norstedt, 1940. On the early development of financial powers see Nils Nilsson-Stjernqvist, *Ständerna, statsregleringen och förvaltningen*, Lund: Gleerup, 1946. On the history of the cabinet system during the early bicameral period see Leif Kihlberg, *Den svenska ministären under*

The rapid gains of the parliamentary principle during the early part of this century have been related in detail in a previous chapter. Its final victory came about, in November 1918, through tacit agreement between the Liberals and Socialists on the one hand and the Conservatives and the monarch on the other. Although the agreement, on the face of it concerned only the introduction of universal suffrage for the two chambers, both sides were fully aware that in closing the traditional gap between the houses they were burying once for all the earlier "honest broker" conception of cabinet government. The Agrarians were too insignificant in 1918 to be included in the agreement, and for more than a decade they remained reluctant to endorse the principle of parliamentarism or to enter a cabinet. In 1930 an Agrarian professor of constitutional law took exception to the statement of a Conservative colleague that all major parties had accepted the new regime;[8] and as late as 1933 a major Agrarian daily advocated "a return to the, so to speak, constitutional method of cabinet formation which prevailed before the victory of parliamentarism."[9] But the Agrarians did not oppose the new system and, under the dynamic leadership of Bramstorp in 1933-1934, completely abandoned their earlier passivity. The total strength of the avowed antiparliamentary parties—Left Socialists, Communists of various designations, Nationalists, and National Socialists—never surpassed 11.2 per cent of the national vote. Both the extreme left and the extreme right, moreover, were badly split in themselves; because of the hurdles that the electoral system interposes, their combined representation has never exceeded 7 per cent in the lower and 3 per cent in the upper chamber. The general acceptance of the parliamentary cabinet regime in the last thirty years has immensely facilitated its operation.

ståndsriksdag och tvåkammarsystem intill 1905 års totala ministerskifte, Uppsala: Almqvist & Wiksell, 1922.

[8] Georg Andrén, "Regeringsmakt och parlamentarism," *Statsvetenskaplig tidskrift*, 33:473 (1930), reporting on a discussion with Carl-Axel Reuterskiöld.

[9] Olle Nyman, *Svensk parlamentarism, 1932-1936*, Uppsala: Almqvist & Wiksell, 1947, p. 52.

GOVERNMENT AND OPPOSITION

Being the fruit of slow, indigenous growth rather than of ready transplantation from abroad, the Swedish cabinet system displays some features that have no exact parallel in other countries. In Sweden, as elsewhere, there are a number of occasions when the government and the opposition engage in a debate of principle covering a wide range of major issues. Ever since 1917 it has been customary for a newly inaugurated government to announce its policies to the riksdag, and a general debate has often followed. Another occasion for the clarification of the political situation comes up every January when, at the opening of the session, the government submits the budget to the chambers. The practice of budget debates developed in early Ruralist days and has been firmly established since the end of the nineteenth century. Because the agenda item under which the debate takes place is the "remittal" of the budget to the appropriations committee they are known as the "remittal debates." The opposition groups generally lead off, in approximate order of their size, and the premier appears as the chief spokesman for the cabinet. The finance minister and financial experts of other parties may discuss the details of the budget. Generally, however, the debate lingers over controversial issues which may bear only remote relation to the budget, and for once the speaker relaxes his vigilance in holding members to the business at hand.[10] The budget debates of the Second World War were as a rule opened by those leaders of the four government parties who did not sit in the cabinet; the Communists got their say only later in the debate. In recent years the opposition leaders have at times determined the order of precedence among them by lot.

At any time during the session, moreover, members of parliament may interpellate the ministers. The rules of the lower chamber have allowed for interpellation since 1867, while the senate delayed the introduction of this French practice until 1912. The interpellant submits his question in writing and must obtain the chamber's approval before it is transmitted to the minister. When the government commands an ample majority,

[10] Edvard Thermænius, "Remissdebatten," in Brusewitz, ed., *Studier över den svenska riksdagens kontrollmakt, op.cit.*, pp. 299–413.

its own followers feel free to interpellate the cabinet; they are more likely to hold their peace when the cabinet relies on tenuous minority support. During the recent war the supporters of the national coalition submitted nine tenths of all interpellations. At all other times the opposition parties have been the most assiduous interpellants.[11] The minister to whom the question is addressed need not answer it but usually does so within a few weeks; courtesy requires that he communicate his answer to the interpellant in advance. In 1938 the chambers introduced a simplified form of interpellation known as "simple questions."[12] But the initial high tide of simple questions has since receded, and it is doubtful whether they will prove an important addition to parliamentary practice.

By contrast with the practice in other countries, the procedures just outlined serve solely as vehicles for criticism, for the exchange of information between government and opposition, and for the clarification of intentions on either side. None of these debates, that is to say, concludes with a vote by which the riksdag would express its confidence or lack of confidence in the cabinet. (The vote at the end of the budget debate concerns a routine decision prescribed in the constitution—committal of the bill—and is taken by acclamation.) There is no equivalent in Sweden to the British custom of "no-confidence amendments to the address," to the French device of "motivated orders of the day," or to the widespread parliamentary practice of "motions of censure." The constitution, which regulates much of the riksdag's work, does not allow the chambers to take any vote that would merely register an opinion without leading to some other kind of action—such as committal of a bill, passage of a law, or adoption of a request to the king for the drafting of new legislation. The ouster of a cabinet by parliamentary resolution is not among the actions contemplated by the constitution.[13]

[11] Elis Håstad, "Interpellationer och enkla frågor," in *Statsvetenskapliga studier*, Uppsala: Almqvist & Wiksell, 1944, p. 391, and Gösta Grym, "Interpellationer och enkla frågor, 1945–1949," *Statsvetenskaplig tidskrift*, 55:249–255 (1952). The veteran Socialist Carl Lindhagen held an all-time record for interpellations.

[12] *Ordningsstadga*, § 20.

[13] Brusewitz, ed., *Studier över den svenska riksdagens kontrollmakt*, op. cit., pp. 252 ff.

There are two instances in which the riksdag has disregarded these constitutional restrictions. The Liberal party, toward the beginning of this century, made a systematic attempt to introduce in Sweden the French procedure of motivated orders of the day. By about 1900, interpellations in the lower chamber had frequently led to a debate, and occasionally members would rise to state for the record their agreement with the interpellant or with the minister interpellated.[14] In 1907 a Liberal interpellant, after a heated discussion with Lindman's minister of the interior, concluded his rebuttal with the following words: "Unfortunately, Mr. Speaker, it is not possible on occasions such as this to demand a vote; but I dare hope nonetheless that if such a vote were possible, the lower chamber would with overwhelming majority [express its disapproval of the government's action]." Upon this signal, forty-seven members of the opposition rose one by one to concur with the interpellant. During the next decade this procedure was used at least five times in the lower chamber, and each time a majority of those present expressed their displeasure with the cabinet's policy. Since 1917, however, these "hypothetical no-confidence votes" have been abandoned. The Conservative cabinets of the early twentieth century had proved quite insensitive to such demonstrations: Arvid Lindman, for instance, stayed in office in spite of four such votes and resigned only after his second successive defeat at the polls. The procedure, moreover, was clumsy when compared with ordinary parliamentary practice in Sweden, which does not rely on time-consuming roll calls or other dilatory techniques. The demonstrations in the chamber, as Professor Brusewitz has remarked, have been impressive but have left little actual imprint.[15]

The other deviation from strict constitutional practice concerns the constitutional committee's examination of cabinet minutes.[16] There have been no impeachment trials since 1854, and since 1874 the chambers have entertained no formal re-

[14] Such statements for the record are explicitly authorized by *RO*, § 52.
[15] This is perhaps the closest equivalent in English of his pun on "*mera effektfullt än egentligen effektivt*," in *Sveriges riksdag, op.cit.*, xv, 259.
[16] On the details of the procedure see *ibid.*, xv, 305 ff., 438 ff., 462 ff., and Brusewitz, ed., *Studier över den svenska riksdagens kontrollmakt, op.cit.*, pp. 1-24, 53-112.

quests for the dismissal of a minister. The committee, nevertheless, continues to undertake its investigation once a year
toward the end of the parliamentary session, and its report to
the chambers may contain critical comments on minor or major
irregularities in the cabinet's activity. After some debate (known
as the "discharge debate," since the report discharges the cabinet of liability to impeachment) the chambers vote to incor-
porate the report into their minutes. Toward the end of the nineteenth century the lower chamber, in taking this vote, occasionally expressed its approval of specific points in the report. Since
in the intention of the constitutional framers the sole purpose of
the discharge debate was to ascertain whether the riksdag was
to request the king to dismiss one of his ministers, a mere
endorsement of the committee's criticism without any such
request seems at first glance absurd. In the senate the speakers
therefore have repeatedly ruled such votes of approval out of
order. The opposition in the lower chamber, however, was
naturally reluctant to risk loss of face in case the senate or the
king chose to disregard a request for dismissal; instead it preferred to express its lack of confidence in a minister by what
amounted to an informal vote of censure.[17] Since the triumph of
parliamentarism the discharge debates have lost much of their
former political significance. Modern cabinet government
presupposes day-by-day agreement between parliament and
ministry, expressed in active cooperation over a wide range of
legislation: a disagreement that becomes apparent only at the
end of a four months' session upon diligent search in the
voluminous cabinet records is likely to be trivial. The cabinet
minutes, moreover, have increasingly come to be filled with
lists of administrative decisions that are reviewed on appeal, so
that the constitutional committee's scrutiny has largely developed
into an investigation of administrative procedure at the cabinet
level.[18] During the interwar period the lower chamber approved
the committee's criticisms on four occasions, and on three of

[17] For a detailed account of an earlier instance see Edvard Thermænius,
Lantmannapartiet, Uppsala: Almqvist & Wiksell, 1928, pp. 281 f.

[18] Otto von Zweigbergk, from his experience as a committee member
in the nineteen-twenties, gives an amusing account of the slow grinding of
"the mills of the constitutional committee" during examinations of the
cabinet minutes; see his *Svensk politik 1905–1929*, Stockholm: Bonnier,
1929, pp. 209–218.

these censure of a minister was clearly implied.[19] In 1929 the chamber's vote caused the resignation of Lindman's finance minister, Nils Wohlin; but this is the only such case on record.[20]

The riksdag, through its power to approve, amend, or reject government bills, has ample opportunity to express its attitude toward the cabinet on concrete issues. On the other hand, once hypothetical no-confidence votes in connection with interpellations had fallen into desuetude and the discharge debates had degenerated into a ventilation of bureaucratic trivia, the riksdag was left with no means of declaring its confidence or lack of confidence in the government in the abstract. Unless it wishes to wield the sledge hammer of an appropriations strike, the riksdag therefore cannot force the resignation of a cabinet that is content to stay despite legislative defeats. Conversely, the cabinet has no effective means of forcing a reluctant chamber to endorse its legislative proposals. This absence of coercion from either side in large part accounts for the smooth functioning of the Swedish system of minority governments from 1920 to 1936.

Cabinets in other countries frequently threaten resignation so as to preserve discipline within a majority party or to cement a brittle coalition. British governments "tend to treat most questions as questions of confidence,"[21] and the French national assembly has had to vote on as many as five confidence questions in a single day.[22] In Britain this strategy is effective because the backbenchers know that the government, if defeated, will dissolve parliament. Dissolution means a strenuous campaign and considerable expense for all of them; for the

---

[19] *Sveriges riksdag, op.cit.*, xv, 453f.

[20] In 1936 several opposition members asked for a vote of censure against Karl Schlyter because of his handling of some administrative detail. Premier Hansson tried to prevent embarrassment by making the matter a question of confidence in the cabinet as a whole. When the chamber called his bluff and carried the motion by a narrow margin no one resigned, and Socialist newspapers were busy explaining that Hansson had not meant what he had seemed to be saying. See Nyman, *op.cit.*, pp. 340ff.

[21] W. Ivor Jennings, *Cabinet Government*, 2d edn., Cambridge: University Press, 1951, p. 458.

[22] John C. Ranney and Gwendolen M. Carter, *The Major Foreign Powers*, New York: Harcourt, Brace, 1949, p. 401.

lonely deserter from his party it means almost certain defeat.[23] In the Fourth Republic, the government's power to dissolve is hedged about with restrictions;[24] in the past, questions of confidence have probably derived what effectiveness they have had from the ever-present possibility that the breakup of the center coalition would sweep into power the Communists or De Gaullists. In Sweden, by contrast, the riksdag has never been dissolved since the advent of parliamentarism; nor has any government been able to plead indispensability, for there has been no acute totalitarian danger. A Swedish cabinet that threatens to resign rarely hopes to compel adoption of its bill; more likely it is tired of responsibility and is seeking a dramatic —or at any rate honorable—retreat. "For our ministries," says Professor Andrén, "a question of confidence has become a way of dying rather than of staying alive."[25]

The Swedish monarch may dissolve either or both houses of parliament, and the only formal restriction on this power is that, if parliament has been dissolved during the session, a second dissolution must wait until the new parliament has sat for at least four months.[26] During the oligarchic period the king used the weapon of dissolution twice against the lower chamber—in the tariff conflict of 1887 and in that over defense in 1914. The senate was dissolved only after the extensions in the local franchise of 1909 and 1919.[27] There are a number of reasons why dissolution has not recommended itself to parliamentary governments in recent decades: (1) The members of the riksdag who are elected following a dissolution do not sit for a full term but merely serve out the terms of their predecessors. A lower chamber election, that is to say, will be held every leap year, whether a dissolution intervenes or not; and the senate, immediately after a dissolution, resumes its ordinary schedule of annual re-

[23] W. Ivor Jennings, *Parliament*, Cambridge: University Press, 1948, pp. 122f.

[24] Cf. Herman Finer, *Theory and Practice of Modern Government*, rev. edn., New York: Holt, 1949, pp. pp. 640 ff., and O. R. Taylor, *The Fourth Republic of France*, London: Royal Institute of International Affairs, 1951, pp. 52 ff.

[25] Andrén, "Regeringsmakt och parlamentarism," *op.cit.*, p. 475.

[26] *RF*, § 109; in 1949 this article was renumbered 108.

[27] *Sveriges riksdag, op.cit.*, x, 51 ff. In 1921 both chambers were dissolved by statute in connection with changes in the electoral system.

placement of one eighth of its membership. A lower chamber dissolution thus is likely to come too close to either the preceding or the subsequent regular election. During the first year of the four-year period it would rarely produce significant changes; during the third or fourth year it would necessitate two costly campaigns in quick succession. (2) Proportionalism makes landslides unlikely. A lower chamber dissolution will seem attractive only if the government party is already close to a majority; for the prospect of gaining merely a somewhat larger minority hardly justifies the trouble and expense of a special election. Hence dissolution was of little use when additional strength for the cabinet was most urgently needed during the nineteen-twenties. (3) While the senate can be dissolved, its electoral colleges cannot. A general election to the senate thus is not an appeal to the electorate; its effects, moreover, can be calculated in advance. A government party will obtain control of the senate by dissolution only if it has just secured a majority in the electoral colleges in a local election, as in 1938 and 1950. (4) Since there is no guidance from recent precedent, it is not entirely clear whether the king would have to grant a dissolution whenever the cabinet asked for one, or whether dissolution remains his personal prerogative.[28]

There have been times when these counterindications did not apply, and it may be that the threat of dissolution helped Hansson obtain passage for his "New Deal" program in 1933–1934.[29] Still, no parliamentary cabinet has ever dissolved a chamber; the possibility of dissolution, instead of being ever present as in Britain, thus seems at best remote. Per Edvin Sköld's remark in 1936 that "The way things are now [i.e. with the requirement of quadrennial elections regardless of dissolution] the Swedish riksdag can practically never be dissolved" may have been prompted by acute disappointment over the legislative defeats of the first Hansson cabinet. Since the statement, however, comes from one of the keenest tacticians of the Socialist party,

[28] On the king's refusal to grant Staaff a dissolution in 1906 see chapter II supra. Hansson in 1932 discussed with the Socialist national committee the possibility of asking the king for a promise of dissolution in case the lower chamber should defeat the cabinet. No promise, however, was in fact obtained; see Nyman, *op.cit.*, pp. 57, 124f., 142; cf. p. 231.

[29] Cf. Per Albin Hansson, *Demokrati*, Stockholm: Tiden, 1935, p. 119, and the passages in Nyman just cited.

we cannot lightly dismiss Sköld's conclusion that "whenever the government cannot carry the parliament along, it has no alternative but to go."[30]

PARTY TACTICS AND CABINET FORMATION

Students of British government have defined a cabinet as a group of leaders of a party or coalition of parties that commands a majority in the legislature.[31] Even in Britain this definition has not always been descriptive of the facts; for whenever the party system has been in process of regeneration minority cabinets have been in office.[32] In countries that have never had clear majority alignments any such statement defines at best an ideal. In Sweden particularly, most cabinet crises have raised a two-fold question: Would it be possible to form a majority coalition? And if not, which of the minority parties would undertake to form the new cabinet?

During much of the oligarchic period the two houses of the riksdag were dominated by solid majorities; yet these belonged to different and at times bitterly antagonistic parties—the Ruralists in the lower house (1868 to 1887 and 1895 to 1902) and the Protectionists and Conservatives in the senate (until 1918). Even before the reforms of 1918–1921 synchronized the political pulse of the two chambers, proportionalism had perpetuated an incipient tendency toward party fragmentation. Thus "at the very moment when the principle of cabinet government was accepted its traditional ground wavered."[33] Only during the four parliamentary sessions from 1941 to 1944 has a single party enjoyed majority control in both houses—and those years coincided with an international conflagration which put a moratorium on the customary processes of cabinet formation. Even if the years of Socialist joint-vote majority (1941,

[30] *Protokoll från Sveriges socialdemokratiska arbetarepartis 15:e kongress*, Stockholm: Tiden, 1937, p. 381.

[31] Ernest Barker, *Reflections on Government*, Oxford: University Press, 1942, p. 38, and Finer, *op.cit.*, p. 576.

[32] E.g. during the transition from Whigs and Tories to Liberals and Conservatives (1845–1852) and when Labor displaced the Liberals as the second major party (1910–1931).

[33] Nils Herlitz, *Sweden: A Modern Democracy on Ancient Foundations*, Minneapolis: University of Minnesota Press, 1939, p. 47.

and 1945 to 1952) be added, it remains true that for most of the cabinet government era Sweden has been bedevilled by the problem of forming cabinets in the absence of parliamentary majorities.

In the thirty-eight years since Edén's inauguration Sweden has had one national coalition (in office for five and a half years); three majority coalitions (totalling nine and a half years); one single-party cabinet with joint-vote support (six years); nine minority cabinets, including one coalition (sixteen and a half years); and two stopgap bureaucratic cabinets (one year). If majority support is the sole measure of the success of a cabinet system, the Swedish variant has clearly been a failure. Yet if duration of cabinets and speedy solution of cabinet crises are the standard, the Swedish record proves superior to that of most Continental countries and does not compare too unfavorably with that of Britain herself: cabinet tenure has averaged two years and four months,[34] and the interval between cabinets has been around six days, in no case exceeding thirteen.[35] Both criteria—stability of support as well as ease of formation and length of tenure—clearly are relevant and, paradoxically, Swedish cabinets would hardly have rated so high on the second scale had they not rated so low on the first. For, given the fluid party situation from 1920 to 1936, a majority coalition would have been much harder to form and apt to dissolve much more quickly than were homogeneous minority cabinets.

The feasibility of minority government over long periods in Sweden requires a word of explanation. When a minority party leader elsewhere on the Continent is asked to form a cabinet he is under strong pressure to bring about a coalition. He needs majority support to pass the initial test of parliamentary confidence, and other parties, thirsting for the perquisites of office, will not lend it unless taken in. No similar contingency arises in

[34] By comparison, tenure in Britain since 1835 has averaged four years (cf. Jennings, *Cabinet Government, op.cit.*, pp. 475 ff.) and in France from 1870 to 1940 and Germany from 1919 to 1933 it averaged eight months (Finer, *op.cit.*, pp. 627, 656; the estimate for France disregards cabinets with less than a week in office). See also *De nordiska ländernas statsråd*, Uppsala: Almqvist & Wiksell, 1935, p. 212, which gives figures for other countries as well.

[35] Perhaps, however, the period of the two caretaker cabinets (October 1920 to October 1921) should be counted as a single protracted crisis.

Sweden, where a confidence vote is not required and where individual ministers have little power over policy and none over appointments. The cabinet, as was shown in the preceding chapter, is above all a body not of administrators but of legislative planners. The game of coalition thus becomes largely a function of legislative tactics.

The relevant tactical considerations can best be understood by distinguishing between the parties at the center (Liberals and Agrarians), who have a choice of aligning with either the right or the left, and the outer parties (Conservatives and Socialists), who can coalesce in only one direction. (The handful of Communists and Nationalists in the riksdag can be disregarded; their support rarely would have affected the majority or minority position of a cabinet, and other parties have been careful not to incur any obligations to them.) The outer parties, eager to commit those at the center to firm support for a common legislative program, have been the chief advocates of coalition; while the center parties, jealous of their freedom of action, have been reluctant to enter any combination. Examples from the 'twenties and 'thirties abound.[36] The Socialists sought to maintain their coalition with the Liberals in March 1920 and to restore it in October 1920, in 1921, 1929, 1930, and 1932. Branting contemplated making a similar offer in 1924 but was dissuaded by his party. Four times the Liberals refused outright; in 1932 they asked for the finance ministry—a stiff price since that was the key post at a time of economic depression— and negotiations broke down.[37] When the Conservatives formed a ministry in 1923 and 1928 they tried to bring about a bourgeois coalition with Agrarians and Liberals and, failing that, one with the Agrarians alone; once again the centrists refused. By contrast, the Prohibitionist Liberals in 1926 and 1930 invited only the Löfgrenites and Agrarians to join. Such a combination, while still far short of a majority, would have strengthened Ekman's hand in his gravitational tactics. The Löfgrenites

[36] See Herbert Tingsten, "Regeringen," in Georg Andrén et al., *Sveriges styrelse*, 2d edn., Stockholm: Victor Petterson, 1945, pp. 107 ff; see also chapter III supra. For a comparative discussion of coalition strategy see Maurice Duverger, *Les partis politiques*, Paris: A. Colin, 1951, pp. 371 ff., where he remarks that "[le] *jeu de bascule ... constitue l'espoir secret de tous les partis du centre*" (p. 374).

[37] Nyman, *op.cit.*, p. 62.

accepted Ekman's offer once, but had cause for regret. The Agrarians clung to their splendid isolation; in 1936 they were ready with a slate of their own even before calling off their perfunctory negotiations with the Liberals.[38] The only exception to the rule during this period was the Conservatives' refusal to serve under Ekman in 1928; in view of their fresh election gains they felt entitled to the premiership and hence refused to bail out Ekman's foundering government.[39]

Constitutional practices and the constellation among the parties being what they were, it was perhaps surprising that majority coalitions formed at all. But even the exceptions confirm the rule. The Liberal-Socialist alliance of 1917 predated the cabinet government system—whose introduction, indeed, was its major objective. The national coalition of 1939 was formed in response to the international situation; significantly its most ardent advocates were the Agrarians, who were growing restive under their commitment to cooperate with the Socialists alone. A coalition of all parties is of course a coalition with no party in particular. When the two Socialist-Agrarian governments took office (1936, 1951) the situation was no longer quite the same. The Socialists, since the 1936 elections, have been the predominant force. Although they did not always have a majority, no one could form one without them: the outer party had expanded until it had captured the center of gravity. Because of their strong position, the Socialists could afford to take in the Agrarians; the latter reluctantly accepted the junior partner role. A preliminary vote in the Agrarian national committee in 1936 was so close that Bramstorp at first suggested breaking off negotiations.[40] When the Socialists, after a slight electoral setback in 1948, proposed another farmer-labor alliance, the Agrarians refused, and a new coalition was not formed until three years later.

The Liberals and Socialists in 1917 were united in the pursuit of a common goal, with differences largely limited to questions of more or less and of timing. Socialist-Agrarian cooperation, on the other hand, has been based on complementary

[38] ibid., p. 442.
[39] Karl Hildebrand, *Gustaf V som människa och regent*, Stockholm: A. B. Svensk Litteratur, 1945–1948, II, 426ff.
[40] Nyman, *op.cit.*, pp. 474f.

rather than identical interests. It proceeded from a pluralist view of society—or, in the less polite phrase of the critics, from "horse trading"—and in turn has done much to advance Sweden on the road toward a pluralist order. While the Liberal-Socialist coalition dissolved once its program had been carried out, the labor-farmer alliance, though not free from friction,[41] has shown remarkable resilience.

Whatever the future of party alignments, it is safe to predict that they will in large part depend on the parties' numerical strength in the riksdag.[42] The Socialists have held their majority or near-majority position for over twenty years, and there is no indication that they will lose it. If and when the bourgeois parties regain a majority, a return to the see-saw policy of the 'twenties under leadership of one of the center groups and to recurrent but fruitless negotiations for coalition does not seem unlikely.

THE KING'S SELECTION OF A PREMIER

The absence of a majority party or coalition during much of the parliamentary government period of necessity has complicated the king's task of selecting a cabinet. Since the late nineteenth century the king's first step in solving a cabinet crisis has been to ask the advice of the speakers in the two houses. Since 1917 these conferences have been supplemented by discussions with the major party leaders. The king's role is chiefly that of a mediator; his final selection depends on the advice he receives. Yet there has been no clear rule to guide the king and his advisers through the tangle of minority party politics—or rather there have been too many conflicting rules. The speakers and party leaders usually have invoked one of the following principles: (1) *The plurality principle.* The aim of cabinet formation being a government with stable parliamentary support, the king, in the absence of a majority party, should call on the party that comes closest to a majority position—i.e. on the plurality party. (2) *The gravitational principle.* The king

[41] See chapter IV supra.
[42] Cf. Jörgen Westerståhl, "Det svenska partiväsendet," in Hal Koch and Alf Ross, eds., *Nordisk demokrati*, Oslo, Köbenhavn, and Stockholm, 1945, pp. 103f.

should offer the premiership to the party at the center of the spectrum, which presumably has the best chance of carrying its legislative proposals. (3) *The culprit principle.* The king should turn to the party primarily responsible for the resignation of the previous cabinet—whether this party has left a coalition or otherwise withdrawn its support from the government, or has had its amendment passed instead of a government bill. Such a party, it is suggested, should demonstrate its ability to form a better cabinet than the one it overturned. (4) *The plebiscitary principle.* If the cabinet crisis follows an election, the king should appoint a ministry from the party that has made the greatest single gain at the polls.

Even more involved arguments have at times been advanced. In September 1932, for instance, the outgoing Liberal premier, Hamrin, insisted that the Agrarians should supply the next prime minister since the bourgeois parties still held a majority and the Agrarians were the only ones among these to gain at the polls. Olsson i Kullenbergstorp, the Agrarian, proposed a bourgeois coalition under Conservative leadership—presumably because the Conservatives held a plurality of bourgeois votes in the riksdag. The Conservatives in turn thought the situation called for a Socialist cabinet, since the Socialists were the plurality party and also had gained more seats in the election than any of the rest. The game of tag came to an end when the Socialists accepted the king's mandate to form the new government.[43]

The contradiction among the four above rules is readily apparent. The plurality principle always supported the Socialists, whereas the gravitational argument pointed to the Liberals and later the Agrarians. The Liberals, because of their position at the fulcrum, also were the most frequent overturners of other cabinets, so that the culprit principle once again would have favored them. The plebiscitary principle, finally, indicated a Socialist government in 1921, 1924, 1932, and 1936, and a Conservative one in 1920 and 1928. Since no one rule was followed consistently, an informal system of rotation among the parties was in fact established.

As the 1932 example shows, a party's willingness or unwillingness to form a government often turned out to be the

[43] Nyman, *op. cit.*, pp. 38 ff.

decisive factor. With so many arguments to choose from, party leaders rarely were at a loss to justify whatever conclusion suited their tactical purposes. Generally only those parties were eager to take office which were at the center of the riksdag spectrum or which had made substantial gains in a general election. In the former situation the possibility of pursuing a legislative program by adroit balancing between right and left beckoned; in the latter the party felt an obligation toward its voters to make at least an attempt at building upon the platform with which it had won popular acclaim. The gravitational and culprit principles won out in 1926, 1930, and June 1936; the plebiscitary one after every election from 1921 to 1936.

There has rarely been any active competition for office among the parties—Trygger's resignation under Liberal and Socialist pressure after the 1924 elections and the rivalry between Lindman and Ekman in 1928 being the two outstanding exceptions. Only once, on the other hand, did each of the larger parties in turn refuse the king's offer to form a government—in February 1921. The solution at that time was the continuation of an administrative caretaker government, such as had already been in office since October 1920. The experience with these two administrative cabinets proved highly unsatisfactory to everyone concerned. Nonpolitical conduct of the highest political office was a phantom—and the younger De Geer's predicament in such a seemingly trivial matter as the coffee excise was apt to dispel any doubts on that score. The parties of the left tended to consider these ministries of higher civil servants Conservative governments in disguise, and the Conservative party resented being saddled with the blame for their mistakes without receiving any credit for their accomplishments.[44] On neither side was there much inclination to resurrect the phantom.

NONPARTISANS IN THE CABINET

Swedish premiers since 1917 have nearly always been party leaders. Plans to entrust the premiership to minor party figures or to a nonpartisan have occasionally been advanced but (except in the cases of De Geer and von Sydow) never carried out. When

[44] Karl Magnusson, *Vid spade och riksdagspulpet*, Malmö: Gleerup, 1950, pp. 199f.

the Social Democrats were forming their first cabinet in March
1920, Hansson, Möller, Sandler, and others urged the appointment of Fredrik Thorsson, heir apparent to the party leader, as
premier. Elections were coming up in the fall, and the party, it
was argued, should not risk the popularity of its leader by allowing him to head a weak minority cabinet. But other counsels
prevailed, and Branting took the premiership.[45] Similar proposals to have the parties form cabinets without fully engaging
their leadership were avdanced at various points—by the
Socialist Engberg in 1920, the Conservative Herlitz in 1929,
and the Agrarian leader Kullenbergstorp in 1933.[46] Such a
course might temporarily have smoothed over the difficulties
of cabinet formation in a multiparty situation. There is no
doubt, however, that the clear connection which was in fact
maintained between cabinets and party leadership facilitated
the gradual reconciliation of party policies which in fact obtained during this period.

Subordinate cabinet appointments, on the other hand, have
not been limited to members of the premier's party. The reasons for this are to be found partly in the constitutional requirement that at least two of the ministers must have had civil service training, partly in the desire to secure wider support for
minority governments, and partly in the inability of the smaller
parties in the riksdag to spare a full contingent of twelve persons
for cabinet work. Trygger's Conservative government included
ten higher civil servants—five of them nonpartisans and one a
member of the Agrarian party. Only five ministers in the second
Ekman and four in the Bramstorp cabinet held parliamentary
seats; the latter also included two Liberals. To date, Branting's
ministries of 1920 and 1921 have been the only ones consisting
exclusively of members of a single party; the second of these
also was the only one recruited entirely from past and present
members of parliament.[47] King Gustaf V frequently tried to

[45] Gunnar Gerdner, *Det svenska regeringsproblemet, 1917–1920*, Uppsala: Almqvist & Wiksell, 1946, pp. 224f.
[46] Herbert Tingsten, *Den svenska socialdemokratiens idéutveckling*,
Stockholm: Tiden, 1941, II, 107; Nils Herlitz, *Svensk självstyrelse*, Stockholm: Geber, 1933, pp. 171 ff.; and Nyman, *op.cit.*, pp. 46, 53.
[47] Sven Linders and Karl Schlyter served in the riksdag both before
and after this period; the 10 remaining ministers were current members of
the riksdag. The figure of 11 past and current members of parliament

"tone down the partisan coloring of the cabinet"[48] even further. Yet his role was limited to advising his advisers, and his personal wishes as to ministerial recruitment rarely were followed. During Branting's illness in 1925 he suggested Östen Undén and Torsten Nothin as candidates for the premiership, and after Ekman's resignation in 1932 he thought of Natanael Gärde.[49] All three were career officials and, though members of parties then in the government, had taken no leading part in their affairs. In 1928 he proposed an "economic-administrative ministry" under the moderate Conservative Sven Lübeck, and in September 1932 a "government of universal civic rally."[50] At other times, finally, he tried to persuade prominent members of one party to enter a cabinet about to be formed by another. He asked the Liberal Eliel Löfgren, long-time member of the Swedish delegation to the League of Nations, to serve as foreign minister under Trygger (1923) and the Socialist foreign minister Rickard Sandler to continue under Bramstorp (1936).[51] On the latter occasion he also urged the Liberal Gärde to accept the justice portfolio, explaining that he would like to see a familiar face in that cabinet of *homines novi*.[52]

DISSATISFACTION WITH THE CABINET SYSTEM

The cabinet's moderation in pursuing the announced aims of the government party and the moderation of the opposition in fighting the government's proposals have given Swedish politics its harmonious quality, which has often been noted by foreign

given in *De nordiska ländernas statsråd, op.cit.*, p. 51, therefore is incorrect. For figures for earlier periods see *Sveriges riksdag, op.cit.*, IX, 236.

[48] Elis Håstad, "Konungen och regeringsbildningen," in *Svensk tidskrift*, 34:372 (1947).

[49] Hildebrand, *op.cit.*, II, 416, and Lars Sköld, "Förfaringssättet vid svenska statsministervakanser efter parlamentarismens genombrott," *Statsvetenskaplig tidskrift*, 51:75 (1948).

[50] Håstad, "Konungen och regeringsbildning," *op.cit.*, p. 371.

[51] *ibid.*, and Nyman, *op.cit.*, p. 439. In 1932 he urged Undén for the foreign portfolio, which Hansson had already promised to Sandler. Nyman, *op.cit.*, pp. 62f.

[52] Gunnar Gerdner in a review of Nyman, *op.cit.*, in *Statsvetenskaplig tidskrift*, 51:193f. (1948). Westman at the time was the only ministerial candidate with cabinet experience. As it turned out, the justice post went to another Liberal, Thorwald Bergquist.

observers. Until the end of the Second World War at least, Swedish government had never been undiluted party government, and even after the war, when the parties out of power have complained with increasing bitterness of "government dictatorship," the cabinet has shown far more consideration toward the opposition than do cabinets in other countries. The largely voluntary character of party discipline, the peculiarities of Swedish legislative procedure, and the moderately partisan composition of the cabinet all have contributed to this result. The very moderation of political warfare, on the other hand, has tended to loosen the ties of responsibility that link the cabinet to the parliament and both of them to the voters. This weakening of responsibility in turn has caused widespread dissatisfaction with the cabinet system so that some dissonant chords can be discerned within the apparent harmony.

In a two-party country such as Britain, control over policy is vested in a single, unified majority party. But the majority faces constant opposition from an equally unified minority party which, in parliament, in the press, and during campaigns, confronts the government with its previous pledges to the public— and at every point stands prepared to give the voters an alternative government.[53] Sooner or later the electoral tide will turn and the roles of government and opposition will be reversed. Through the device of a two-party system, no major section of the public is permanently excluded from the government; and with both parties constantly competing for public favor, the electorate exercises as complete control over policy as is consistent with a representative system.

It was advantages such as these that made a system of cabinet government attractive to its early Swedish advocates.[54] Yet almost as soon as the system was introduced it became clear that the Swedish version differed from the ideal in almost every particular. During the 'twenties and early 'thirties no government had the support of a parliamentary majority; responsibility for policy was divided among the four major parties; and legislative initiative was largely in the hands of the parliamentary

[53] Jennings, *Cabinet Government, op.cit.,* pp. 15 f., and Barker, *op.cit.,* p. 38.
[54] See Karl Staaff, *Det demokratiska statsskicket,* Stockholm: Wahlström & Widstrand, 1917, passim.

committees, where a small Liberal group had the decisive word regardless of which party had formed the government. In the last two decades the cabinet has been restored to a strong and leading position; yet the opposition continues divided and there is little prospect for that regular alternation between government and opposition which the theory of parliamentary cabinet government envisages.

Criticism of the governmental system in Sweden thus has followed two distinct lines, the first predominant until the nineteen-thirties, the other during the more recent period. Looking back on the minority government period, a leading Socialist commented somewhat facetiously: "Our parliamentary democracy in Sweden has had a remarkable fate. Shortly after its birth . . . it assumed the questionable form of minority governments based on unstable and changing parliamentary alignments."[55] Others did not mince their words in condemning the "accursed system" of shifting majorities, "under which no Swedish citizen ever knows what will happen next."[56] The proportional multiparty system, a Liberal editorialist complained, had given rise to a situation where no general election gave a clear mandate to any party. "We might just as well let the parties toss coins to determine who is to occupy the government chancellery."[57] And a Conservative political scientist blamed the multiparty system and the attendant weakening of governmental responsibility for the "glaring discrepancy between the unrealistic and impracticable ideas expressed in party programs and a governmental policy based on thoughtless compromises. No one pays much attention to the ideas since they are not to be carried out anyway. Why, then, trouble to revise these ideas that are doomed to a miserable existence in programs ever forgotten?"[58] Finally, it has been suggested that to call such a system one of parliamentary cabinet government was an outright misnomer since the Swedish system as it developed during

[55] Ernst Wigforss, "Demokrati, parlamentarism och klasspolitik," in *Ett genombrott*, Stockholm: Tiden, 1944, p. 21.

[56] O. W. Lövgren at the national convention of 1928; see *Protokoll över Sverges socialdemokratiska arbetarepartis trettonde kongress*, Stockholm: Tiden, 1928, p. 115.

[57] Otto v. Zweigbergk, *Svensk politik 1905-1929*, Stockholm: Bonnier, 1929, p. 341.

[58] Andrén, "Regeringsmakt och parlamentarism," *op.cit.*, pp. 482f.

this period implied "a negation of the very concept of parliamentarism."[59]

Other observers gave the system of "shifting majorities" their qualified endorsement. Conservatives, who until 1918 had strenuously opposed any attempt to subject the government to the control of popular majorities, discovered that it was "not such a bad arrangement that the parliament should lack solid majority blocs and instead include a number of different parties which combine to form now one kind of majority and now another, according to the circumstances."[60] Some of them saw in the minority party system a continuation of the time-honored Conservative principle of checks and balances and added confidently that the new balance, based as it was on the social structure of the electorate, might outlast the defunct checks once embodied in the constitution.[61] They might have added that, to the extent that proportional representation had reinforced existing tendencies toward a multiparty system, the new balance was a direct result of Conservative policy. The Liberal Prohibitionists, of course, had no reason to quarrel with a system that permitted them to dictate major legislative decisions, and even an occasional Socialist thought that it moderated the "obvious ruthlessness" of government by a majority party.[62]

THE CASE FOR PERMANENT NATIONAL COALITION

The return since 1933 and 1936 to strong cabinets with stable support in the riksdag closed this first phase of the debate. In 1938 the Socialists, for the first time in the history of any party since the adoption of universal suffrage, obtained a majority of the popular vote. It became increasingly clear in the following years that in view of the traditional stability of voter

[59] Fredrik Lagerroth, "Staaff eller De Geer? Till frågan om vårt levande statsskicks typologi," *Statsvetenskaplig tidskrift*, 47:31 (1943).

[60] Herlitz, *Svensk självstyrelse, op.cit.*, p. 175.

[61] Georg Andrén in *Sveriges riksdag, op.cit.*, pp. 611f. Professor Andrén's praise in 1935 of a system which he had sharply condemned only five years earlier (see note 58 supra) reveals a certain ambivalence in the Conservative attitude. The circumstance that on the second occasion a Socialist cabinet was in office, on the first a Conservative one, may have played its part in this change of heart.

[62] Rickard Lindström, *Om kompromiss*, Stockholm: KF, 1932, p. 30.

alignments and the unlikelihood of landslides under PR there was little reason to expect any early or major swings of the pendulum. A single party thus might gain permanent control of the government, whereas the opposition might find itself in a minority for an indefinite period. There was widespread agreement that such a situation ill accords with the fundamental preconceptions of democracy, and the fact that Socialist predominance rested on an exceedingly small margin—at times on a mere plurality—accentuated the feeling of dissatisfaction.

The second phase of the debate was opened by none other than the leader of the majority party itself. At a Socialist party congress in June 1940 Premier Hansson declared that "a situation in which the opposition is always doomed to remain in opposition is actually quite absurd... An opposition which senses the hopelessness of its struggle and to which [the majority] does not listen cannot take the place which belongs to the opposition in a good democratic system." Hansson added that a permanent national coalition of all major parties, such as the one formed in December 1939, might be the best way out of the impasse.[63]

Many political leaders and observers were ready to accept Hansson's major premise. As the Conservative leader Gösta Bagge put it: "The exercise of exclusive power by a permanent majority party is incompatible with democracy and popular government."[64] The solution suggested by Hansson (i.e. a permanent coalition of all parties with the exception of the Communists) has also been accepted by a number of prominent figures in various camps, while others have rejected it as unsatisfactory. The proposal that the government be permanently entrusted to all major parties together has found its chief advocates in Herbert Tingsten, an ex-Socialist and since 1946 editor of the largest Swedish newspaper, the Liberal *Dagens Nyheter*, and in Elis Håstad, a prominent member of the Conservative party.[65] Even a spokesman for the Agrarian party,

[63] *Protokoll, Sveriges socialdemokratiska arbetarepartis 18:e kongress*, Stockholm: Tiden, 1940, p. 65.

[64] Gösta Bagge, *Tal 1941-1943*, Stockholm: Högerns Riksorganisation, 1943, p. 287, Cf. the official commentary on the Conservative program of 1946, *Frihet och framsteg*, Stockholm: Högerns Riksorganisation, 1946, p. 36.

[65] For Tingsten's position see his pamphlet *Problem i svensk demokrati*,

which otherwise contributed little to the debate, declared in 1949 that "the system of a permanent national coalition ought to be given a try."[66]

The proponents of permanent national coalition have argued that under such a scheme the government would be more fully representative of the entire population, and hence more democratic, than under a system of one-party government; that representation of all major groups of the population within the government is a Swedish tradition dating back to the estate period; that their postulate is but a logical consequence of the principle of proportionalism which demands that all parties, including the minority parties, should be represented in the government; and that only a government with the broadest possible parliamentary support can assert its authority against increasingly powerful economic organizations. They have generally admitted, at least by implication, that a national coalition might have difficulty in maintaining the necessary unity within the government,[67] that there would be no organized opposition in parliament, that the government might therefore become irresponsible, and that the electorate would lose control of the government. They have argued, however, that under a national coalition all parties in parliament could afford to relax party discipline, so that latent disagreements *within* each party could be aired more fully than is possible under the traditional system. Furthermore, they have urged that a permanent coalition sys-

Stockholm: Tiden, 1941, esp. p. 17; his book *Argument*, Stockholm: Bonnier, 1948, pp. 196–216; and a series of articles "Reform av statsskicket," *Dagens Nyheter*, Stockholm, July 20–22 and August 3–5, 1947. Håstad has treated the question in a number of articles published in *Svensk tidskrift*: "Den svenska 'korporatismen,'" 27:675–684 (1940); "Samlingsregering eller partiregering?" 30:323–236 (1943); "Samlingsregéringen och samarbetsidén," 32:233–235 (1945); "Konungen och regeringsbildning," 34:367–373 (1947); and "Samlingsregeringen och dess problematik," 35:108–120 (1948). Nils Herlitz advocated a national coalition as a permanent institution as early as 1929; his article entitled "Regeringsproblemets svårigheter" is reprinted in his *Svensk självstyrelse*, pp. 171–191.

[66] Karl Lindegren, "Regeringsproblemet," *Politisk tidskrift* (1949), p. 325; Lindegren became national secretary of the Agrarian party in 1941.

[67] This was the experience of the wartime national coalition. Cf. Fritiof Domö, "Ett års samlingsregering," *Svensk tidskrift*, 27:646–650 (1940); and Per Albin Hansson, "Ministerstyrelse och regeringssamarbete," *Tiden*, 37:390–393 (1945).

tem be combined with extended provisions for direct popular participation in legislation through referendum and initiative;[68] and they have pointed to the experience of Switzerland as proof that an all-party government with referendum and initiative can be both strong and democratic.[69]

In spite of the many arguments that have been advanced in favor of a permanent national coalition in peacetime, it does not seem likely that any such plan will be adopted in the near future. There has been considerable opposition to the plan not only among the Social Democrats but also among the bourgeois parties.[70] By 1944 the leaders of the bourgeois parties in the wartime coalition had become convinced that continued cooperation with the Socialists would be impossible after the end of the emergency. In July 1945 Per Albin Hansson, who himself had started the public discussion about an all-party government in peacetime, agreed to a dissolution of the coalition. Since Tingsten's conversion to Liberalism in 1945 and Hansson's death in 1946 the plan has found no prominent supporters among the Socialists. So far, therefore, the very preponderance of the Socialists, which first gave rise to demands for peacetime national coalition, has rendered that scheme impracticable. It is

[68] Cf. Tingsten, *Problem i svensk demokrati*, *op.cit.*, pp. 27f., and "Reform av statsskicket," *op.cit.*, July 22, 1947. The Socialist-Agrarian government, in a bill of April 1954, took a first step toward permitting wider use of the referendum. According to the bill a consultative referendum must be held, upon request of one third of the membership of both houses, on any legislation exccept appropriations, treaties, and matters which the riksdag labels urgent. The liberal-Conservative opposition has advocated a decisive (rather than consultative) referendum.

[69] See Tingsten, *Problem i svensk demokrati*, *op. cit.*, pp. 68f., and Håstad, "Samlingsregeringen och dess problematik," *op.cit.*, p. 111. Håstad has presented a study of Swiss government and politics in his monumental *Regeringssättet i den schweiziska demokratien*, Uppsala: Almqvist & Wiksell, 1936. Note that in Switzerland the members of the federal council are elected by parliament for three-year terms rather than appointed by the chief executive; no one seems to have advocated such an arrangement for Sweden.

[70] For Socialist opposition see, e.g., Torsten Gårdlund, "Samlingsregering som normal ordning," *Tiden*, 35:129–133 (1943), and Arne Björnberg, "Samlingsregeringen, ett utkast till eftermäle," *Tiden*, 37:24–25 (1945); the latter title, significantly, translates: "The National Coalition—Notes for an Obituary." Gösta Bagge, Conservative leader until 1944, was one of the most outspoken opponents of the plan; see his *Tal 1941–1943*, *op.cit.*, pp. 281ff.

possible that gradual changes in the social structure—notably
the steady gain of the white collar element at the expense of
industrial worker[71]—may redress the balance in favor of the
bourgeois parties; yet a fuller mobilization of traditional non-
voters among the working class might offset any such gains.
Furthermore, the recent alliance of Socialists and Agrarians
(1951), if maintained in the future, may enable the former to
retain their key position even in the face of a further reduction of their present plurality. There appears, on the other
hand, to be widespread support for a system of national
coalition among the electorate;[72] and if the international situation should markedly deteriorate, the parties may well overcome their reluctance to reenter a broad coalition.

THE PROBLEM OF MAJORITY RULE

The recent Swedish debate on cabinet government and
majority rule has centered upon two broad and intimately related problems. The first was clearly stated by Professor Herlitz,
when he wrote that "one of the most important political questions today" was to discover to what extent the majority principle will be accepted as equitable by the minority within a democratic nation. Herlitz himself suggested that the principle was
likely to find acceptance (1) if, in passing legislation "unity can
be obtained among a large number of members of parliament"
and (2) "if elections lead to continual changes so that one and
the same majority does not remain in power for a long time"
and if in parliament itself "now one and now another majority
is formed."[73] The dissatisfaction that has arisen in Sweden because of narrow margins of party dominance and inflexible
voting alignments indicates that, as far as it goes, this analysis
is entirely correct. The experience of other countries, nevertheless, might point to additional variables. Thus a fuller investigation might show that acceptance of the majority principle is directly related not only to the size of the majority and the

[71] See Fritz Croner, *Tjänstemannakåren i det moderna samhället*, Uppsala: Geber, 1951.
[72] Elis Håstad et al., *"Gallup" och den svenska väljarkåren*, Stockholm:
Geber, 1950, pp. 246, 309, 312, 313f. 317f.
[73] Nils Herlitz, *Svenska statsrättens grunder*, Stockholm: Norstedt, 1940.

flexibility of alignment, but also to the felt need for unity; and inversely related to the felt importance of the issues subject to majority decision.[74] The psychological emphasis of the Swedish discussion contrasts with the tenor of the recent debate on majority rule in the United States. Can, or should, majority rule be combined with minority rights? Are some such rights (especially the freedom of today's minority to propagate its opinions in speech and writing in the hope of becoming to-morrow's majority) presupposed by the very rationale of majority rule? And if so, should these rights be guaranteed by institutions other than majority rule? Such have been the questions in the foreground of attention in the United States. There has been no suggestion in Sweden that conditions making the majority principle palatable to the minority should be imposed by any agency other than the decision of the majority itself. Few American writers, on the other hand, seem to have pondered that to be told they are legally free to become majorities is no effectual antidote to "the forlorn hope of constant minorities."[75]

The other main focus of the recent Swedish debate has been the question of responsibility. In fact, as long as the present inflexible alignment persists, Swedish advocates of responsible

[74] One or another of these variables has occasionally been pointed to in the literature; see, e.g., Robert Bierstedt, "The Sociology of Majorities," *American Sociological Review*, 13:705 (1948); Finer, *op.cit.*, p. 82; Carl J. Friedrich, "One Majority against Another," *Southern Review*, 5:47 (1939/1940), and the same author's *Constitutional Government and Democracy*, Boston: Ginn, 1946, p. 587, and rev. edn., 1950, p. 165; Pendleton Herring, *The Politics of Democracy*, New York: Norton, 1940, pp. 46, 51, 133; and Willmoore Kendall, *John Locke and the Doctrine of Majority-Rule*, Urbana: University of Illinois Press, 1941, p. 122. There appears, nevertheless, to have been little systematic discussion since Rousseau's *Contrat social* (esp. IV, 2, and II, 3).

[75] To borrow Burke's phrase (quoted by John MacCunn, *The Political Philosophy of Burke*, London: Longmans, 1913, p. 19). For recent contributions to the American debate see Edwin Mims, Jr., *The Majority of the People*, New York: Modern Age Books, 1941; Henry Steele Commager, *Majority Rule and Minority Rights*, New York: Oxford University Press, 1943; Herbert McCloskey, "The Fallacy of Absolute Majority Rule," *Journal of Politics*, 11:637–654 (1949); and Neal Riemer, "The Case for Bare Majority Rule," *Ethics*, 62:16–63 (1951). Herlitz's question, on the other hand, has been raised by Willmoore Kendall ("On the Preservation of Democracy for America," *Southern Review*, 5:63 [1939/1940]), and the authors cited in the preceding note all suggest at least partial answers.

government are facing a serious dilemma: If the traditional cabinet system is maintained, the government, immune from electoral defeat, will at best be responsible to little more than half the electorate. If the traditional system is abandoned in favor of all-party government, responsibility will be diluted in proportion as it is broadened. Premier Hansson, in his speech of 1940, chose the second horn, while Social Democrats since that time have preferred the first.

CHAPTER VIII

THE POLITICS OF COMPROMISE

THE politician has been called "the man who deliberately faces both the certainty that men must live together, and the endless uncertainty on what terms they can live together, and who takes upon himself the task of proposing the terms, and so of transforming the unsuccessful human group into the successful group."[1] The strength and nature of unifying and disruptive forces delimit the politician's task and mold the character of political parties in any community. The basic unity of Swedish society makes compromise possible. Its engrained diversity makes compromise necessary. The resulting political process in turn reshapes the social setting from which it arises.

Sweden, as we have seen, has a small and remarkably homogeneous population. Nearly all the inhabitants speak the same native language and belong, at least nominally, to the same Lutheran state church. The small Finnish border population and the even smaller groups of nomadic Lapps have not become active as political minorities. The only sizable denominational minority groups—the Protestant dissenters—have been very active in politics, especially in the Liberal and Prohibitionist parties. Yet high-churchmen, sectarians, and agnostics are found in each of the major parties, and religious questions have never aroused partisan controversy. Nor are there any sharp regional contrasts. The country's natural resources are not distributed evenly. Yet there is forest everywhere; there is agriculture in the extreme South and in the North; there is mining in the far North and in the Center; and manufacturing spreads along a wide belt across the country. Above all, there is no consciousness or memory of political ambitions or grievances that would set one region against the other.

History has cooperated with ethnology and geography in creating conditions favorable to self-government. Although

[1] William Ernest Hocking, *Man and the State*, New Haven: Yale University Press, 1926, p. 13.

democracy in Sweden is a recent phenomenon, the tradition of popular representation and of government by law dates back, without significant interruption, to the Middle Ages. The transition from oligarchy to democracy was accomplished peacefully and the circle of politically active citizens extended gradually. Parliamentary government benefits from time-tested procedures and retains much of the intimacy typical of an earlier period when the rulers were members of a small elite bound together by ties of personal friendship and family.[2] Since 1814 Sweden has enjoyed a continuous period of peace, and the effects of the Great Depression, though severe, were far less devastating than in many other countries.

In the absence of pronounced ethnic, religious, and regional cleavages, party distinctions have followed occupational differences. In Sweden as elsewhere, groups dissatisfied with prevailing social conditions have supplied the original impetus for party formation.[3] The early annals of Swedish parties, nevertheless, suggest a modification of the hypothesis advanced by Robert Michels that "Organization...is the weapon of the weak in their struggle with the strong."[4] Social groups strongly entrenched in their political position remained unorganized, to be sure, until their control was challenged. Yet neither did those who were hopelessly weak or outnumbered compound their predicament by tying themselves to a rigid discipline. The contrast between the bureaucratic-agrarian-industrial oligarchy and the farmers erupted into open conflict not in the senate, where representation was heavily weighted in favor of the former, but in the lower chamber, where forces stood about evenly divided. Again, the lower middle and working classes

[2] "To this day the remnants of aristocratic organization retained by English society exert a profound influence upon the political life of the nation. The absence of this traditional aristocratic basis of the English parliamentary government has had a good deal to do with the failure of European systems presumably modeled after the English pattern." Carl J. Friedrich, *Constitutional Government and Democracy*, rev. edn., Boston: Ginn, 1950, p. 179. In this respect, as in the history of cabinet government itself, Sweden has evolved a pattern of her own closely paralleling that of Britain.

[3] Cf. Ludwig Bergsträsser, *Geschichte der politischen Parteien*, Mannheim: J. Bensheimer, 1921, p. 1.

[4] Robert Michels, *Political Parties*, Glencoe, Ill.: Free Press, 1949, p. 21.

founded the first national parties at a time when a secular rise in money wages was helping them in ever-greater numbers to cross the plutocratic franchise barriers. Parties formed not among the most depressed classes but among those already in ascendance.[5] Political inertia gave way to party activity where the increment of strength to be derived from organization promised to make the difference between success and failure. The Ruralist decline after 1888 and 1895, the Liberal-Socialist divorce of 1920, and the Liberal splits of 1914 and 1923 point to a well-known corollary: Once the major aims of a political movement are attained it is prone to disintegrate.[6]

These generalizations, nevertheless, do not apply to a later period when partisan activity had come to be taken for granted. The modern Agrarians clearly were undismayed by the impossibility of attaining full political control. Like the Ruralists in their period of decline, but even more purposefully, they were striving to safeguard the particular interests of the farmers by temporary alliances with other parties. Extremist groups, responding to psychological needs of their own, have appeared on the stage (and one of them has remained there for over three decades) though their chances of reaching any of their stated goals, by revolutionary or legal methods, have been infinitesimal. Limited-purpose parties such as the Agrarians and particularly the extremists thus have not conformed to Max Weber's well-known definition of the aim of a political party. According to Weber, "The end to which [a party's] activity is devoted is to secure power within a corporate group for its leaders in order to attain ideal or material advantages for its active members."[7] Reconverts from Communism, such as Lindhagen, Höglund, and Kilbom, knew that they were in a far better position to participate in the exercise of power and to secure such advantages as members of the Social Democratic party; yet many others remained in the Communist fold.

[5] For an analogous hypothesis concerning the origin of revolutions see, e.g., Crane Brinton, *Anatomy of Revolution*, New York: Norton, 1938, pp. 44, 46.

[6] Maurice Duverger, *Les partis politiques*, Paris: A. Colin, 1951, pp. 333f.

[7] Max Weber, *The Theory of Social and Economic Organization*, New York: Oxford University Press, 1947, p. 407.

Older parties in the course of time have acquired a purely organizational momentum. Founded originally as vehicles for the pursuit of specific demands, they now rarely consider a new program or policy without first pondering its impact on the party's growth and survival. This subtle inversion of means and ends can go far toward counteracting the corrosive effects both of sudden victory and of prolonged defeat. Thus the three bourgeois parties continue to expend much of their energy upon competition with one another. Yet there are today no fundamental political differences between them (or at any rate between the Conservatives and Liberals), and it is likely that a complete merger would have put them in a far better position to stem the Socialist electoral tide. Nor has the Socialist party shown any signs of decay. It is the oldest, largest, and most elaborately structured of the present parties. Also, despite its political predominance throughout the last two decades, its program remains largely unfulfilled. Critics who dismiss demands such as complete nationalization as irrelevant mistake their true import. The Social Democrats, to be sure, made no attempt to socialize after 1920, after 1932, or after 1945—any more than they had prepared a revolution in the eighteen-nineties. The party did not serve its program; yet the program served the party. Major portions of the original socialist ideology continue as a source of inspiration, while a liberal welfare program provides guidance for action. When Tingsten demonstrated that the party had long since repudiated in practice every important program point and shared its present political principles with all the other major parties he was met with cries of indignation.[8] Three years later (1944) the party proceeded to refurbish its socialist eschatology. The chiliastic promise has been effective just because it has not been put to any pragmatic test.

The desire for economic improvement has been an important motive in the rise of political movements. But the quest for

[8] See Herbert Tingsten, *Den svenska socialdemokratiens idéutveckling*, Stockholm: Tiden, 1941, II, 409 and passim; the critiques in *Tiden*, 33:229, 278, 343, 377 (1941); and Tingsten's rebuttal, *Tiden*, 33:542. Torsten Gårdlund, one of the few friendly critics, a few years later resigned the editorship of *Tiden*. In withdrawing from the party's activities he did not, however, follow Tingsten into the Liberal camp.

political power and social status has been an even more potent force. Throughout the late nineteenth century—and long before that—the difficulty of adjusting material interests was compounded by disagreement over the procedures by which adjustment should be sought. At least twice, at the time of the suffrage controversy between 1902 and 1907 and during the tense closing days of the First World War, this political conflict threatened to erupt into violence. Its resolution proved to be at once more painful and more lasting than the mere removing of any material grievance could have been.

The recent constitutional history of Sweden may be interpreted as a constant ebb and flow between two opposite principles. On the one side have stood those who would domesticate political power by concentrating it in the hands of representatives accountable to a wider circle of citizens; on the other those who would render it innocuous by splitting it up and setting each part against the other. In their rebellious youth most political movements have favored concentration of responsibility. Once satisfied, they have been more receptive to the diffident doctrine of checks and balances. The conversion generally has come soon enough to stave off each subsequent attempt at unified control. The bourgeoisie of the nineteenth century, who fought to subject Karl XIV's ministers to parliamentary supervision, later supported De Geer's bicameral equipoise. Whereas the early Ruralists had hopes of adapting French parliamentarism to Swedish practice, their heirs forty years later helped thwart Staaff's scheme of party government. And Staaff's successors in the nineteen-twenties became the chief beneficiaries of the new proportionalist balance. Up to the time of the Second World War no single political movement thus exercised undivided power. When the Socialists did gain full control their policies had become so moderate as to belie earlier predictions of "one-sided class rule."

Swedish politics, then, has consistently faced situations where positive decisions could result only from compromise. Branting once in a querulous mood called Sweden "*ett kompromissarieridetland*"—"a compromiser-ridden country."[9] In Sweden perhaps more than anywhere else the technique of compromise has been an essential ingredient in the art of propos-

[9] *Tal och skrifter*, Stockholm: Tiden, 1927–1930, III, 214.

ing the terms on which men can live together. Many of her outstanding politicians—Gustaf Boström, Gottfrid Billing, Arvid
Lindman, Carl Ekman, and Per Albin Hansson—have been
accomplished masters of that technique. The structure of compromise has varied with the nature of the initial difference.
Where conflicting programs have offered no area of overlap, an
inclusive compromise has been the logical answer. The dispute
over taxes and conscription was settled in 1885 and 1892 when
each chamber conceded the other's demand. The political
triangle of the nineteen-twenties, on the other hand, favored *exclusive* compromises: Conservatives and Socialists could carry
only such proposals as found favor with the Liberals. Where the
question was financial, the Liberals might in addition offer to
split the difference now with the right and now with the left. The
Socialist-Agrarian alliance, finally, has brought a return to *inclusive* compromises—which indeed provide the natural foundation for any pluralist order. The three types of compromise here
distinguished may be symbolized as follows (the terms before
the arrow representing the initial positions, the one after it the
resulting settlement):

$$a, b \longrightarrow a+b \qquad \text{(inclusive)}$$

$$a+b, b, b+c \longrightarrow b \qquad \text{(exclusive)}$$

$$a, b \longrightarrow \frac{a+b}{2} \qquad \text{(split the difference)}[10]$$

To classify is one thing, to evaluate quite another. Some hold
with Burke that "All government, indeed every human benefit
and enjoyment, every virtue, and every prudent act, is founded
on compromise."[11] Others condemn compromise as rank cow-
ardice and shallow opportunism. A better view, perhaps, would
distinguish a lower form that appeases all without satisfying
any (of which logrolling is the prototype) from a higher one
that fully reconciles the initial differences.[12] Any such distinc-

[10] In Swedish committee parlance the three forms are known respectively
as "invitation," "amputation," and "compromise"; see chapter VI supra.
[11] "Speech on Conciliation with America" (1775), in *Works*, 12 vols.,
Boston: Little, Brown, 1877, II, 169. For a Swedish eulogy on compromise
see Rickard Lindström, *Om kompromiss*, Stockholm: KF, 1932; 2d edn.,
Stockholm: Tiden, 1938.
[12] Harold D. Lasswell, "Compromise," in *Encyclopaedia of the Social
Sciences*, New York: Macmillan, 1930–1935, IV, 147–149, calls the higher

tion, of course, is easier to formulate in the abstract than to apply to concrete instances. Politicians anxious to compose a serious divergence of interest will be happy if they secure the minimum of votes required to carry the final proposal. Inevitably its supporters will place the resulting decision nearer the top, whereas its antagonists will place it nearer the bottom of such a scale. Policy indeed is often nothing but "the product of political compromise dressed in the language of justification by the philosophers of the winning side."[13] But a policy can last only if it does not long divide the community into winners and losers, if it embodies a standard of justice acknowledged by all sides. Any evaluation must account not only for the conditions under which a decision comes about but also for the future situation to which it applies. A pattern of politics must be viewed together with its total consequences and presuppositions.

As a result of successive compromises the area of political controversy in Sweden has narrowed considerably since the first emergence of parties. The early conflicts between Ruralists and senate oligarchy, between protectionists and upper class free-traders by the turn of the century had been composed sufficiently to make possible a joint front against the suffrage movement. Sixty years ago the Conservatives staunchly defended the oligarchic *status quo*, the Liberals demanded universal suffrage, and the Socialists were still under the spell of Marxist revolutionary dogma. The farsighted recognition by a few tories that some modification of the *status quo* was inevitable, the prudent calculation by Socialist leaders that violence was too high a price for equality if the aim could be achieved at lesser cost, and the innate aversion of the Liberals to close association with any extreme position created the preconditions for a peaceful settlement. Once agreement on the basic constitutional issues was reached in the compromises of 1907 and 1918, the way was free for a further *rapprochement*. The Socialists overcame their dislike for the

type "integration" and only the lower "compromise." Cf. John Morley's distinction between "legitimate" and "illegitimate" compromise (*On Compromise*, London: Chapman & Hall, 1874, p. 159), and Rousseau's between the "general will" and the "will of all" (*Contrat social*, II, 3 and passim).

[13] Pendleton Herring, *The Politics of Democracy*, New York: Norton, 1940, p. 40.

monarchy, the state church, and an organized army. For their ideal of a planned nationalized economy they substituted the practice of social welfare and security. The Conservatives accepted democracy in good faith and recently have proposed its elaboration through legislative referenda. Once opposed to joining the League of Nations, they now endorse Sweden's accession to the United Nations. While defending free enterprise they concede that public or private control of any specific economic activity "must always be a question of expediency."[14]

The parties have not hesitated to ransack the tenets of their rivals. The Socialists under Per Albin Hansson inscribed upon their banner Kjellén's young-conservative slogan of "the people's home."[15] Bertil Ohlin has developed a program of "social liberalism" and asserts that his Liberals rather than the Social Democratic party are the true champions of "economic democracy."[16] The Conservatives remain loyal to the state church but see in nonconformism an equally valid expression "for the determination of our people to live within a Christian society."[17] The Socialists are the only major party that makes no reference in its program to Christianity; yet a Christian Socialist association formed in its midst in 1929, and today several ministers of the state church sit with the Socialist riksdag delegation.[18] The Liberal party no longer advocates prohibition; yet all the parties agree on the continued need for fighting alcoholism. Although the Agrarian party claims to be the sole spokesman for the farmers it has in fact no monopoly on the advocacy of rural interests. Only the Communists remain outside the ever-widening pale of political agreement.

Throughout the recent history of Swedish parties compromise and consensus thus have laid the fondation for further compromise and closer coincidence of views. The same principle of

[14] *Frihet och framsteg*, Stockholm: Högerns Riksorganisation, 1946, p. 179; on the referendum see *ibid.*, pp. 39 ff.
[15] See, for example, Hansson's speech entitled "Folkhemmet, medborgarhemmet," in his *Demokrati*, Stockholm: Tiden, 1935, pp. 19–32. On Kjellén cf. chapter II supra.
[16] *Socialliberal samhällssyn*, Stockholm: Folkpartiet, 1948, pp. 57 ff.
[17] Conservative program of 1946, article 14, section 5.
[18] Cf. Tingsten, *op.cit.*, II, 318 ff., and Raymond Fusilier, *Le parti socialiste Suédois*, Paris: Les Editions Ouvrières, 1954, pp. 291 ff.

cumulation[19] can be observed in the concrete achievements of
Swedish politics. The last 100 years have brought the liberation
of successive social groups from traditional restrictions, and a
progressive equalization of political rights and economic opportunities. Each step along this road has led to new demands for
freedom and equality, thus adding to the original momentum.
The reforms of the mid-nineteenth century lifted paternalistic
restrictions on economic enterprise and guaranteed freedom of
association to the lower classes. The Ruralists succeeded in
removing the remnants of feudalism in agriculture, and during
the present century the large masses of rural proletarians have
settled on land of their own or moved to the city. Military service
now is a duty of citizenship rather than the special burden of a
single class. The government derives its major revenue from an
income tax rather than from tolls and excises, and the rates for
the higher incomes have been stepped up sharply. The suffrage
has been transformed from a plutocratic privilege into a democratic right. Union organization and continued prosperity have
brought an unprecedented rise in nominal and real wages.
Having for some decades assumed responsibility for the unemployed and for indebted farmers, the government now concen-
trates on preventing rather than curing economic depressions.
Sweden today maintains one of the highest national standards
of living and affords her citizens one of the most inclusive systems of social welfare and security.

While the earlier reforms tended toward individualism, this
direction was reversed as soon as full political equality was
achieved. The adoption of proportionalism was the first important step toward pluralism, and social and economic policy
since the nineteen-thirties has brought a rapid advance along
the same road. Today the worker's wage and the industrialist's
profit, the price of farm products and the consumer's cost of
living depend increasingly on collective and political bargaining. With her parties based almost exclusively on occupational
distinctions, Sweden today closely approximates the corporativ-
ist ideal.[20] The numerical recording of the voter's choice, more-

[19] On this principle, of which the well-known "vicious circle" is the
negatively valued subcategory, see Gunnar Myrdal, *An American Dilemma*, New York: Harper, 1944, appendix 3.

[20] Gunnar Heckscher, *Staten och organisationerna*, 2d edn., Stockholm:
KF, 1951, pp. 184f.

over, cuts the Gordian knot of all pluralist political theory[21]—
the apportionment of representatives among the occupations.
Some doubt remains, however, whether pluralism in any form
can in the long run be squared with traditional democratic
presuppositions. One of these presuppositions demands that in
selecting its rulers a sizable portion of the electorate attempt to
judge the merits of candidates and programs. In Sweden the
number of voters whose judgment is fettered by enrollment in a
political party is large, and among the rest a change of party is
as rare as a change of profession. A politician attempting to
forecast the long-term trend of the party vote will be concerned
with statistical data on the increasing ratio of white collar to
manual labor rather than with government policies or opposition platforms. The reservoir of potential voters who do not go
to the polls is rapidly dwindling. The partisan struggle increasingly assumes the character of dugout warfare.

The rigid voting alignment, strongly favored by the Swedish
version of proportional representation, has prevented any regular alternation between ins and outs such as a two-party system
might have produced. During the nineteen-twenties, to be sure,
the multiparty system institutionalized compromise and there
was a quick procession of Socialist, Conservative, and Liberal
ministries. Meanwhile, however, the smallest among these
groups, the Liberals, determined policy. For several decades
the electoral system prevented the emergence of a majority
party. Yet once the Socialists had surmounted all or most of
the hurdles, they were assured of a far longer period of unchal-
lenged predominance than they would have enjoyed under
plurality elections. There is no apprehension that the government will abuse its power so as to stifle opposition. But the
prospect of continued one-party preponderance has given rise
to acute dissatisfaction with cabinet government in its traditional form.

Every human achievement has its price. To list some of the
costs of the politics of compromise is not to deny the genuine
benefits it has rendered. There is one other item of cost intimately connected with the very human attitudes that have made
institutionalized compromise possible. The political man not

[21] See, e.g., Francis W. Coker, *Recent Political Thought*, New York:
Appleton-Century-Crofts, 1934, pp. 297f.

only seeks to find the terms upon which he can live with others; he also strives after power and glory. In Sweden any open pursuit of such goals is severely inhibited by strong social disapproval. But, as an analysis of the legislative process has shown, these inhibitions do not abolish power competition within the political arena. Instead competition assumes a more subtle and often insidious quality. Compromise at best removes the substantive causes of conflict, but it does little to satisfy the ambition or to dissipate the resentment—in short to relieve the psychological tensions—engendered by the conflict.

An eminent participant observer of the Swedish political scene went so far as to designate a widespread feeling of frustration and disappointment as the distinguishing mark of genuine compromise. In an interesting article Rudolf Kjellén—professor of political science, theorist of geopolitics, Conservative politician, and leader of the "Young Conservative" school—compared the decision of 1865 which replaced the estates with a bicameral parliament with that of 1907 which introduced manhood suffrage modified by proportional representation. To Kjellén the popular reaction to these two measures constituted a "psychological proof" that the second one was, and the first one was not, a true compromise. "A real compromise solution where everyone must pay an appreciable price for his gain will be received, as was the decision of 1907,...with silence and utter indifference. The very enthusiasm in 1865...testifies conclusively that the reform that time was very close to the heart of the one side."[22] Whether this emotional cost of compromise appears as a large or small item on the ledger will depend largely on the temper and mood of the accountant. The different and often catastrophic effects of habitual intransigence are all too evident in the recent history of other Continental countries to require comment.

Whatever its merits or defects the politics of compromise is firmly rooted in tradition. The recent "progressivism" of

[22] Rudolf Kjellén, "1866 och 1909," in *Historiska studier tillägnade Harald Hjärne*, Uppsala: Almqvist & Wiksell, 1908 [*sic*], pp. 679f. Kjellén participated in the riksdag's decision of 1907. Bishop Henning von Schéele, one of the few members of the riksdag present both in 1865 and in 1907, drew a similar contrast between the popular reception of the two measures. See Åke Thulstrup, *När demokratin bröt igenom*, Stockholm: Bonnier, 1937, p. 65.

social reform in Sweden should not obscure the conservatism of her politics. "The King shall maintain and further justice and truth, prevent and forbid iniquity and injustice; he shall not deprive anyone, or allow anyone to be deprived of life, honor, personal liberty or well-being without legal trial and sentence; he shall not deprive anyone, or permit anyone to be deprived of any real or personal property without due trial and judgment in accordance with the provisions of the Swedish law and statutes."[23] These clauses of the present constitution, which have been called the Swedish bill of rights, repeat almost word for word the ancient formula of the coronation oath, first recorded in the fourteenth century. Sweden's riksdag is the oldest national legislature except for the British parliament, her fundamental law the oldest written constitution after that of the United States. Representative government and freedom of speech and press, the administration's independence from direct political supervision and its right to participate in policy making, the publicity of administrative decisions and the citizen's right to appeal them—all these are securely and historically established. The future of monarchy in Sweden seems assured—at least so long as the present royal house has eligible heirs. From earlier periods of oligarchic rule Swedish democracy has inherited traditions of intimacy, good manners, and mutual respect among parliamentary representatives; and these habits continue to temper the legislative process at a time when the more mechanical checks and balances have disappeared from the constitution. The anomaly of hierarchical patterns of deference to rank and social position in a professedly egalitarian society is further evidence of the strong grip of custom and tradition. The essence of that tradition is a strict and often meticulous regard for law and legal procedure, expressed in the old adage *"Land skall med lag byggas"*—"Country shall be built with law."

[23] *RF*, § 16; English translation according to Amos J. Peaslee, *Constitutions of Nations*, Concord, N.H., 1950, III, 96 ff.

APPENDIX

APPENDIX

TABLE 5

THE POPULAR VOTE IN SWEDEN, 1911-1954

Year	Chamber	Potential Voters in % of Population	Actual in % of Potential Voters	National Socialists	Nationalists	Conservatives	Agrarians	Liberals	Social Democrats	Left Socialists	Communists	Others
1911	L	19.3	57.0	.	.	31.2	. .	40.2	28.5	.	.	.1
1914[a]	L	19.5	69.9	.	.	37.7	. .	32.2	30.1	.	.	.0
1914[b]	L	19.7	66.2	.	.	36.5	. .2[c]	26.9	36.4	.	.	.0
1917	L	19.5	65.8	.	.	24.7	3.1[d] 5.3	27.6	31.1	8.1	.	.1
1919	U	49.1	63.3	.	.	24.9	6.3 6.9	25.4	30.5	5.8	.	.2
1920	L	20.4	55.3	.	.	28.1	6.2 7.9	21.8	29.6	6.4	.	.0
1921	L	54.2	54.2	.	.	25.8	11.1	19.1	36.2	3.2	4.6	.0
1922/3	U	48.0	38.2	.	.	31.8	11.9	17.1	32.9	1.8	4.5	.0
1924	L	55.6	53.0	.	.	26.1	10.8	3.9[e] 13.0[f]	41.1	.	1.5[g] 3.6[h]	.0
1926/7	U	49.1	49.8	.	.	28.9	11.7	3.2 12.9	39.0	.	. 4.1	.2
1928	L	57.6	67.4	.	.	29.4	11.2	3.0 12.9	37.0	.	. 6.4	.1
1930/1	U	51.4	58.2	.	.	28.4	12.5	2.5 11.0	41.4	.	4.0[h] .	.2
1932	L	60.0	67.6	.6	.	23.5	14.1	1.9 9.8	41.7	.	5.3 3.0[i]	.1
1934	U	53.3	63.6	.9	.	24.2	13.3	12.5	42.1	.	4.0[j] 2.8	.2
1936	L	62.8	74.5	.7	.9	17.6	14.3	12.9	45.9	.	4.4 3.3	.0
1938	U	63.1	66.0	.8	.	17.8	12.6	12.2	50.4	.	1.9 3.8	.5
1940	L	64.8	70.3	.	.	18.0	12.0	12.0	53.8	.	.7 3.5	.0
1942	U	67.8	66.8	.	.	17.6	13.2	12.4	50.3	.	.1 5.9	.5
1944	L	66.1	71.9	.1	.1	15.9	13.6	12.9	46.6	.	.2 10.3	.3
1946	U	69.5	72.0	.	.	14.9	13.6	15.6	44.4	.	. 11.2	.2
1948	L	68.8	82.7	.	.	12.3	12.4	22.8	46.1	.	. 6.3	.1
1950	U	68.2	80.5	.	.	12.3	12.3	21.7	48.6	.	. 4.9	.2
1952	L	67.7	79.1	.	.	14.4	10.7	24.4	46.1	.	. 4.3	.1
1954	U	70.3	79.1	.	.	15.7	10.3	21.7	47.4	.	. 4.8	.1

L = Lower chamber election.
U = Election for upper chamber electoral colleges.
[a] March 1914 (dissolution election).   [b] September 1914 (regular election).
[c] Bondeförbundet.   [d] Jordbrukarnas Riksförbund.
[e] Löfgren Liberals.   [f] Prohibitionist (Ekman) Liberals.
[g] Höglund faction.   [h] Kilbom faction.
[i] Sillén faction.   [j] Socialist party (Kilbom-Flyg).
Source: The figures are compiled (in part calculated) from the official election statistics.

TABLE 6

Distribution of Seats in Parliament, 1912–1955

Session	Lower Chamber							Upper Chamber					
	Nationalists	Conservatives	Agrarians	Liberals	Social Democrats	Left Socialists	Communists	Conservatives	Agrarians	Liberals	Social Democrats	Left Socialists	Communists
1912	.	64	.	101+1	63+1	.	.	84+2	.	51+1	12	.	
1913	.	64	.	101+1	63+1	.	.	87+1	.	49	13	.	
1914, Jan.	.	64	.	101+1	63+1	.	.	87+1	.	49	13	.	
1914, May	.	80+6	.	71	72+1	.	.	87+1	.	47+2	13	.	
1915	.	82+4	.	55+2	87	.	.	88+1	.	47	14	.	
1916	.	82+4	.	56+1	87	.	.	86+4	.	46	13+1	.	
1917	.	83+3	.	55+2	71+1	15	.	86+3	.	44	16	.	
1918	.	56+1	5[a]	9[b] 61+1	85+1	11	.	86+2	.	45	16	1	
1919, Jan.	.	56+1	5	9 62	86	11	.	84+2	.	43	19	2	
1919, Aug.	.	55+1	6	9 62	86	11	.	36+2	8[a]	10+1[b] 41	49	3	
1920	.	55+1	6	9 61+1	86	11	.	36+2	8	9+1 41	49+1	3	
1921	.	70	10	19+1 47+1	75	5	2	36+1	9	9+1 40	50	0+1	3
1922	.	61+1	21	41	93	6	7	40+1	18	38	50	1+1	
1923	.	62	21	41	93	6	7	39+3	17	38	50	2	
1924	.	62	21	6[c] 30+5[d]	99	.	7	42+2	17	14[c] 20+2[d]	52	.	
1925	.	65	23	4+1 27+1	104	.	1[e] 4[f]	42+2	18	13 20+2	52	.	
1926	.	65	23	4+1 28	105	.	4[f]	44+3	16	9 24+1	52	.	
1927	.	65	23	4+1 28	105	.	4	46+3	16	8 23+1	52	.	
1928	.	65	23	4+1 28	105	.	4	48+4	14	7 23+1	52	.	
1929	.	73	27	4 28	90	.	8	47+2	17	7 23+1	52	.	
1930	.	73	27	4 28	90	.	8	47+2	17	6 23+1	52	.	
1931	.	73	27	4 28	90	.	8	48+2	17	5 22+1	54	.	
1932	.	72+1	27	4 28	90	.	8	46+3	19	4 21+1	55	.	
1933	.	58	36	4 20	104	.	6[f] 2[g]	47+3	18	4 18+1	58	.	
1934	.	56+2	36	4 20	102	.	8[h] 2	46+3	19	2 17+1	61	.	
1935	3	52+1	37	25	102	.	8 2	46+2	20	19	62	.	
1936	3	52+1	37	25	101+1	.	8 2	44+2	22	16	65	.	
1937	.	44	36	26+1	112	.	6 5	43+2	22	16	66	.	
1938	.	44	36	27	115	.	3 5	41+2	23	17	67	.	
1939	.	44	36	27	115	.	3 5	40+1	24	15	69	.	
1940	.	44	36	27	115	.	3 5	37+1	24	15	72	.	

			Lower Chamber						Upper Chamber			
Session	Nationalists	Conservatives	Agrarians	Liberals	Social Democrats	Left Socialists	Communists	Conservatives	Agrarians	Liberals	Social Democrats	Left Socialists	Communists
941	.	42	28	23	134	.	3	34+1	24	15	75	.	1
942	.	42	28	23	134	.	3	34+1	22	15	77	.	1
943	.	42	28	23	134	.	3	31+1	21	15	81	.	1
944	.	42	28	23	134	.	3	30+1	20	15	82	.	1
945	.	39	35	26	115	.	15	29+1	21	14	83	.	2
946	.	39	35	26	115	.	15	27+1	21	14	84	.	3
947	.	39	35	26	115	.	15	25+1	21	14	86	.	3
948	.	39	35	26	115	.	15	24+1	21	16	85	.	3
949	.	23	30	57	112	.	8	24+1	20	18	84	.	3
950	.	23	30	57	112	.	8	22+1	23	20	81	.	3
951	.	23	30	57	112	.	8	21+1	25	20	79	.	4
952	.	23	30	57	112	.	8	20+1	24	21	80	.	4
953	.	31	26	58	110	.	5	19+1	25	22	79	.	4
954	.	31	26	58	110	.	5	15+1	25	27	79	.	3
955	.	31	26	58	110	.	5	13+1	25	30	78	.	3

Note: Figures after + sign indicate independents. Horizontal lines indicate general elections.

a Jordbrukarnas Riksförbund.
c Löfgren Liberals.
e Höglund group.
g Sillén group.
b Bondeförbundet.
d Prohibitionist Liberals.
f Kilbom group.
h "Socialist" party.

Source: *Lagtima riksdagen* (Stockholm, annually); some figures corrected.

TABLE 7
PRIME MINISTERS SINCE 1876

Date of Appointment	Name of Prime Minister	Party Composition of Cabinet
1876 March 20	Baron Louis Gerard De Geer[a]	.
1880 April 19	Count Arvid Posse	.
1883 June 13	Carl Johan Thyselius[b]	.
1884 May 16	Oskar Robert Themptander[b]	Free Trade
1888 Feb. 6	Baron Gillis Bildt	Free Trade–Protectionist
1889 Oct. 12	Baron Gustaf Åkerhielm	Protectionist
1891 July 10	Erik Gustaf Boström (I)[b]	Protectionist
1900 Sept. 12	Fredrik Wilhelm von Otter[b]	.
1902 July 5	Erik Gustaf Boström (II)	.
1905 April 13	John Ramstedt	.
1905 Aug. 2	Christian Lundeberg	Conservative-Liberal
1905 Nov. 7	Karl Staaff (I)	Liberal
1906 May 29	Arvid Lindman (I)	Conservative (Proportionalist)
1911 Oct. 7	Karl Staaff (II)	Liberal
1914 Feb. 17	Hjalmar Hammarskjöld	Conservative (Independent)
1917 March 30	Carl Swartz	Conservative
1917 Oct. 19	Nils Edén	Liberal-Socialist
1920 March 10	Hjalmar Branting (I)	Socialist
1920 Oct. 27	Baron Gerard Louis De Geer	(Administrative)
1921 Feb. 23	Oscar von Sydow	(Administrative)
1921 Oct. 13	Hjalmar Branting (II)	Socialist
1923 April 19	Ernst Trygger	Conservative
1924 Oct. 18	Hjalmar Branting (III)	Socialist
1925 Jan. 24	Rickard Sandler[b]	Socialist
1926 June 7	Carl Gustaf Ekman (I)	Liberal (Prohibitionist-Löfgrenite)
1928 Oct. 1	Arvid Lindman (II)	Conservative
1930 June 7	Carl Gustaf Ekman (II)	Liberal (Prohibitionist)
1932 Aug. 6	Felix Hamrin[b]	Liberal (Prohibitionist)
1932 Sept. 24	Per Albin Hansson (I)	Socialist
1936 June 19	Axel Pehrsson i Bramstorp	Agrarian
1936 Sept. 28	Per Albin Hansson (II)	Socialist-Agrarian
1939 Dec. 13	Per Albin Hansson (III)	Socialist-Agrarian-Liberal-Conservative
1945 July 31	Per Albin Hansson (IV)	Socialist
1946 Oct. 11	Tage Erlander (I)[b]	Socialist
1951 Sept. 30	Tage Erlander (II)	Socialist-Agrarian

[a]Minister of state for justice since May 11, 1875 (and previously, April 7, 1858 to June 3, 1870).

[b]Change of prime minister only.

TABLE 8

Potential Majority Combinations in Parliament since 1906

Years	Lower Chamber					Upper Chamber					Joint Votes				
	Conservatives	Liberals	Agrarians	Socialists	Communists	Conservatives	Liberals	Agrarians	Socialists	Communists	Conservatives	Liberals	Agrarians	Socialists	Communists
1906–1911		*		*		*					*				
	*	*													
1911–1919		*		*		*							*		*
	*	*									*	*			
1919–1921+		*		*				*		*			*		*
	*	*				*	*				*	*			
1922–1924		*		*				*		*			*		*
	*	*	*			*	*				*	*	*		
1925–1931		*		*				*		*			*		*
			*	*		*	*				*	*	*		
	*	*	*												
1932		*		*				*	*			*		*	
	*	*	*			*	*			*	*	*	*		
1933–1936+		*		*				*		*		*		*	
			*	*				*	*				*	*	
	*	*	*			*	*	*			*	*	*		
1937–1938		*		*				*		*			*		*
			*	*				*	*				*	*	
				*	*	*	*	*		*	*	*	*		
1939–1940		*		*				*		*		*		*	
			*	*				*	*				*	*	
				*	*	*	*	*	*					*	*
1941–1944+			*					*					*		
1945–1952	*		*					*					*		
			*	*											
				*	*										
1953–		*		*				*				*		*	
			*	*									*	*	
	*	*	*										*		*

Asterisks indicate parties whose support was required to form a majority; the asterisks on each line represent one potential majority combination.

The symbol + indicates periods for which the combinations for both chambers were identical.

TABLE 9

Cabinets since 1905: Composition, Parliamentary Support, and Causes of Resignation

Appointment	Premier	Party Composition	Parliamentary Support			Cause of Resignation	Resignation
			Lower Chamber	Upper Chamber	Joint Votes		
8- 2-1905	Lundeberg	7C 2L 2I	226:4	150:0	376:4	Purpose of coalition achieved	10-28-1905
7-11-1905	Staaff	7L 4I	106:124	0:150	106:274	Conflict with monarch	5-25-1906
5-29-1906	Lindman	4C 1L 6I	1906—109:121 1911— 92:138	150:0 133:17	259:121 225:155	Election (−28)	9-30-1911
10- 7-1911	Staaff	10L 1I	102:128	52:98	154:226	Conflict with monarch	2-10-1914
2-17-1914	Hammarskjöld	4C 7I	1914— 64:166 1915— 86:144	88:62 89:61	152:228 175:205	Defeat on joint vote	3- 5-1917
3-30-1917	Swartz	5C 6I	86:144	89:61	175:205	Election (−24)	10- 2-1917
10-19-1917	Edén	7L 4S	1918—148:82 1919—148:82	62:88 90:60	210:170 238:142	Coalition breaks	3- 6-1920
3-10-1920	Branting	11S	86:44	50:100	136:244	Election (−1)	10-22-1920
10-27-1920	De Geer	1C 11I	Nonpartisan			Defeat in LC; cabinet disagrees	2-14-1921
2-23-1921	von Sydow	1C 11I	Nonpartisan			Election	10- 5-1921
10-13-1921	Branting	12S	93:137	50:100	143:237	Defeat in UC	4- 6-1923
4-19-1923	Trygger	6C 1A 5I	62:168	42:108	104:276	Election (+3)	10-14-1924
10-18-1924	Branting-Sandler	11S 1I	105:125	52:98	157:223	Defeat in both chambers	6- 2-1926

TABLE 9, CONT.

Appoint- ment	Premier	Party Com- position	Parliamentary Support			Cause of Resignation	Resigna- tion
			Lower Chamber	Upper Chamber	Joint Votes		
6- 7-1926	Ekman	4PL 3LL 5I	33:197	34:116	67:313	Election (−1); coaliton breaks	9-26-1928
10- 1-1928	Lindman	8C 4I	73:157	49:101	122:258	Defeat in both chambers	6-2-1930
6- 7-1930	Ekman-Hamrin	8PL 4I	28:202	24:126	52:328	Election (−8)	9-19-1932
9-24-1932	Hansson	12S	104:126	58:92	162:218	Defeat in both chambers	6-15-1936
6-19-1936	Pehrsson i Bramstorp	9A 2L 1I	37:193	22:128	59:321	Election (−1)	9-23-1936
9-28-1936	Hansson	7S 3A 2I	148:82	88:62	236:144	International crisis; coalition formed	12-13-1939
12-13-1939	Hansson	4S 2A 2L 2C 3I	1939—222:8 1941—227:3 1945—215:15	149:1 149:1 148:2	371:9 376:4 363:17	Coalition breaks	7-31-1945
7-31-1945	Hansson-Erlander	12S 4I	1945—115:115 1951—112:118	83:67 79:71	198:182 191:189	Coalition formed	9-30-1951
9-30-1951	Erlander	8S 4A 4I	1952—142:88 1953—136:94	104:46 104:46	246:134 240:140		

Abbreviations: A[grarians], C[onservatives], I[ndependents], L[iberals], L[öfgren] L[iberals], S[ocial Democrats]. LC = Lower chamber. UC = Upper chamber. Italicized figures indicate majority support, figures in parentheses seats lost or gained by the government.

247

Figure 1. Party Genealogy

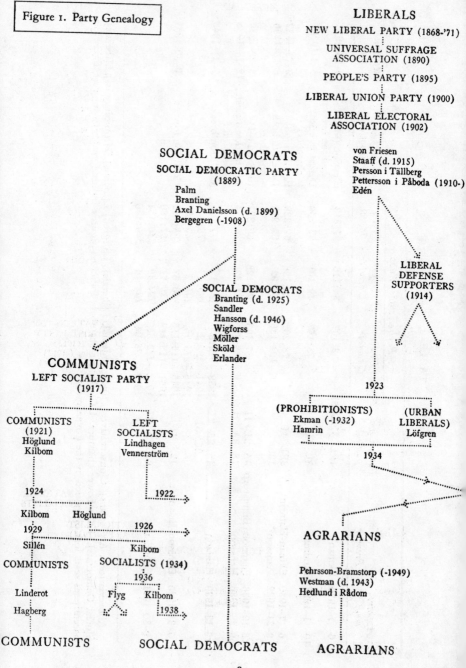

LIBERALS
NEW LIBERAL PARTY (1868-'71)

UNIVERSAL SUFFRAGE
ASSOCIATION (1890)

PEOPLE'S PARTY (1895)

LIBERAL UNION PARTY (1900)

LIBERAL ELECTORAL
ASSOCIATION (1902)

SOCIAL DEMOCRATS
SOCIAL DEMOCRATIC PARTY
(1889)
Palm
Branting
Axel Danielsson (d. 1899)
Bergegren (-1908)

von Friesen
Staaff (d. 1915)
Persson i Tällberg
Pettersson i Påboda (1910-)
Edén

LIBERAL
DEFENSE
SUPPORTERS
(1914)

SOCIAL DEMOCRATS
Branting (d. 1925)
Sandler
Hansson (d. 1946)
Wigforss
Möller
Sköld
Erlander

COMMUNISTS
LEFT SOCIALIST PARTY
(1917)

1923

COMMUNISTS
(1921)
Höglund
Kilbom

LEFT
SOCIALISTS
Lindhagen
Vennerström

(PROHIBITIONISTS)
Ekman (-1932)
Hamrin

(URBAN
LIBERALS)
Löfgren

1934

1924

1922

Kilbom   Höglund

1929   1926

Sillén   Kilbom
COMMUNISTS   SOCIALISTS (1934)
              1936
Linderot   Flyg   Kilbom

Hagberg   1938

AGRARIANS

Pehrsson-Bramstorp (-1949)
Westman (d. 1943)
Hedlund i Rådom

COMMUNISTS   SOCIAL DEMOCRATS   AGRARIANS

248

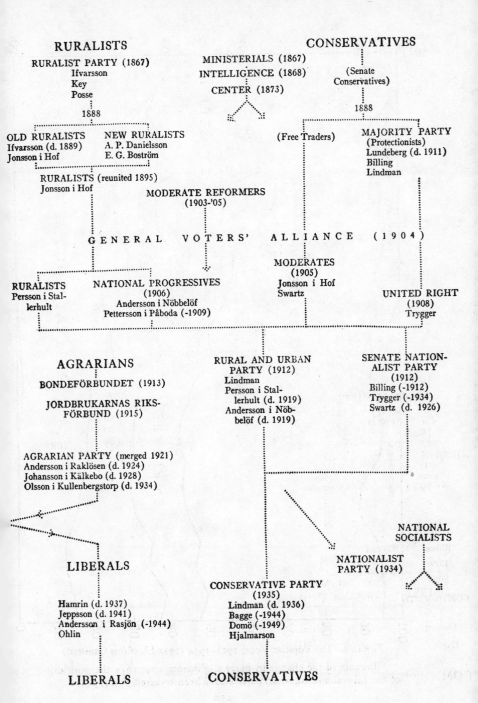

RURALISTS
RURALIST PARTY (1867)
  Ifvarsson
  Key
  Posse
1888

CONSERVATIVES
MINISTERIALS (1867)
INTELLIGENCE (1868)
CENTER (1873)
(Senate Conservatives)
1888

OLD RURALISTS
Ifvarsson (d. 1889)
Jonsson i Hof

NEW RURALISTS
A. P. Danielsson
E. G. Boström
RURALISTS (reunited 1895)
Jonsson i Hof

(Free Traders)

MAJORITY PARTY
(Protectionists)
Lundeberg (d. 1911)
Billing
Lindman

MODERATE REFORMERS
(1903-'05)

GENERAL VOTERS' ALLIANCE (1904)

RURALISTS
Persson i Stallerhult

NATIONAL PROGRESSIVES
(1906)
Andersson i Nöbbelöf
Pettersson i Påboda (-1909)

MODERATES
(1905)
Jonsson i Hof
Swartz

UNITED RIGHT
(1908)
Trygger

AGRARIANS
BONDEFÖRBUNDET (1913)
JORDBRUKARNAS RIKS-
FÖRBUND (1915)

RURAL AND URBAN
PARTY (1912)
Lindman
Persson i Stallerhult (d. 1919)
Andersson i Nöbbelöf (d. 1919)

SENATE NATION-
ALIST PARTY
(1912)
Billing (-1912)
Trygger (-1934)
Swartz (d. 1926)

AGRARIAN PARTY (merged 1921)
Andersson i Raklösen (d. 1924)
Johansson i Kälkebo (d. 1928)
Olsson i Kullenbergstorp (d. 1934)

NATIONAL
SOCIALISTS

LIBERALS

Hamrin (d. 1937)
Jeppsson (d. 1941)
Andersson i Rasjön (-1944)
Ohlin

CONSERVATIVE PARTY
(1935)
Lindman (d. 1936)
Bagge (-1944)
Domö (-1949)
Hjalmarson

NATIONALIST
PARTY (1934)

LIBERALS   CONSERVATIVES

249

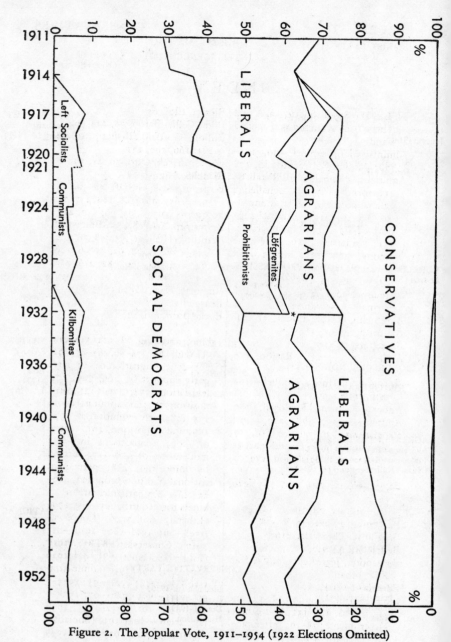

Figure 2. The Popular Vote, 1911–1954 (1922 Elections Omitted)

* Because of the change in party alignments after 1932 the positions of the Liberal and Agrarian parties have been reversed at this point.

INDEX

N. B.: The Swedish letters å, ä, and
ö have been arranged as if spelled
a and o.

administration, cabinet and, 175–
178; publicity of records in, 178
Agrarians, compared to Ruralists,
41; form party, 75; challenge
Liberal position, 104; and Socialists, 102, 105, 107; electoral support of, 118, 139; membership,
151; leadership, 159; discipline
among, 168, 171; and cabinet
government, 200, 220–221; limited purpose of, 228
agriculture. *See* farmers, Swedish
Farmers' Association
Åkerhielm, Gustaf, Count, 38, 244
Åkerman, Assar, 169
Åland, 101
Andersson, Gustaf, i Rasjön, 110,
157, 172
Andersson, Hans, i Nöbbelöf, 64,
72n., 166n.
Andersson, Johan, i Raklösen, 170n.
Andrén, Georg, 178, 206, 219n.
associations, prevalence of, 7;
growth of, 46–47; and parties,
153–157; and legislation, 179

Bagge, Gösta, 110, 161, 163, 220,
222n.
Berg, Fridtjuv, 57, 162
Bergegren, Hinke, 49, 77–78
Bergquist, Thorwald, 216n.
Bergström, David, 47, 57, 162
Bernadotte, Jean Baptiste. *See* Karl
XIV Johan
Bernadotte dynasty, 65
bicameralism, adoption of, 17; and
parties, 18, 130–131; and cabinet
government, 78–79; attenuated
by committees and joint votes,
186, 195–196

Biesèrt, Elof, 65
Bildt, Gillis, Baron, 38, 244
Billing, Gottfrid, Bishop, 59, 64,
163, 166, 190, 231
von Bismarck, Otto, 20, 25, 39
Blanche, August, 28
Boström, Erik Gustaf, 38–40, 55,
59, 64, 65, 69, 74, 80, 188, 231, 244
bourgeois parties, 95, 96, 210, 229
Bramstorp. *See* Pehrsson-Bramstorp
Branting, Hjalmar, 51, 58, 61, 62,
63, 69, 76, 77, 78, 92, 95–96, 160,
162, 163, 164, 169, 182, 216, 230,
244
Braunias, Karl, 125, 153
Brusewitz, Axel, 203
Burke, Edmund, 21, 231

cabinet, and king, 38, 212–216; and
riksdag, 66, 78–80, 83–85, 92,
201–206; resignation of, 80, 205;
party support of, 169, 209; and
legislation, 174, 179–180; composition, 175; and administration,
175–178; early evolution of, 197–
199; and opposition, 201; tenure
of, 209; nonpartisans in, 215;
moderation of, 216–217; formed
by minorities, 218; permanent
national coalition proposed, 219–
223. *See also* parliamentarism
cabinets formed in: 1905—65; 1906
(Liberal)—66; 1906 (Conservative)—69; 1911—80; 1914—82;
1917 (Conservative)—83; 1917
(Liberal-Socialist)—83, 92; 1920
(Socialist)—92; 1920 (administrative)—93, 214; 1921—95; 1923—
96; 1924—96; 1926—97; 1928—
99; 1930—101; 1932—103; 1936
(Agrarian)—108; 1936 (Socialist-
Agrarian)—108; 1939—110; 1945
—113; 1951—115, 223

251